LOCO in YOKOHAMA

BAYE McNEIL

A HUNTERFLY ROAD BOOK

Published by: Hunterfly Road Publishing
604 Macdonough Street, Brooklyn, New York 11233
718-701-8241

Copyright © Baye McNeil, 2013
All rights reserved

ISBN 978-0615885117

Original Cover Art by J.J. McCullough
Book Design by Miki Hayashi

No part of this publication may be reproduced, stored in, or introduced in a retrieval system, or transmitted, in any form, or by any means (electronic, mechanical, photocopying, recording, or otherwise) without the prior written permission of both the copyright owner and the above publisher of this book.

For more information on book or author go to: www.locoinyokohama.com
Or send email to: loco@locoinyokohama.com

To Yokohama,
my home away from home, be it ever so humble. . .
And to Mrs. Betty
for reminding me how to love

TABLE OF CONTENTS

Acknowledgments --- 7
Introduction: A Portrait of Promise ------------------------------------ 11

1   This is Loco --- 29
2   On Bonding, Bullying and Betrayal ------------------------------ 41
3   A Cursed Smile --- 61
Interlude: Chikan Chicanery -- 73

4   Bipolar Bear Hug --- 81
5   Effluvium --- 101
6   Are You African? --- 117
Interlude: You Ain't Gotta Explain Shit To me --------------------------- 139

7   One Moment Please --- 143
8   Protocol -- 161
Interlude: You Had Me at Sumimasen ------------------------------------ 171

9   The Makings of Mrs. Betty ------------------------------------- 177
10 Is Loco-sensei a Nee-Gah, Too? -------------------------------- 189
Interlude: On Reading, Writing and Alchemy --------------------------- 197

11 Manzai of the Onani Brothers --------------------------------- 209
12 Yes I Am -- 217
Interlude: By the Time I Get to Yokohama ------------------------------ 227

13 Hurricane Betty -- 233
14 Long Live The King -- 245
Interlude: You're Too Kind -- 255

15 Forever Cute --- 265
16 Apeshit -- 277
17 So, This Is Christmas . . . In Yokohama ----------------------- 293
Interlude: Small Accomplishable Goals --------------------------------- 305

18 Loco Wuz Here --- 309
19 Mental Instagrams --- 319
20 Distant, Aloof, but Alive --------------------------------------- 333

About The Author -- 343

ACKNOWLEDGMENTS

Doffing my baseball cap, I salute my editor, *Shari Custer*. A remarkable woman who, at the time of this book's publishing, I have yet to meet in person, have only heard her voice once via SKYPE, and resides on another continent, but has managed to be my most significant other throughout this process. While unorthodox, this is far from a phenomenal feat. Current technology is capable of so much more. What does have the feel of the phenomenal, at least for me, is the trust we've placed in one another, despite these minor hindrances. She has brought not only her many years of editorial and writing experience to bear, but her lifelong love and respect of books, readers and writers, her in-depth knowledge of psychology, as well as her understanding of Japanese culture, language and people. Her feedback and suggestions have made the whole editorial process joyful, enlightening and educational. From the depth of me, thank you, Shari. Your portrait is in my soul's hall of fame.

I also owe a tremendous debt of gratitude to my homeboy in the UK, the incredibly knowledgeable and generous *Kaz Obuka*, for helping me with the proofreading as well as providing some deft and insightful editorial tips that, without a doubt, improved the overall quality of this book. My Man!! I also owe, BIG time, my homegirl, the brilliant and talented *Kimberly Tierney*, who not only helped with the proofreading, but gave me some great ideas on how to promote this book and some invaluable leads in that respect to boot. Hugs and kisses!!

This book's cover is a testament to the talent and creativity of two people: The first was, once again, *J.J. McCullough*. J.J.'s artwork, as was the case with my first book, Hi! My Name is Loco and I am a Racist, is kick-ass, and sets the tone for the book impressively. Thanks, JJ! And then there was the beautiful and gifted Miki Hayashi who helped me pull it all together with her exceptional eye for design, transforming it from a cover I was happy with to one I am overjoyed to be associated with. She's been my rock, and I can't imagine this book would have been as true to my vision as it is without her by my side. Thank you, Miki-chan!

And to all the people who supported my first book—in particular, *Hikosaemon*, *Kateria Niambi*, *Kemba Mchawi*, *Ashley Thompson*, *Sandra Barron*, *Michael Peckitt*, *Douglass Reed*, *Marie Brown*, and *Amanda Taylor*—and helped make it the monumental first step it was, my long-term LIY blog readers, my Facebook, Twitter, Instagram, Tumblr and Google+ followers, my family and friends, thank you for the encouragement and ongoing support. I do my part on the creative end, work my butt off, sacrifice and lay it all on the line to the best of my ability, but without your "likes", "retweets", "shares", reviews and, most importantly, your full-throated word-of-mouth endorsements helping to spread the word, it might all be for naught. Aluta Continua—The Struggle Continues

"Teachers teach and do the world good!"
—KRS 1, *My Philosophy*

"You love hard, and you hate hard, and that's the measure of a full emotional life. Anybody tells you different is a saint or full of shit!"
—Mrs. Betty

Introduction

A Portrait of Promise

Spring break was no vacation.

Almost every day of it found me at an internet cafe writing, editing, and revising the book you're about to read. And, after months of false starts and trial and error, I'd finally figured out the central theme and general tone, and was getting to a point where I felt comfortable announcing publicly that I was in the homestretch. An autumn release was looking very promising.

But then there was the question of how to introduce this work. On that front, I was stumped.

Years of writing have granted me a bit of faith in the process, though, so I don't panic as much as I used to. I no longer think of it as a crisis and, above all, I refrain from getting all dramatic and attaching debilitating labels like "writer's block" to it. I've come to believe that if one remains open to the possibilities, that inspiration, moments of clarity, and occasionally even brilliance—what I call the muse—will come. She (and, yes, the muse is a "she" to me) often appears when I least expect her, at inconvenient times and from unexpected directions, but I count my blessings that she comes at all.

And this time was no different.

It would have been nice if she had arrived during my spring vacation when I'd set aside the time to entertain her, take her on a guided tour and show her the sights. But standing there in the terminal waiting, as ho-hum and mediocrity sauntered by, sometimes winking at me and even showing a little leg, I had to accept the fact that she'll come when she's good and damn ready. This time around she actually waited until *after* my vacation had ended to show up at my front door in the middle of the night, rousing me from a fitful slumber, and saying, "Don't act like you ain't glad to see me. Just give me some love!"

And I did—plenty of it.

There's nothing more arousing than when the muse makes an appearance.

★ ★ ★ ★ ★

Here in Japan, the new school year begins after the spring break, unlike back in the U.S. where it begins in autumn. It took a while for this concept to *grow* on me, pun intended, being that that's how this practice won me over. The idea of beginning a new year while new life is springing up all over the place just works for me now. Those cherry blossoms that Japan is famous for are still flourishing at the start of each semester, allowing the kids to have their class photos taken beneath a splash of pink petals in bloom, the very portrait of promise. There's something felicitous about that scenario.

I arrived at my school at about 8:30, and it was already bustling with activity, from both students and staff. Though it was my first day back, it was hardly theirs. The Japanese teachers in a public junior high school don't really have much of a spring vacation. Whether the students are there or not, the teachers must show up and make whatever preparations go into the new school year. Since I'm neither a direct employee of the school nor of the Board of Education here in Yokohama, but rather a contractor employed by a middleman—which I will refer to as *The Company* from this point on—and not required to participate in said preparations, I generally return from spring holiday to a semester already underway.

There were several new faces in the office. A fact I noticed as soon as I opened the door. First among them was the vice-principal, seated at the traditional VP desk nearest the door. He started at my entrance and sprung from his seat. I slid the door closed behind me and grinned as I made my way towards him.

"You must be Loco-sensei!" he said in Japanese.

I dusted off my Japanese, filthy from almost two weeks of disuse, and replied, "Yes, I am. And, you must be the new vice-principal?"

"Correct!"

"It's very nice to meet you," I said, bowing my head and almost hitting the hand he'd extended for a shake. Half a second later he flipped to Japanese mode, looking a little stilted and amused, as if he were thinking "N*ow if that don't beat all! A bowing gaijin!*" and behaving the way an adult might if he were expected to formally shake hands with an eight-year-old prodigy who insisted on being acknowledged as a potential business partner.

"Your Japanese is very good!"

"Not really," I said through a practiced smile. "But, I think I've got this greeting thing down pat."

I winked, and he laughed. He might have even got it.

Just then, last year's VP strode out of the principal's office and took a look at some documents on the new VP's desk, and I could tell at a glance that he'd been promoted. His demeanor confidently declared *the buck stops here. . . now*! It's funny, but even his gait favored the previous principal's, the one whose beck and call he'd been at the whole time I've known him. His erect posture made him appear to have grown a couple of inches. His suit had been upgraded, giving him a sheen I'd never seen him flaunt before. Last year he always seemed to have a film around him, like chalk dust or like "Pig Pen" from the Peanuts comic strip. In fact, his whole aspect had been upgraded and had become sharper, more competent, and seasoned. He'd been more than ready for this transition and it was clear he was relishing every moment of it.

And I was happy for him. I didn't know his name, but I was happy for him.

In Japanese schools, the principal and vice-principal are rarely referred to by their given names. Much like the president of a country, they're known simply by their title. And so, though I'd probably been told his name at some point, because I'd never used it, I'd never committed it to memory. He was simply *fuku-kouchou-sensei* (vice-principal). And from this day forward, judging from his new swagger, I was pretty sure I'd be dropping the *fuku* and calling him *kouchou-sensei* (principal).

He looked up from a document, noticed me, and grinned.

"Welcome back, Loco-sensei," he said, coming around the desk to face me without any obstacles between us.

"Thank you!" I said. "Principal?"

"Yes, that's correct," he said, beaming with an expert mix of timidity and pride, like a man on his honeymoon running into the concierge—emerging from his hotel suite after a solid three days and nights of "Do Not Disturb" being posted on the door.

"Congratulations!" I said, and bowed deeply. I realized at that moment that I *was* really proud of him. From what I could see, he'd definitely earned it!

The VPs with ambition for the school's top slot are generally very sharp people, and over the course of the seven years I've been teaching in junior high schools in Yokohama, I've met quite a few. They are the ones that truly manage the office. It's virtually impossible to fake the funk as a VP. You've either got it or you don't. Besides, you're under constant scrutiny from above and below, within and without. While the principal has a private office he can duck into, close the door, and go undisturbed for hours on end, the VP has no such sanctuary. His desk is at the head of the open bay where all the teachers work. He's the first stop for all visitors and the voice on the other line most often when the school receives a call. He, or she, is the point person for most problems and issues that arise over the course of the day. He literally has enough duties to keep him and two other people up to their necks in tasks and paperwork.

He formally returned the bow and thanked me, looking very moved by my gesture, like he'd sensed its sincerity. We chatted for a moment before I turned and faced the office.

Actually, there were quite a few new faces, maybe 20 or so, and they all stared at me with varying degrees of *"wow, take a look and see what just breezed through the door!"* After years of this kind of reaction to my presence practically everywhere I go in this country, it's hardly off-putting any more. Besides, I knew from experience what was coming next.

Though I've been bounced around to a number of schools during my tenure, this was not the first time I returned for a second or even third year with the same school. And one thing that has been consistent is that there's an explicit change in the behavior of the teachers that remain behind from the previous year—positively explicit!

Maybe the previous year they hadn't said two words to me the entire time, or our conversations were limited to greetings and *extended* greetings—including inquiries about health or a prolonged discussion of the weather or seasonal changes, and little else. But, suddenly, upon my return for a second tour, those same people tend to treat me like we've gone through hell together, and survived! I've come to think of it as a show for the incoming teachers to somehow, and for some reason that evades me, impress upon the new lot that *this gaijin of ours is alright with us. He's part of our team, our family and, by God, we adore him!*

Of all the quirky behavior I've encountered in Japan, this is a quirk I've actually come to like because it's essentially founded on truth. In most cases the schools *are* incredibly challenging and we have *indeed* gotten through some hellish moments. And, these have brought me closer to some really awesome people over the years, and has given me more material as a writer than I could possibly commit to prose in a lifetime, (but I'm gonna try, nonetheless, starting with this book). The only part of this situation that is disingenuous is the implication, in most cases, that we've done anything *together* or had a direct relationship beyond inhabiting the same space and greeting one another every day.

Case in point, here came one of the teachers, God knew what her name was, whose only utterance to me last year—the same on a number of occasions—was a not particularly gentle reminder to place my order for one of the hot lunch boxes the school orders from a delivery service *before* the 9:30 deadline. I'd forgotten to do so several times, causing her to have to call the service and amend the order after the fact, a troublesome task taking her away from her other troublesome tasks. Today, I actually thought she was going to hug me based on the way she approached me, with open arms and smiling broadly. At the last moment her arms swung to her sides and she stopped and bowed. It was still pretty nice of her, though. After her greeting I snapped my finger, pantomiming that I'd just remembered something. I turned and went and checked the box next to my name on the lunch box order sheet. When I turned back to her, she was laughing and let several other teachers in on our private joke.

Most of the teachers that weren't transferred behaved similarly, demonstrating a *much* higher degree of fondness and ease with my presence than they had even two weeks earlier when the previous school year ended. There were pats on the back, aggressive handshakes, fluent Japanese blasted at me—as opposed to the baby talk littered with broken "Japlish" they'd mollycoddled me with the previous year—a couple of hugs—yes, *actual* physical contact—one rather intimate moment where a teacher imparted to me their sadness over so-and-so sensei's transfer, and another teacher, on the down low, bemoaning their being sent back to our hellhole of a school.

As I said, I'd expected it, but this school was the biggest I'd ever worked at, with about a thousand kids and over 60 teachers plus the maintenance staff, nurses and office clerks. So there was a *whole* lotta "love" in the air, or rather the Japanese facsimile thereof, which too often is the best you're going to get in these parts. It's a love I've struggled to place my trust in, because I've found you can rarely ascertain its depth, or distinguish it from ostentatious decency and customary kindnesses. It generally appears suspiciously superficial as it is expressed through an endless supply of saccharine smiles, cloying trinkets, bean tarts, and rice cookies—the Japanese equivalent of Hallmark Cards and Forget-me-nots.

Only now, there was more of that, more than there'd ever been in my career.

I suspect that after years of wallowing in skepticism, I've undergone some involuntary assimilation, some self-preserving soul alterations for survival's and sanity's sake, and now accept this affection at face value more often than I used to. I took my time working my way around the office, too, wallowing in the warmth of this welcome, for a change.

I also appreciated the effect this behavior was having on the new teachers. I knew it would inhibit most of them from experiencing the customary malaise and that infernal Japanese discomposure for as long a period as they would without the benefit of this tolerably duplicitous demonstrative display of inclusiveness.

There had been seven Japanese English teachers last year. Three of them, including the former head Japanese English teacher, were transferred to other schools this year, as is the practice in Yokohama public schools. The Board of Education routinely rotates the teachers around the school circuit every three years or so, which meant three replacements, including a new jack fresh from university, had rotated around to our school.

Abe-sensei met me after I'd made it about half-way through the spacious yet overcrowded office, and showed me to my new desk—which was actually my old desk moved to a new location. He informed me that he was the new head English teacher.

Abe was a really cool guy, and definitely did not fall under the description of those other teachers who had previously relegated themselves to salutations and the daily climate clambake. He and I had had extensive conversations on a number of topics, including some of the heavier subjects covered in my first book, *Hi! My Name is Loco and I am a Racist*. On the strength of these talks, he'd actually gone out and bought it, had me autograph it, and had been reading it little by little over the course of the entire year—his English being passable but far from fluent.

"The new English teachers have classes this period," he informed me. "So I'll introduce you to them later, OK?"

"Cool!" I said, and we got down to business. "For today's lesson I was thinking we could do the same thing that we did last year. I'll do my self intro. And, then have the kids do theirs and then we'll play a game in which I'll quiz them on my intro. What do you think?"

"Perfect!" he said.

I've introduced myself to thousands of kids during my tenure so I didn't need much preparation. I had laminated photos of my family and hometown to show them and a game I was sure they'd get a kick out of. I was all set.

While I waited for my first class, a couple of new teachers of other subjects came over to my desk and introduced themselves . . . in fluent Japanese! It seemed I was already reaping the rewards of the second-year illusive love fest.

★ ★ ★ ★ ★

Come second period, I went up to the class Abe and I were to teach a solid five minutes early, marched into the room—shocking the hell outta the kids and silencing their racket—took a seat at the front desk where they're accustomed to seeing only Japanese faces, smiled and nodded at a couple of them, and whipped out my iPad.

The topic of every conversation shifted to me then. And the prudence of some of the kids, this being their first close encounter with an alien race, meaning non-Japanese, could not help them resist the tug of their curiosity as it dragged them inexorably towards me.

Most, I could see plainly in their shifting attentions, were struggling to decide which was more fascinating, me or the iPad. Several decided I was, but for most it was a no-brainer, the iPad! This was especially so once I'd flipped its case open. There were "oooos" and "ahhhhs" all around.

Anxiety dispelled, which had been my plan.

"Do you have any games?" came the first brave voice, in Japanese.

"Yes, I do," I replied, also in Japanese. "Have you ever heard of miniature golf?"

"No, what's that?" several asked.

I opened up my favorite miniature golf application and began playing so they could see. By the time I got to the second hole, half the class was crowded extremely close around me to catch a glimpse of it, just as I had anticipated.

"Have any of you ever played miniature golf?"

I realized I'd never seen a miniature golf course in Japan, so I was curious.

"I have," one kid replied, very naturally. "In Hawaii!"

"I mean, in Japan," I said, laughing, letting them all get a full dose of my humanizing mirth.

Then I glanced at the clock on the wall above us, as did the students. There were seconds left until the bell would ring. I abruptly closed the iPad and stood up, and the students raced to their seats. Abe-sensei arrived just then and a few moments later the bell began to ring. By the time the Westminster chimes had finished, all of the kids were seated and looking attentive. Abe and I smiled at each other as we were no doubt having the same thought. We both knew this kind of discipline wouldn't last long. By next week, the knuckleheads would begin to surface. First there'd be one, then two, then as many as five kids running into the classroom at the last minute, or even after the chimes had stopped.

This wasn't cynicism. This was experience.

He turned to the class and one student seated in the rear commanded the class to attention. Then, everyone in unison, Abe-sensei and I included, bowed.

"Good morning, class," Abe-sensei said.

"Good morning, Abe-sensei!" the class replied.

"How are you, today?"

"I'm fine, thank you, and you?" they each sang, having been taught this earlier in the week while I was still savoring the last hours of my vacation. Some may have even learned it in elementary school.

In Japanese, Abe-sensei then said to the students, "And this gentleman standing beside me is Loco-sensei. He is an English teacher."

He paused for a second and I was about to jump in and cut him off because I had an introduction all planned out and didn't want him giving away too much information about me and spoiling my game.

But, then, surprising the shit outta me, he added, "He is also a writer. He's published a brilliant book about life in Japan for a black man. I read it recently and I really can't express how remarkable an experience it was. It made me laugh and cry and think about a lot of things I'd never thought about before. Things *we all* need to think about. We are so fortunate to have such an esteemed colleague as he, and you are very lucky students to have him as your teacher, so pay attention to what he has to say and do your best!"

As he was saying these things about me, and as I kept alternating my attention between him and the students, one person kept popping into my mind, Mrs. Betty.

God, I miss her.

She was everything I love about this place wrapped up in one sage, aged, yet irrepressible package. She was the epitome of humanity. And, through her exuberance, Yokohama was transformed before my eyes from a city I could say I lived in to a place I could call home.

It was Abe's words that had conjured her up. And, if their faces were any indication, the students were affected by his words as well.

Then Abe turned and faced me, and jarred me from my remembrance when he said, "So sorry, you can start now." He gestured grandly to indicate that the class was all mine. I could tell he didn't think I quite caught everything he'd said, and he was right. There were a few words in his introduction I couldn't make heads or tails of. But, I got the gist, and then some.

I didn't know what to say or even what I was feeling at that moment. It was as if my emotions had overloaded and something had short-circuited. I think I might have nodded or something in his direction and turned back to face the class.

They each looked at me bearing expressions I don't think I'd ever seen on Japanese teen faces before, at least not with me as the cause or at the center of it.

A girl seated in the front row looked up at me, and I just knew she was a reader; a reader for joy, for knowledge, for fun. I don't know how I knew. But I was certain that due to the profound diversion and rapture books had given her, this 14-year old girl had elevated this entity known as "writer" to a magical, almost mythical, plateau. And here she was, seated not before some black foreign guy who'd left his home and come across the sea to fill her head with English, but before an entity who takes mere words and transforms them into the stuff that swells the shelves in the library of her soul and fills in the folios of her imagination with fancy, color and endless possibilities.

There was a boy, seated off to my right, with stickers of characters from a popular manga series, *One Piece,* on his notebook. And I could read in his expression that he had made the connection between this entity known as *writer* and his beloved anime as well. I was able to somehow intuit from the language his body spoke that, at that very moment, while Abe was telling them all that I was a writer, this boy's imagination had soared between and beyond Abe's words. It had moved from "he is a writer" to "someone sits down at a keyboard and actually writes *One Piece* with only his imagination as his guide" to "I think of great ways to expand on *One Piece* stories all the time, but choose to play soccer instead because all of my friends do" and arrived at "but, to be a writer for *One Piece* would be the greatest job in the world!"

Maybe it was just my imagination playing tricks on me, but this was how I perceived the energy in the room, and I'm generally pretty perceptive.

It made me think about something I hadn't thought about directly in quite a while—my *ultimate* bucket list. It is not just a lifetime "to-do" list, but that semi-morbid list of goals and ambitions I want to accomplish before I kick the bucket.

On that list resides items such as taking a year and driving or cycling across America, visiting various countries like South Africa, Kenya, Ghana, Brazil, Mexico, etc. for extended periods of time, conquering my irrational fear of roaches and rodents, quitting smoking—which might even extend the amount of time I'll have to do the other things on the list—learning how to fly, perhaps even buying my own plane, and learning to play the piano proficiently—one of the things I gave up upon coming to Japan for some reason.

But, at the pinnacle of that list, I remembered as I stood before 40 beaming youths, are two things: *being a published writer* and *being acknowledged as an author.*

★ ★ ★ ★ ★

I published my first book, *Hi! My Name is Loco and I am a Racist* in 2012, and the reviews started rolling in soon after. It was a critical hit and people began to acknowledge me as a serious, *bona fide* writer. Actually, even before I published the book, back when I was only blogging, recognition was given. But, I never fully embraced it.

At first, I'd convinced myself that I wasn't a *real* writer because, after all, I was a blogger, and the generally held idea is a blogger is to a writer as static cling is to lightning. And even after I published the book, I still secretly felt a little inadequate to the title because I had *cheated* the process. I hadn't sent my manuscript off to editors and agents and waited for them to validate my work with their response as most of my predecessors and literary idols had. I skipped over that risk of rejection, by-passed the gatekeepers, forewent what some would call the process by which professionals keep the market from being saturated with amateurish and unpolished garbage.

Then there was my belief that I hadn't done anything that *anybody* couldn't do to contend with. It was like when my friends back home would tell me that they admired me for having left the U.S. and moved overseas—something they couldn't see themselves doing or for whatever reason haven't been able to do. To me, those always felt like platitudes. If you *really* wanna do something, you just set your mind to it and do it, success or failure be damned. And, embracing such a maxim can hardly be thought of as admirable. It's borderline common sense, like exercising to improve your health or studying to improve your mind.

Nothing special whatsoever.

In fact, once I'd finally got off my ass and did it, I kind of felt like I'd set the bar too low; it was the equivalent of having "try every type of beverage at Starbucks, and collect Starbucks coffee mugs from every prefecture in Japan" on the top of my bucket list. I actually felt kind of embarrassed to have such low expectations of what I could accomplish in this lifetime.

So, perhaps to redeem myself, I pretended that writing and publishing a book and acknowledgment as a writer were trifles that had never been on my bucket list, and proceeded as if the bar had never been that low; that it had always been my ambition to build a successful writing career and publishing company, write a best-seller or two, get a story of mine turned into a film, and win a Pulitzer prize or NAACP Award.

I told myself that all I'd done was go shopping and pick up some ingredients. I hadn't even started cooking, yet.

★ ★ ★ ★ ★

It was not until I saw myself through the eyes of these kids, and through Abe-sensei, that I realized what others had been thinking and feeling about my work, about me, and much more importantly how *I* felt about me. I *had* done something worthy of at least a pause for the cause and a spiritual "attaboy"—if from no one else but me.

So, a year after the fact, I finally felt fully empowered to accept the title of writer. My timing could have been better though, as my emotions that had abandoned me just moments before suddenly came rushing back like a tsunami. These feelings were intensified by the fact that I wouldn't be able to share this moment of self-actualization with Mrs. Betty. She'd seen this in me before I even had an inkling and without reading a single thing I'd ever written. And, as I greeted this class filled with children I'd never met before, but who'd somehow managed to help me—as did Abe—to recognize what I am through *their* recognition of what I am, I fought back tears.

However, by the third class in a row, all of which had begun with Abe doing a similar introduction as he had for that first class—and the kids responding similarly—I was over myself. And, I began to take note of the various personalities among the kids, which is what I'd usually do on the first day in years past.

While Abe was doing his little spiel about my being a writer, I noticed one boy sitting in the front row of the class had not responded as most of the kids had. He was not impressed in the slightest, or hid it damn well. He sat there with a precocious little gleam in his eye and a not-so-subtle challenge in his demeanor. He reminded me of some of the so-called "salarymen" I see on the train who, upon finding themselves in my vicinity, respond to the *notion* of me they have swimming around in their heads as opposed to anything I've done or said to them. By virtue of being whatever I am in their stereotype and misinformation-plagued imaginations, I have made a conscious and aggressive effort to intimidate them, and *expect* them to be intimidated by me, and so they feel the need to assert that they are *not* intimidated by me in the slightest. This *confrontation* of sorts usually results in some unwarranted and uncharacteristically aggressive behavior on their part.

I can't tell you if this complex is caused by my race, size, or simply because they don't like my face or energy. Maybe it's just an alpha-male thing. Whatever it is, whatever its cause, that's what I intuited in this kid! I could see it written all over his posture and expressions; he was going to challenge me directly!

He reminded me of a student I'd met three years earlier—a kid I'd never met the likes of in Japan— and haven't done so again since. And, I've been searching and waiting for the next one like him!

One thing I've realized about teaching here, and perhaps it's the same everywhere, is that it seems the "same" kids keep coming and going. Or, I should say, the same personality types and characters and even physical appearances keep popping up. I used to think it was due to Japan's historical isolation, that the gene pool is fairly shallow on this island, so there really isn't that much diversity in "breed". Compound that with the identical dogma and indoctrination most kids are exposed to, and the same limited access to "outside" stimuli and propaganda, and you sometimes feel like you're working in a clone factory.

I didn't want to get my hopes up, but the energy I was getting from this new kid had me calling off the search, and partially convinced that after a three-year absence perhaps I was to be blessed once again with another Matsui-kun.

Good lord, has it really been three years?

Matsui was one of several Japanese people who came along at a time when I was struggling in every way imaginable and about to write off Japan and, in particular Yokohama, as a lost cause and an utter waste of my time, talent and energy. I believe to this day that they were godsends, these folks, especially Matsui-kun and Mrs. Betty. They were little miracles placed in my path to challenge every argument I was making against this place, much the same way Aiko—to whom my first book was dedicated—had before I came to live in Yokohama.

And this book is about this unforgettable time when Yokohama finally and permanently endeared herself to me through the remarkable people I've come to know here.

This book is for them.

I'm not big on gratuitous gushing or even showing my appreciation too overtly. But I want to share with them and with you guys the impact they've had on this man's life, and I hope they all will have a chance to read this.

I have, of course, changed all names, locations, and various other details and circumstances so much so that it might take some effort for even the folks being discussed to recognize themselves in my stories. But know that I have dedicated this book to them, and to Yokohama, this beautiful city of ours, with love and undying gratitude.

★ ★ ★ ★ ★

This book begins in 2009, when I was teaching at two junior high schools in Yokohama: Mendokusai Junior High and Syouganai Junior High. I was alternating two weeks of work at each. It was my third year at Mendokusai, my first at Syouganai, and my fourth year overall of teaching in Yokohama.

It was about that time that I started documenting and recording for future purposes what was going on around me. And, thank God I did, because I'd hate to have to depend solely on my memory to share these stories with you.

Some of these tales and anecdotes have graced the pages of my blog, *Loco in Yokohama*. The blog posts were written almost in *real time* as part of a blog-bound literary reality show; it was a series that ran on a regular basis for over two years! I had challenged myself, as an exercise to increase efficiency and become more prolific, to write and publish each story the same day it occurred, and I called this project *Live From Locohama*. It was a huge hit, much like the series that evolved into my first book, *Hi! My Name is Loco and I am a Racist*. However, this series had very little in common with that one aside from its author.

Readers of the first book may recognize that one of these stories, in Chapter 2, was previously published in *Hi! My Name is Loco and I am a Racist*. I included it in that book as a sort of literary trailer for this one. I had always planned to have these stories traditionally published one day, but now that I've gone ahead and started my own publishing company with a bang, thanks to the first book, I've decided to solidify my *own* tradition and publish them myself.

So, without further ado, Hunterfly Road Publishing presents *Loco in Yokohama*

Author's Notes

The majority of the following tales take place at two different schools: "Syouganai" Junior High and "Mendokusai" Junior High.

The stories under the Syouganai Junior High heading occurred during my first and only year teaching at that school. This was a year during which I met two of the most influential people in my life here in Yokohama, Akiyama-sensei and Mrs. Betty, as well as a number of other "characters" who were entertaining, enlightening, and provocative, including Yamada-sensei and Okubo-sensei.

The stories under the Mendokusai Junior High heading occurred during the last of my three years teaching there. It was a challenging and eventful period in which I met the "characters" that most of these tales revolve around, some of whom would become permanent fixtures in my life in Yokohama. Others have left an indelible imprint on my soul and thus are recurring characters in these stories. They are as follows: Kawaguchi-sensei, Takahashi-sensei, Matsui-kun, and Mika-chan.

The remaining tales fall under the heading of "Interlude".

Since there is much more to life here in Yokohama than what happens inside the school, under the "Interlude" heading I've included several anecdotes, errant thoughts, conversations, and tales that occurred outside of the school. Some of these interludes take place on trains, in cafes, and on the streets of this lovely city I've adopted as my home.

1
This is Loco
(Syouganai Junior High)

"Good morning, class."

"Good morning, Yamada-sensei," the class sang.

"This morning I want to introduce you to two new English teachers," Yamada said, in Japanese. "This is Akiyama-sensei. Please say good morning to her. Ready, go. . ."

"Good morning, Akiyama-sensei!"

"Good morning," Akiyama replied to the students.

"And we also have a very special guest! This is Loco. Say good morning to Loco. Ready, go!"

"Good Morning, Loco!"

"Please, Loco, introduce yourself to the students."

I stood there for a moment, rendered speechless. It was a long moment during which I contemplated telling Yamada-sensei why I'd been dumbstruck right then and there in front of the class. But, as a result of a second thought, I didn't.

That second thought being. . .

You know what? I'll come back to that.

Once my shock had worn off and I realized that 40 or so confused young faces were watching and waiting for me to speak, I went into my introduction routine. It was the one I'd been honing since I began teaching in public schools several years earlier. I have to whip it out and dust it off every year at this time for incoming students. It's a critical moment in which I make my first impression, establish what they can expect from me, and what I expect from them. By the end of the intro, most students have a pretty good idea of what they'll be in for over the course of their time with me. They'll know I expect them to make an effort to learn the English I present, or at least participate and go through the motions without being disruptive to those who might want to learn. They'll know I ain't above a little goofiness and some fun and games, within reason. And, they'll know I give respect and expect it in return.

But, this time, my routine lacked the zest and interactivity it usually had. "This is *Loco*" kept echoing in my ears, drowning out everything else.

After the class, back in the teacher's office, I sat at my desk waiting for Yamada-sensei to appear. She didn't. I sat beside Akiyama-sensei, and she was there.

"Akiyama-sensei, where is Yamada-sensei?"

"She is helping out another teacher now. Why, what's up?"

She had a look on her face like she already knew what was up, though.

I liked Akiyama. Actually, I liked her almost from the moment I'd first met her two days earlier. And it wasn't because she'd studied in the U.S. so was not immediately—and, in most cases, perpetually—uncomfortable around me. Nor was it because once she'd learned I could speak Japanese a little, she had no problem using it when we spoke; which was something most Japanese, regardless of English ability, often seem resistant to do. Nor was it because she hadn't asked me if I could use chopsticks, eat sushi, or stomach fermented soy beans.

Nope.

It was simply because, from jump, she proceeded to treat me as just another new teacher at the school—no differently than she'd treat any new acquaintance. And that may sound like a small thing, but unfortunately it wasn't. It was huge. In fact, it was something that hadn't happened since I started teaching in Japan. Something I'd long since written off as beyond Japanese capacity.

We eyed one another, neither flinching. I was sizing her up trust-wise. I wasn't sure exactly what was going through her mind at that loaded moment, but I was pretty sure it was along the same lines.

Experience got the better of me, though. My people instincts had proven to be untrustworthy in Japan a number of times, and I had the scars to prove it.

"Nothing. I was just wondering," I sighed.

"You were wondering why she introduced you as 'Loco' instead of 'Loco-sensei,' right?" she asked, with a smile so lavish with understanding that I felt almost ashamed to doubt her. But, still I held my ground. In addition to the scars of betrayal, I also had fairly fresh wounds still on the mend.

"She did?"

"You know she did! I saw your face when she said it. You looked. . . let's just say, 'surprised'."

If this were some elaborate ruse on her part to exude trustworthiness and get me to open up, it was working.

Hesitantly, ever so carefully, I inched past the danger sign posted at the pond's edge and placed a foot on the ice that covered its surface, increasing the amount of weight I put on it incrementally while listening and scanning for cracks.

"Why would she do that?"

"I don't know. I was surprised, too," Akiyama-sensei said. She'd said this gently, but the words were laced with ambivalence that rivaled my own.

Both feet were firmly on the potentially treacherous ice, now. And it was bearing my weight, seemingly solid as cement.

"I mean," I added. "Would any teacher ever introduce another Japanese teacher by their first name?"

"I've never seen it," she said, bravely joining me upon the ice. Her eyes were wary but she seemed less cautious than me. Her seasoned ice skates dangled harmlessly over her shoulders, but the slightly serrated blades looked ominous and lethal. "Not in over ten years of teaching."

I shrugged.

Then, in a leap of faith, I sat down on the ice and laced up my skates—as did she almost simultaneously. We sat there and gave each other a meaningful look, laden with promise. And, like that, it was done. We were in this together.

Pretty soon we'd be figure-eighting our way toward a lasting friendship.

★ ★ ★ ★ ★

Akiyama-sensei was a new teacher at this school as well. These forty-some odd people bustling around us were strangers to her, too.

Moreover, though she shared ethnicity, language and culture with them, I suspected her time abroad had altered her consciousness just enough to make being a full-fledged, card-carrying Japanese insider not so much an absence of choice, but a matter of choice. And I think some of the others in the office were aware of that which, to them, probably translated into she has options we don't—not to mention being able to communicate fairly fluently in that fornicating foreign tongue with that outsider, whispering and conspiring with him, laughing and giggling to jokes we don't understand—which suggested she wasn't quite as "Japanese" as the rest of them. Having had relationships with several women who'd found themselves in this unenviable position, I'd learned it was a risk any Japanese who had spent a great deal of time in the West had to face.

Akiyama hinted that this was the case at our first meeting when I'd told her I was a writer, and that I was working on a book about some of the challenges of living in Japan as a non-Japanese.

"Really?" she'd asked. "A writer? That's impressive. What *are* some of these challenges?"

"Well, er. . ."

"Come on, tell me," she urged, sensing my misgivings. She'd glanced around to check if the coast was clear, suggesting to me that whatever I said would be kept in confidence.

But, I wasn't ready.

"It's not really a secret," I said, deciding to keep it light. "One of these challenges is . . . at least for me, it is, the, umm, the effort it takes to, er, to not, er, dislike Japanese people."

"You think you need to, ummm, be a foreigner to, er, dislike, er, Japanese people?" she replied, without any hesitation

Our eyes locked, hers sparkling with repressed hilarity. Then we both exploded into raucous laughter that drew inquisitive eyes and a bit of scorn from the rest of the office.

When she could breathe again she said, "You know I'm just kidding."

Like hell she was, and she knew I knew she wasn't.

She'd almost won me over with that disclosure, especially after she'd mocked me. That was showing a level of informality that is rare in these parts and taking the kind of liberty that only friends grant one another.

★ ★ ★ ★ ★

That first week I managed to impress my Japanese co-workers by doing something I'd never done before. I learned all of their names. It's not that it was difficult, but I simply hadn't committed myself to doing it previously.

Why?

Long ago, I discovered that, aside from the English teachers, my co-workers didn't expect me to know their names. This was either because there were too many of them to memorize or because Japanese names are too difficult for foreign brains to retain and for foreign mouths to say—at least that's the implication or sometimes the direct assertion. They'd say such things overtly or imply them by always indicating the person they were talking about by pointing, by offering a description, or re-confirming that I knew the person who belonged to the name they'd used several times. They'd make statements of conjecture like they're hard cold facts, such as, "My name is Shoutarou, Shou-ta-rou. I know Japanese names are difficult for you gaijin, so you can call me Tarou." It's actually pretty annoying because it makes you feel like they think you're mentally challenged. So, this time around, I proceeded with a little homegrown proactivity in order to abort that annoyance before it manifested itself in my new workplace.

On day one, I was provided a seating chart with all of the teacher's names in kanji (Chinese characters). Some of the kanji characters I knew, but most I didn't.

It was my new acquaintance, Akiyama-sensei, who'd given me the chart. And when she did, she wasn't wearing the strained expression I was accustomed to when I received such things. Usually, it was a face prepared for my inevitable failure to understand anything on the page before me. On the contrary, Akiyama-sensei handed them to me with a look that hinted at a challenge. Not that she had expected me to succeed, but she certainly didn't expect me to fail.

This was a good sign of things to come.

What Akiyama didn't know is that Yamada had given me the same sheet earlier, only she'd taken the time to write the names in romaji (Roman characters, English, for all intents and purposes) beneath the kanji version.

Once Akiyama had gone away, I focused on the list Yamada had provided. Syouganai Junior High was almost three times the size of my other school, Mendokusai, and had many more teachers as well as kids. It was a truly intimidating list. I'd struggled to retain teacher names at schools in the past, but the expectation was so low sometimes I concluded, "Why the hell should I bother?" But, this time, I set my mind to it, and used all the mnemonic devices at my disposal.

I associated the person's name differently when spoken than I did when I saw the kanji characters. There were just too many kanji characters with the same pronunciation, but completely different looks and meanings. So, it was easier to remember Yamashita-sensei because he was an overgrown boy built like a human paper weight. It was easy to imagine him as the base of a mountain. "Yama" means "mountain" and "shita" means "under" or "below". And, Tanigawa-sensei? Her mouth ran like a river—mouthing an endless stream of "saas" and "nanikas"—like the Japanese version of a valley girl. (Tani means "valley", gawa means "river"). And so on and so forth.

By the end of my third day, I had everyone's name committed to memory, and put Yamada's list away in my desk drawer while keeping Akiyama's atop the desk.

"Really?" Akiyama said in disbelief, upon learning of my feat of memory. Perhaps the speed with which I did it would even have been impressive if I were Japanese.

"Yep," I said, flushed with pride, and proceeded to call out the teachers' names by face.

"Oh my god!" she cried out, and called all of the other teachers in our area over to witness my little parlor trick.

The greatest satisfaction came from the stumped look on their faces when they saw, live and uncut, that their language was no great unfathomable mystery. Uh-uh, not to *this* western mind! It was *both* memorable and pronounceable by *this* gaijin . . . albeit unreadable.

Akiyama-sensei, though, once the others had been properly impressed and returned to their business, tested me on the down-low.

"That's really impressive! Can you read this one, too?" she asked, writing down a name in kanji. She'd stumped me, of course, and got a big kick out of it.

"Bet you're feeling pretty full of yourself right now, aren't you?"

"I knew it was a trick! I used the same kinds of tricks when I was studying English in the states. You can't trick a trickster!"

"Who is this?" I asked, pointing at the characters.

"Her—over there by the door," she said nodding her head towards a woman about to walk out of the office.

"Oh," I snickered.

"What?"

"Nothing," I said. I still hadn't gotten past my 'first impressions don't mean jack in Japan' jitters with Akiyama—at least not enough to share with her that I had remembered that woman's name, Hasegawa, because she was one of only two hotties in the office, young, with long shapely legs, and a badunkadunk!

Nah, Akiyama and I definitely weren't there yet.

She looked at me like she was a little injured by my continued misgivings. I didn't know how to explain to her what was going on with me. I guess I could have just called it trust issues and left it at that, though.

I certainly wouldn't have minded having a buddy in the workplace, though. It got pretty lonely there sometimes. The loneliness was compounded by the disquiet of being surrounded by some of the kindest, friendliest people on the planet, and knowing that this kindness was mostly due to custom and manners and a social equality I had virtually no chance of ever being a full-fledged part of. This was for a number of reasons, most of which were either beyond my control, objectified me ridiculously, or went against any number of principals I'd been raised to believe were essential for a better world. And the worst part was knowing—from experience—that any relationship I succeeded in creating would hinge on a relatively obscure and exclusive cultural contract fraught with pitfalls. In other words, it could come crashing down at any time for any number of reasons and there was a strong chance I'd never understand satisfactorily what had gone wrong.

★ ★ ★ ★ ★

"Maybe the ALT she worked with at her old school didn't mind, so she probably thought it was OK," Akiyama said in response to my poser about Yamada. "Or maybe she thinks that foreigners don't like all the fuss and formality of life in Japan."

"You think *actual* thought went into this?" I asked. "I was giving her the benefit of the doubt that she'd done it without thinking at all."

"Huh?"

"I mean, she actually thought to tell the students to drop 'sensei' and even 'mister' and to call an adult and a teacher, by his *first name*? Without even considering consulting the adult in question about it?"

"You know what? You're right!"

"Am I overreacting? I mean, is there something I don't know? Is there some kind of gaijin guidebook floating around I don't know about that says—"

"No," she said, laughing. "At least I don't think so."

"May I ask a favor of you, then?"

"Ummm, yes?" she said suspiciously, like we'd known each other for years and she knew that whenever I formally asked for a favor it was always a doozy.

The three of us were due to teach a class again the following period, and there'd be another chance for Yamada-sensei to introduce me. In fact, over the course of the next two days, she would have six more chances due to the size of the school.

Something had to be done.

"Can you *please* tell her? I don't have a problem speaking up for myself but I'm not good at confronting people here. I've done it several times and I'm afraid I might . . .," and this was the second thought I'd had in the classroom, "I might scare her."

She laughed, and then snapped, "Oh, hell, no!"

She said it goodheartedly though.

"C'mon, I'll owe you one," I cried, but I could tell by her obstinate tone that I was just wasting my breath. "She'll see right through me. Trust me, I'm speaking from experience here. I've scared teachers before!"

"I can be scary, too, sometimes," she said.

I believed it. I could hear it in the way she'd refused my request.

"Not as scary as me. C'mon, please, hook me up! "

"No way," she said. "I've got my own problems!"

"Great."

"Sorry."

Some of the best people I've met here were people who could say 'no' definitively, probably because it was so rare.

By the end of the day, we would exchange email addresses and phone numbers, and I'd be calling her by her first name, "Yoko".

★ ★ ★ ★ ★

The next period we met at the classroom and Yamada-sensei went through her routine again.

"Good morning, class," she sang.

"Good morning, Yamada-sensei," they chorused.

"This morning I want to introduce you to two new English teachers. This is Akiyama-sensei. Please say good morning to her. Ready, go . . ."

"Good morning, Akiyama-sensei!"

"Good morning," Akiyama replied to the students, already grinning in my direction.

"And we also have a very special guest! This is Loco. Say good morning to Loco. Ready, go . . ."

"Good Morning, Loco!"

I glanced over at Akiyama-sensei. She had a plastic smile shining on her face. But I could see her real smile peeking out from beneath it, like rice through saran wrap. She was eating this up! More cool points for her.

"Please, Loco, introduce yourself to the students."

"Sure thing!" I said to Yamada, and then turned to the class full of cheery faces. "Good morning. My name is Loco but you may call me "Mister Loco" or "Loco-sensei.""

Smiles were fading fast.

I repeated it in Japanese, adding, "Saying Loco without "mister" or "sensei" is a no-go! Now everyone repeat after me, "Good morning, Loco-sensei!"

They did.

I tried not to look directly at Yamada-sensei during the entire class. I didn't know how my indirect reproach was playing out with her. The class went so well, and she was so cheerful throughout though, that I wondered if she'd even picked up on it. But then, alas, in the middle of the class, she referred to me as Loco minus any title. "Give your papers to Loco once you're done," she'd said. And again, later in the period, "repeat after Loco," she said, so I knew I hadn't gotten through.

So, once the bell rang for the end of class, and as we were gathering our materials, I took a deep breath and called her over. Akiyama discerned with a glance what was about to go down and smiled as she eased her way out of the classroom, winking at me at the door.

Here goes nothing.

"So, Yamada-sensei, I wanted to tell you before class, but I didn't have a chance . . ."

"Tell me what?" she asked.

I had already dragged my feelings—kicking and screaming—into the cell where I keep them in situations like these, but I was concerned they might escape through my eyes or tone. I could have used some sunglasses right about then.

"I just wanted to tell you that, um, that I prefer to be called "mister" or "sensei". You know, like all the other teachers in this school."

"Eeeee!" she said like I was bringing up something so far removed from her reality as to be incomprehensible.

"Don't get me wrong," I said, trying to dial it down a bit, not that English idioms were useful in this regard. She probably had no idea what "don't get me wrong" meant. "Using my first name is OK, if you must, and of course, "mister" is OK too, but, er, unless the title of sensei is reserved for Japanese—"

"Oh my God!" she almost shrieked, drawing the attention of several students in the hallway. "I'm so sorry! Please forgive me, Loco! I mean, Mr. Loco-sensei, I mean, I, I don't know what to say."

She babbled in panic-filled broken English for a few more seconds.

"It's not a big deal," I said, trying to calm her down and stop her from bowing without restraining her physically from doing so. "I just don't want the kids to think of me as one of their buddies, you know? There's a respect factor. I think there have to be certain boundaries, don't you?"

"Of course, of course, you are so right! I have no excuse! I . . ."

"No need for an excuse," I said, and hesitated to continue. Maybe I had said enough for one session. But, why prolong this? Just get it over with. "Also, I don't think the kids should think of me as a very special guest. I'm their English teacher, right? I'm not a visitor here."

"Oh, my God! I'm so sorry."

This went on for about two more minutes.

She was out sick for the next two days.

Great.

2

On Bonding, Bullying and Betrayal

(Mendokusai Junior High)

My eye caught the hand movement and spotted the projectile as soon as it left its source, Matsui-kun.

Takahashi-sensei—the other half of my teaching team—was writing something on the board with her back to the class, so she didn't know she was a target. She probably couldn't imagine being the target of anything thrown by a student. I, along with most of the class, watched this object sail across the room in slow motion on a beeline for Takahashi, only to fall short of its target. It landed somewhere between the first row and the teacher's desk and rolled towards Takahashi's feet.

She never saw it. But I did. And, immediately after, I saw red.

It was the first time I'd felt rage directed at a student. As far as I was concerned, what Matsui did—even if done playfully—amounted to attempted assault and battery. And to make it worse, it was done practically in my face as if to say *you don't even matter in my world, Loco-sensei* confirming my suspicions about how many people here consider my feelings, and I suspect dislodging some other deep-seated insecurities, as well. On top of that, I realized I had about as much tolerance for that kind of shit as my teachers in my elementary school had for it. Zero!

And, before I knew it, before I could consider the ramifications of such an act, I hurled the piece of chalk in my hand across the room and hit Matsui square in the chest. If I had been holding a coffee mug then that too would have been sent flying his way. Perhaps anything as big as a dictionary would have grown wings in my hand.

Why? A little background . . .

First—about Takahashi-sensei—she was still relatively new at this teaching thing. She had been at it for only a year so she was essentially still an apprentice. She behaved very kindly, she was smart, and her English was not awful. But, unfortunately for her, something about her rubbed her co-workers the wrong way. At least, that's what I thought. I mean, I couldn't imagine that the stern treatment, the accusatory tones, and harsh criticism she had been receiving were simply hazing. Hell, I had been working with these same people for almost two years when she arrived and they had—with a few exceptions—from the start shown me a great deal of patience and consideration. It continued even after my "gaijin honeymoon (special treatment and allowances granted because I was a foreigner)" was over.

Even my closest friend in the school, Kawaguchi-sensei, who I'd never heard even raise her voice, so couldn't imagine her doing so, treated Takahashi worse than samurai treated burakumin (Japanese lower caste). Every conversation any teacher, and in particular the female teachers, had with Takahashi seemed to be at the brink of exasperation—like at any point they might either storm away, spit in her face, or drop-kick her.

At first, I thought it was simply jealousy. After all, all of the teachers aside from Takahashi were well over 40 and some over 50, while Takahashi was in her early twenties, fresh from university, bright-eyed and bushy-tailed, cute, and fashionable. What was more, to kick them all while they were down, she'd been blessed or cursed with bountiful breasts and favored tight-fitting cleavage-accentuating sweaters, or at least she used to. But, I couldn't believe it was that simple. Whenever an answer was arrived at without much thought, I questioned it. It was my habit.

So, I asked my buddy Kawaguchi—who seemed quite beside herself sometimes when she interacted with Takahashi—what the deal was. She told me, in no uncertain terms, that Takahashi was a fuck-up and lied to cover up her fuck-ups. I was shocked, but not at the prospect of Takahashi fucking up. She was a new jack. There were bound to be fuck-ups. And I was not even surprised about her lying about it. Hell, there are approximately two ways to deal with having fucked something up—face the music or duck blame. Most people, in my experience, duck blame if possible.

No, what surprised me was Kawaguchi's venom and total loss of decorum. She'd usually hedge around harsh declarations. With her, nothing was ever *absolutely* wrong. It was always a little wrong or different to her way of thinking. Nothing tasted like shit to her. The taste was always just a little odd. She even used fairly formal Japanese when she was addressing students—something very few teachers do. So, who the hell was this woman, I wondered.

She told me about how, on several occasions, Takahashi would screw up such and such a report and lie about it, or she'd be late for meetings and pretend not to have been informed about such and such and blah, blah, blah. While she was talking, I just kept searching her face for some sign of the woman that was there before Takahashi had joined the staff. The woman I knew wasn't petty or malicious at all. Then again we had only worked and sat side by side for a year or two. How well does anybody know anybody anyway? Not to downplay the seriousness of these misdemeanors Takahashi was accused of—and being punished for—but Kawaguchi was going off the deep end over them.

In her first year, Takahashi was the homeroom teacher of a third-year class, but this year, she'd been given a class of first-year students. I actually thought it was a great break for her. The third-year students knew all the ropes and I figured they'd drive her crazy. Just last year, one of the crazier third-year students had hauled off and slapped fire out of the homeroom teacher, but that student had been certifiable—an actual future mental patient—and by no means represented the student body. The first-year students last year had been *so* sweet. You could just eat them up. They spent half the year shy and obedient and the second half just as obedient, but also fun and eager to learn.

This year's deposit of first-year students, however, was another story. It was like there was some kind of rotation equally dispensing the worst of the worst from the worst elementary school in the area among all of the junior high schools in Yokohama,—and it was our school's turn to take on the lot from *that* elementary school.

Poor Takahashi. It was bad enough that she was being bullied by her colleagues, but now she had to figure out how to get a class of future nine-fingered yakuza, hostesses, and pachinko (Japanese Gambling) parlor employees to appreciate studying anything, especially something as utterly useless as English. I started feeling sorry for her, despite my suddenly schizoid buddy's admonitions about her. I hadn't even realized at first that I had become Takahashi's ally. Maybe I commiserated because I saw some parallels between our predicaments. Like me, here she was in an environment where the natives treated her with hostility for reasons mostly beyond her control.

Or, maybe I was just a sucker for a pretty face and bodacious assets.

Sometimes she came to school looking like she was one harsh word away from losing it. What she would do then, who knows. In America, emptying a .45 automatic into your boss or several magazines of M-16 shells into everyone in the office, or simply quitting might be option "A". Here in Japan, people in her situation—who were disliked, and treated like shit, even due to the standard hazing at a new job—have been known to off themselves; suicide seemed to be option "A" and "B". So, I became really concerned about her. I really didn't want anything like that to go down on my watch knowing I could have done something about it.

Sometimes Takahashi and I would have private moments together, like those in the recording studio when we were preparing tests for the students and we needed to record English conversations. We'd be alone in the booth behind closed doors and she'd give me some deep eye contact and say, "Tsukarechatta (I'm tired)."

I'd heard that word used that way several times before—like when I broke-up with my ex-girlfriend. She'd begun using that phrase in reference to our relationship months before as our relationship slowly deteriorated. The nuance being more of "I've exhausted all options," than simply "I'm tired." At those times I'd share little anecdotes about my teaching experiences with Takahashi. I'd tell her stories from my first year at Mendokusai and how trying it was, and continued to be, and how little by little—after I had made efforts to try to fit in—it had gotten more bearable. I'd end these stories with a "so, let's hang in there" so she'd feel less alone.

Whenever I spoke to Kawaguchi about Takahashi, I never failed to mention how well she was coming along and would give her examples of how she'd handled a particular problem or resolved an issue in the class. Kawaguchi was beyond appeasement, though. She'd listen to me, not knowing where I was coming from nor realizing that I had taken on the task of being Takahashi's advocate, and counter every accolade I offered with some slander.

I couldn't really argue with Kawaguchi, though. I too noticed that, though Takahashi was clearly qualified to teach English, she lacked certain other skills necessary to manage a classroom. She was at the bottom of the totem pole in the office and scolded constantly, and it seemed the students—these *worst of the worst* students—sensed her feelings of powerlessness and instability. Instead of seeing someone they should handle with kid gloves, they saw easy pickings. Walking into her class was like walking onto the set of a new TV series called "Kids Gone Loco." Whenever I joined the class and once they saw my face—a face they didn't see everyday due to my schedule, but once every two weeks or so—a ripple of uncertainty would course through the room. "Should we continue to act like we ain't got no sense in our heads or comport ourselves in a respectful manner?" The majority would go with the latter, but there were two kids who opted, unfailingly, for the former.

LOCO in YOKOHAMA

One was Satou-kun, a 13-year old future henchman or "yes man" for some yakuza boss. He didn't have a bone of leadership in his body. He'd just sit quietly waiting to see which way things would go. He took his cues from another student, the boss . . .

Matsui-kun.

★ ★ ★ ★ ★

A little about Matsui-kun . . .

I remember the first time I met him a couple of weeks earlier. I came to the class prepared to do my usual introduction lesson in which I talk about myself—in the simplest English possible— while showing pictures of my family back home in the U.S. In most cases, this is their first interaction with a foreigner so I try to make it a pleasant experience and as entertaining as possible by hamming it up a bit. I used to withhold the fact that I knew Japanese because once they learned that, well, "what's the sense of trying to speak English," some of them would always conclude—that is, those who hadn't come to that conclusion before they even walked in the room.

But, inevitably, I'd slip up by responding to something said in Japanese unwittingly or saying something in Japanese only someone fluent in Japanese would say, or even behaving the way that speaking Japanese modifies one's behavior. Kids pick up on the slightest things.

Matsui picked up on it first.

Matsui was the smallest and had the happiest disposition of anyone in the class. In fact, he was happier than any student I'd ever met, and energetic to the Nth degree.

At first glance you got the impression that he was trying to compensate for his stature with his character, like some Japanese-version of the Napoleonic complex. Only, he did it with a great deal of charm. You find yourself rooting for him and wanting him to be successful. He laughed and joked non-stop and only spoke with the volume on max. He was one of those kids you'd sooner use gentler terms like "rascal" or "mischievous" to describe than "menace" or "delinquent".

Everything except his size reminded me of someone I knew.

It was clear from that first day who the leader of this class was going to be. Most of the students knew each other already having come from *that* elementary school, and Matsui had probably been the leader back there, too. I didn't think about any of this that first day, though. I was too busy trying to make a good first impression and to seriously assess the students' learning styles and abilities. But, Matsui? He was assessing *me*, aloud!

"Loco-sensei! You can speak Japanese, can't you!" he yelled, in Japanese, with the kind of joviality that is hard to resist and expressing joy in every word.

"A little," I said, giving my pat answer.

"You're lying!" he snapped with a raucous giggle. Then, he jumped out his seat and started addressing the class. "Hey everybody, this guy can speak Japanese—better watch what you say!"

Takahashi-sensei was there beside me. This was her homeroom, but I could see in her demeanor that she had already relinquished control of the class. Somehow, in the week before this first lesson with me, Matsui had pulled a coup d'état. While she remained the figurehead lame duck empress, he was shogun. But, this kind of thing was not unusual. In Japanese schools, the teachers pretty much let the kids do as they please and—because of those filial piety elements in the culture—generally that meant study hard and behave accordingly in order to make sure you didn't bring shame to your parent's name. But, maybe 10% of the time, at least in my experience, there were classes who decided that they'd rather run amok.

"Loco-sensei, how did you learn Japanese?" he asked in Japanese, an earnest inquisitive expression on his face.

Since the cat was out of the bag, I replied in Japanese, "I've been living here for several years so—"

"You got a *Japanese* girlfriend, right?"

"What? That's none of your business. Listen, sit down and let's—"

"Loco-sensei's a horny sleazebag! Ha, ha, ha, ha, ha, ha!"

Everybody laughed. I glanced at Takahashi-sensei, again. She turned bright red and started scolding Matsui. Her scolding fell on deaf ears, though. Half the class was held enthralled by Matsui's audacity at insulting this huge, black foreigner while the other half seemed embarrassed or too scared not to laugh. Matsui scanned the room while he held forth from his throne. He apparently siphoned energy from his audience.

Then, he turned to me wearing an expression I could hardly read, somewhere between pity and regret.

"Loco-sensei, I'm sorry," Matsui cried at the top of his voice. He jumped up out of his seat again, ran towards me, and leaped in my arms. I caught him instinctively, and he gave me the warmest, most affectionate hug I'd ever gotten from a student—even warmer than some of the girlfriends I've had in Japan. I was dumbfounded. Here was this little rascal in my arms, hugging me about the neck like it was the most natural thing in the world; I actually thought he was going to kiss me on the cheek. He was light as a toddler and I didn't let him down immediately. It was a moment. We had bonded, somehow.

At least I felt something.

And, I realized just then who he reminded me of. . .

He reminded me of *me,* when I'm drunk.

★ ★ ★ ★ ★

From our first meeting on, this had become our routine. I'd come to the class a little early and catch him rattling windows with his vociferous screeching and menacing of other students. Upon noticing me, he'd stop whatever he was doing and holler, "Loco-sensei!" Then, he'd run-jump into my arms—all hugs and an irresistible quality.

Having routines with students was not unusual. I have about a couple dozen students with whom I have a greeting routine, many consisting of some variation of the pound, high-fives, and handshakes they've seen black people do in movies. But, Matsui simply liked leaping into my embrace, like a loving son might do upon his beloved father's return from a prolonged business trip abroad, or a chimpanzee might do when his favorite trainer shows up with a tasty treat. I think that was the feeling he tapped into, something paternal and protective.

Yep, he'd found my weak point and charmed the hell out of me.

His charms didn't work on Takahashi, though. She saw right through him for the terrorist that he was. He was a non-conformist—something the American in me found admirable—but Takahashi called "trouble" almost from the start. It took me a little while to see what she meant though. I saw Spanky, not Damien.

But it wasn't long before I spied the "666" mark on his scalp.

The following week, he decided that English class was recess, the classroom was the playground, his classmates were his flock, and that Takahashi was the jungle gym, the see-saw, and the swings—*almost* metaphorically speaking. I mean, he didn't actually ride Takahashi—not physically anyway—and his classmates weren't exactly overly willing participants, but the rest is a non-metaphorical description. All learning or even pretense at doing so basically came to an abrupt halt.

I'd been teaching for a few years then, but I'd never had a class like this. At the monthly company meetings, my co-workers would tell horror stories and I'd be like, "That happened in *Japan*! Stop exaggerating! C'mon, that's bullshit! Ain't no student spit at a teacher! Get outta here with that!"

Periodically *The Company* would remind us teachers of certain guidelines on reprimanding and disciplining students. And, to put it simply, the rule was, "Don't!" Don't touch them. Don't scold them. Don't even think about touching them or scolding them. That's not your job. Leave that to the Japanese teachers.

During my first year at the school, there was an isolated incident in which one student who was being bullied by another finally had had enough and went after him in the middle of the class with a pair of scissors. As I approached the student with the scissors stealthily from behind, the Japanese teacher practically dived in front of the damn things to stop him from slicing the other. The way he had thrown himself into the fray led me to believe that maybe the Japanese teacher's guidelines say something to the effect of, "in the event of an altercation, if there is bloodshed, it had better be yours, or heads will roll!"

So, I walked into the Ringling Brothers Barnum and Bailey Circus, and saw Takahashi trying to go through the motions of teaching a class while it was going berserk. She was almost on the brink of tears or collapse and, according to my guidelines that came down from on-high, I should have allowed it. But, fortunately, I didn't have to, at first, because most of the students were a little intimidated by me. By virtue of my maleness, my height and girth, or perhaps even my blackness was a factor—whatever it was—it kept the kids in check. But, one day, it didn't matter anymore, and it only took me a moment to realize how I'd been neutralized.

Yep, you guessed it. It was Matsui, with all his running and leaping and hugging, he'd shown all who'd been intimidated that Loco-sensei ain't nothing but a great big teddy bear. Like Pooh-San (Winnie the Pooh), only *a sleazebag*!

You gotta give him credit, though. He was a bright kid, and pretty courageous.

One of the advantages of not being afraid to be in the limelight and having a very big mouth and no reservations about saying anything that comes to your head to anyone—students and teachers alike—is you're uncommon—in Japan anyway. You're damn near a working-class hero. Add to that the fact that Matsui was naturally charismatic with a joie de vivre, was daring and funny. It's no wonder that half of the class was wrapped around his little finger and the rest kept their mouths shut.

And, if challenged, he was merciless, before, during, and after classes.

Once, in the middle of my lesson, while I was getting the students to repeat some English phrases, Matsui kept taunting another student who was twice his size and sitting clear across the room by telling jokes and making insults. Most of the class was laughing and the rest wanted to.

At one point, the target of his derision said something I couldn't understand. To be honest, I can't understand much of what they say—maybe 50% at best—because the kids speak in code and slang and sometimes the Japanese equivalent of Pig Latin, so it's virtually impossible to catch everything unless you're a 13-year-old Japanese student. But, whatever he said must have rubbed Matsui the wrong way because, at that point he got up, stood on his chair, and threw his pencil-case with a little mustard on it at the other student. He took the blow upside the head like he'd had it coming to him as his comeuppance for challenging Matsui. Then Matsui asked politely, at volume 10, for the student to return the case. And, don't you know, he got up and brought it back to him! Matsui accepted it and thanked him with a nod and a bow, like this was just the way it was and there was nothing either of them could do about it.

Then he looked at me. I'll never forget his eyes that day. He was smiling that same 1000-watts-of-love smile he always shined on me, but in his eyes, there was something there, like wisdom. It was not like an adult's wisdom, but definitely wiser than I feel comfortable with any child around me being. That precocious stare frayed the bond between us a bit, I think—at least for a while it did.

The next day when he saw me in the hallway and came a-running, I side-stepped his leap. He landed on his feet like a cat, turned on me, and the smile had a blackout, revealing something that was always there, but somehow I'd missed it before. It was something dark, unforgiving, and calculating. It was only there for a moment, though, like a glimpse beneath his mask.

Then he turned away and ran down the hallway like the incident had never occurred.

The next day he threw something at Takahashi-sensei, and I threw a piece of chalk at him.

★ ★ ★ ★ ★

"Oooooooooh!" the entire class exhaled aloud. As shocking as it was for me to see something being thrown at the teacher, it was even more so for the reverse. Students looked like I had taken a dump on him. Their looks were so shell-shocked I actually got scared and thought *"Oh fuck, what have I done now?"*

Takahashi turned around from the board at the sound of the students and asked, "What? What happened?"

None of the students said anything, not even Matsui.

Life here in Japan had slowly but surely re-wired my sensibilities as well as my expectations of people, and in particular, kids. So that now, what wouldn't have even caught my attention in the past sets off all kinds of bells and whistles—things like people dropping trash in the street, talking loud, talking on cell phones on the train, drivers blowing their car horns, etc. According to my old sensibilities, these were all misdemeanors, but with my sensibilities re-wired by living in Japan so long, they've been upgraded to punishable felonies.

As was Matsui's throwing stuff at Takahashi.

Looking out at the crestfallen faces of my students, I regretted my overreaction and wondered how it could have come to be. Yes, I was in defensive mode, practically on suicide watch when it came to Takahashi. I didn't know if having things thrown at her by students would push her over the edge, but it couldn't have helped—that's for damn sure. Besides, I believed it was important for us to present a united front against the unruly masses and to show that we had each other's backs. It was especially the case now because, to me, the object tossing represented an unacceptable escalation in bad behavior, and needed to be put down severely and deterred. He had to be made aware that that kind of thing was not going to be tolerated, and Takahashi certainly wasn't going to do a damn thing.

Someone had to do something.

But, aside from the power struggle going on, to be honest, I was a little hurt. I mean, he had really won me over. The bond I felt was real! I liked his hugs the way my mother likes my hugs. I really like physical affection. I loved the way he ran and jumped in my arms when he saw me. It made me feel more human, and in Japan—which has a tendency to be a really dehumanizing society for foreigners—I had, without really noticing it, looked forward to it every time. I didn't care that he was a knucklehead and liked power. I like knuckleheads, and I like power, too. Some of my best friends were knuckleheads at some point or another, but either grew out of it or learned how to put it to good use.

So, I guess you could say I kind of missed him already.

Matsui stared at me for a long time after that, his face frozen in an odd expression somewhere between befuddled and despondent. He was really starting to worry me. Maybe the shock had been too much for him. Or, maybe, he was simply plotting his revenge. After all, he'd lost face big time and he knew that the class was waiting to see how he would handle this. Perhaps he'd never even been challenged before by a teacher. His henchman, Satou, watched Matsui with an open-mouthed gape, then focused his eyes on me. The darkness they held was startling and it took an effort not to squirm beneath their intensity. I made a mental note to watch my back around that one.

Takahashi was walking around the class checking notebooks while I stayed up front trying to look relaxed and pretend like everything was normal. I was hoping this whole situation would just blow over and be forgotten and pretending that all the tension I felt and the drama playing out in my head was just my imagination. I do that sometimes. Call it a survival instinct.

However, when Takahashi reached Matsui, she must have realized that he, and in fact the entire class, had been silent for going on two minutes or so, which was unprecedented. She looked around the room at the various students then at Matsui's frozen stare at me and asked him what was wrong.

"Loco-sensei pss pss pss pss pss pss," he whispered, another first.

Takahashi's face dropped. She turned to look at me, then back at Matsui, then down at the floor where the yellow piece of chalk lay, now crushed—no doubt beneath Matsui's slipper. Then, she looked back at me. The light in her face went out, and I knew that whatever ideas I had about a united front were mine alone.

When she rejoined me at the head of the class, she whispered, "Loco-sensei? Matsui says you threw chalk at him?"

Her tone was incredulous. It was not like she didn't believe him, but like she couldn't believe what I'd done. She was as shocked as the students. Though it was hardly a question, I almost denied it. She probably still would have believed him.

"Yeah," I said, after a moment's hesitation. Then added, "But only after he threw something at you!"

I'd said this in English and hoped she understood it was done in her defense. But her tone was all, "*Say it isn't so, Loco,*" laden with shock and disgust and laced with guilt. It was like she hadn't even heard anything after my affirming I'd done it.

I peeped over at Matsui as the chimes sounded for the end of class. He was still sullen and looked on the brink of tears. I felt pangs of panic-tinged regret coursing through me.

What the hell have I done?

I collected my unused teaching materials, lost in the contemplation of going and apologizing to him. I *had* been out of line, after all.

Then, I caught a glimpse of movement in front of me and looked up. It was Matsui.

"Loco-sensei, I'm very sorry I made you angry," he cried, at a barely audible volume.

"What?"

"I made you angry, right?" he said a little louder, his Japanese spoken like a toddler's. "And . . .I'm sorry. It's my fault."

"Uhhh." Just then I caught a movement behind me in my peripheral vision and I wheeled around swiftly. Satou was back there, but he also wore a mask of shame. He didn't say anything. He never did. He just stood there with his head down.

"I'm the one who should apologize," I said, turning back to face Matsui. "I'm sorry."

"No, no." He bowed and gave me a hug without looking up, his tiny head resting against my gut. Then he turned and marched out of the class into the hallway, Satou in tow, without even a glance back. I stood there trying to figure out if this was a ploy or if his apology had been genuine. Had I neutralized him with a piece of chalk? Was a brief flash of my anger enough to make him rethink his position?

As I made my way downstairs to the teacher's office, I felt like a heavy burden had been lifted off of me.

When I got to the office, I noticed that Takahashi was already there. And, as was becoming a common sight, she was being chewed out by Kawaguchi. I wondered what the matter was but I had learned to keep my distance from my buddy when she was getting in Takahashi's ass about something. She was like a different person, and it was kind of spooky. I felt sorry for Takahashi, as usual. She looked like she was being bitch-slapped by a pimp for giving out freebies. The other teachers in the office were pretending not to notice this, but it was like not noticing a total solar eclipse at midday. It was the Tyrannosaurus Rex in the room.

From what I could gather, Takahashi-sensei had handed in some report late causing "blah, blah, blah" to be "blah, blah, blah-ed". It was more of the same shit. Kawaguchi-sensei ended her harangue with an awful funky and malicious "Da yo ne (and you know I'm right)!" and walked away from her. Takahashi-sensei took her leave of the office, probably to run to the bathroom and weep her eyes dry.

Poor thing.

My desk is next to Kawaguchi-sensei's, so as she passed by I put my head into a textbook and acted like I didn't even know she was there.

"Loco-sensei," she whispered. "Come with me for a second."

I followed her out of the office and into the conference room across the hall. Kawaguchi-sensei usually did this when she had something important to tell me that she didn't want the rest of the staff to know about.

She sat me down.

"You know, Takahashi-sensei, she told me about what happened with the student in her class."

"She *did*!"

"Yeah, she told me that you threw a piece of chalk, and it hit Matsui-kun. Is that what happened?"

"Yeah, basically. He threw something at her and I kinda lost my—"

"He threw something at Takahashi-sensei?"

"Yeah."

"She didn't tell me that part."

"It's not important anyway. I was wrong. I shouldn't have done it."

"Yes, please be more careful!"

"I will."

"Ah! I get it now!" She snapped, and laughed.

"What?"

"Ne, ne (check this out)," she whispered in the echoing conference room we were in, looking around like she was about to let me in on a great secret. "She told me about that when I brought up her latest fuck up. I tell you she is a sneak and a liar, but I know you never believed me, right? Hora (See)! She was trying to use you to get me off her back!"

"You really think so?" I asked.

Kawaguchi just smiled.

I'd like to think that I was the kind of person who wouldn't be fazed by shit like this. I mean, I shouldn't have expected her *not* to tell anyone, right? Hell, I might have been a danger to the students, having taken to throwing things at them. Of course she would feel it was her responsibility in the name of student safety to report it. But, I have to admit that I *was* fazed. I *did* feel betrayed.

And next time my little buddy Matsui gets into one of his tyrannical states, and even if he starts to launch larger objects at whatshername, the dime-dropping fuck-up with the big tits—I won't worry if she's a hazing episode or two from a suicidal date with fate via the front of some speeding commuter train—that bitch is on her own!

★ ★ ★ ★ ★

The following week, I got a call during lunch time. When I saw *The Company's* name on my cell phone, I knew it was something bad or, at best, neutral news. They never called for good news. And then when I heard *him*, it all but confirmed my suspicion that something was amiss.

"Loco, my man," came Tony's silky voice.

Tony had been a manager at *The Company* longer than I'd been working there, and from the first time I'd heard his voice, I knew how he'd obtained and maintained his position. He'd bamboozled the pants off of *The Company,* selling them an image of being smooth and cavalier and possessing utter competence. It was all in his voice. I respected him for having the wherewithal to do it, but that didn't stop me from hating his voice and the mind that engineered it.

"Yeah?"

"How are you today?" he asked, his words ringing hollow from overuse. Like maybe I was his hundredth call that day. But his silk, despite my best efforts, always triggered defensiveness and self-preservation.

"I'm good, what's up?" I said, matching his desire to dispense with the pleasantries and cut to the chase.

He sighed accidentally before swallowing it beneath what passed for his proactively positive voice. But, I'd heard it, without a doubt. Perhaps he'd even intended for me to hear it, an attempt to share a bit of his life with me. The sigh was heavy, laden with hassles he'd rather not spend his life sorting out, but I could hear subtext in that sigh: 'this is how I make a decent living here, while my friends and family back home in the States are getting laid off left and right in a plummeting economy that hasn't found bottom yet, so I do what I gotta do.'

"We've just received some feedback from one of your schools."

I assumed it was related to what had transpired at Syouganai with Yamada-sensei and her failure to insist that the kids show me the proper respect that a grown-ass man deserved. So, unintentionally responding to his sympathy-seeking sigh that had been preempted by the business at hand, I blurted out, "At Syouganai, right? Yeah, I know what it's about, but what was I supposed to do? I handled her with kid gloves, but—"

"Actually, this feedback is from Mendokusai," he interrupted.

"Oh."

"I don't need to know what happened at Syouganai?" he asked, like it were a rhetorical question that he would've ended with the tag question "do I" if he hadn't been sitting in an office filled with his fellow office workers.

"No," I said once I'd pulled my size-13 Timberland boot outta my mouth. "Not at all."

Everything was going well as could be expected at Mendokusai, so I couldn't imagine what he was calling about. Kawaguchi-sensei and I were tight, and if she ever needed or had a problem with anything, she spoke up. That was one of the things I really dug about her from the start—and such candor is, unfortunately, rare here. And, Takahashi-sensei, though she had shown me that she had no qualms with smiling in my face while she twisted a knife into my back—I'd yet to give her reason to give me a bad review. Or, had I?

Oh, Jesus, not again!

"Well, there were a couple of answers to our feedback questions that we felt we needed to forward to you so that you can make the necessary changes in order to remedy the situation."

"I see. Such as?"

"Now, don't get upset."

"I'm not upset," I snapped in my defense. "I'm just. . . anyway, what were the questions?"

He ran off a list of questions that *The Company* sent to the Japanese English teachers for them to answer with "excellent", "very good", "needs improvement," or "poor". Though I hadn't received any "poor" marks, I had received several "needs improvement" marks. One was in the area of spending time with the students outside of the classroom.

I was shocked!

"You mean, aside from the tennis and basketball club activities I join regularly?" I asked sarcastically.

"That's what it says here," Tony said. "It says you don't spend time with the kids."

"Well, that's some bullsh . . . some nonsense!" I said, just as what the issue was exactly hit me like a roundhouse kick in the jaw. The tennis club was mostly second-year and third-year students and so was the basketball club. I hardly participated in any club activities with the first-year kids because . . . Well, just because.

"What?" Tony asked, sensing I had something to add.

"Nothing," I sighed.

"As you know, spending time with the students outside of the classroom is useful for helping maintain a positive atmosphere inside the classroom."

"Yeah, I know. . ."

"And the Japanese teachers will *really* appreciate the effort," he chanted, almost like he'd joined some bizarre management training cult and had been reciting these lines repeatedly for 24 hours straight. He sounded like he needed a break badly, like if he had to repeat these lines to one more teacher he was simply going to snap. "I've even found that the kid's behavior improves exponentially when they see the ALT as someone they can relate to in and out the classroom."

"I got you, Tony. I'm on it," I said.

"Thanks," he sighed, almost gratefully. "Now, you know I can't tell you the teacher's name, but I need to know what your thoughts are about the review and what you intend to do to rectify the situation."

I was picturing my big-titted, dime-dropping colleague filling out this questionnaire, trying to urge *The Company* to urge me to take control of her first-year class so that her life could be easier.

"Loco, you there?" he asked, 'cause I'd gone silent, fuming.

I explained to him that, obviously, I planned to spend more time with the kids—meaning Matsui-kun, Satou-kun and company—and take part in their club activities. I was thinking of things like, oh, who can throw the biggest rock at the teacher, who can design the best tattoo on the bathroom wall, or who can get the most squeeze money from the other students—but I told him that I would do whatever I could do to make She-Who-Must-Not-Be-Named-sensei's life easier.

"That's the spirit, bro," Tony said, silky as a samurai's kimono.

3
A Cursed Smile
(Syouganai Junior High)

LOCO in YOKOHAMA

Official observations of my teaching had a tendency to be nerve-racking, especially when done by a representative from the Board of Education here in Yokohama. But the woman tasked to do these performance reviews understood very well what foreign teachers had to go through living in Japan and working at Japanese schools, as she was a foreigner herself, all appearances to the contrary. Though she wasn't Japanese, I really couldn't tell what ethnicity she was, and after our third or fourth meeting it ceased to matter to me. She looked like a cross between Lena Horne and Pocahontas. I imagined in Japan she was probably often mistaken as a genetic aberration of Japanese descent.

She spoke Japanese fluently, of course, understood their customs and had adopted most of their mannerisms. This was so much so that the Japanese teachers and administrators, upon meeting her for the first time, seemed to respond initially as if she were an interloper wearing Japanese cultural camouflage that didn't quite disguise her foreignness. However, when combined with her ethnic ambiguity and the fact that she was there in the capacity of representing an entity whose authority they were not in the practice of questioning, it forced them to exercise their judgments a bit more judiciously than they normally would with your run-of-the-mill foreigner.

This was an annual review, making this the third time she had come to watch me do my thing and, as usual, I'd had a month's advance notice of her visit, so I wasn't especially tense. At least I wasn't until the beginning of the week, a week during which I had planned to prepare this lesson carefully with Yamada-sensei. However, she had been out sick, again, this time with a cold, or something. She had spent Monday and Tuesday in bed, as per her doctor's orders, and was unable to speak apparently. Her mother conveyed all of this to the school by phone. This left me with no clue about what grammar point we would be teaching, nor had she left word with Akiyama-sensei or any of the other English teachers.

Also, unlike the other English teachers I'd worked with over the years, Yamada liked to make her own lessons. At least I believed this to be the case because she always had. I'd come to the school and there'd be a lesson on my desk that she had taken from some textbook (not our school's) or some internet site. Or, she'd pull me to the side and ask me what I thought of a lesson she'd put together from scratch.

Well, Wednesday came around and Yamada returned to work, just in time for my review. I'd been concerned about her on Monday, as teachers at this school didn't generally call in sick unless they were deathly ill. And two days in a row meant she was dotting the "I"s and crossing the "T"s on her will. By Tuesday afternoon, once I knew I was going to be heading into a lesson to be reviewed by the Board of Education half-cocked thanks to her, my disposition had made the leap from "hope she's alright" to "bet that bitch is at the beach!" However I did manage to smile when I said good morning and asked after her health.

I had a full schedule that day so I didn't have time to meet with her, except for a few minutes before home room and a few minutes after lunch. With no time to plan a proper lesson, I suggested we do a game in which the kids break up into teams and construct sentences using sentence fragments found on slips of paper. The team to construct the most sentences correctly wins. Yamada was cool with that. She probably would've been cool with group meditation on English. She looked like she'd been dragged bodily to the office, like death warmed over wearing a surgical mask.

Well, it wasn't a traditional lesson but the BOE lady wasn't disappointed with it. In fact, my observation went rather well, all things considered. She told me I clearly had a rapport with the students and handled them with care and professionalism.

"You could dish out a little more praise though. The kids really need it," she added.

"That's true. They do respond well to praise," I responded.

I took notes dutifully during the feedback and asked questions to clarify her remarks.

"You have an incredible smile, Mr. Loco," she said, looking at me like, contrarily, she'd said something I ought not to place too much stock in. "A powerful smile, which is both a blessing and a curse."

"Can you clarify that statement please?" I asked, diligently, pen in hand.

"Well," she began. "Your smile is radiant! I mean, I meet and observe a lot of teachers all over this city, and I remember little things about each one. And the one thing I remember about you is that smile of yours. I actually looked forward to seeing it today!"

"Thank you," I said, feeling a little embarrassed. Of course I'd heard such things about my smile before, but rarely had I received such flattering remarks in a professional setting. I suddenly felt a red flag go up. . . right up my spine via my rectum! She was setting me up like the pro she was, cushioning the fall with a little misdirecting sweet talk.

"Your smile lights up a room," she said through a well-maintained set of pearly whites. "But, it also has the effect of turning that light off when it's absent. You know what I mean?"

"Yeah, I guess," I replied nervously, still waiting for the other shoe to drop. "I need to smile more, right?"

"Yes! Even if it's fake. A fake smile is better than no smile, especially for you!"

"My curse," I sighed.

"Exactly," she said, with a finality that almost made me think she was wrapping up. I was about to put my pen away when she Lieutenant Columbo'd me with a, "One other thing . . ."

Ah, here it comes. . .

"Uh huh?"

"A little earlier we had a short meeting with Yamada-sensei, poor thing," she said, and she was no longer smiling. Pearly whites became pursed lips set in a grim grin. Lasers from her eyes scorched my eyelashes. "She had some complaints, no, I shouldn't say complaints. She had some concerns."

"Concerns?"

"Yes. Just the one concern actually."

"Concerning?" I asked, but regretted it immediately. I was getting defensive. I heard it in my tone. And if I heard it I knew she heard it, too.

"Everything is fine, Loco. No need to get upset," the BOE lady said like, despite appearances, she was on my side and we were in this together. It was in her tone.

We were sitting in the principal's office having this meeting. Rather large black & white framed photographs of every principal of Syouganai from the school's inception during the American occupation after WWII up 'til now on the wood-paneled walls surrounded and looked down on us as we sat on leather sofas facing one another. There was a fancy coffee table between us, a lovely coffee service atop it, with little porcelain coffee cups and delicate saucers with ornate and flowery designs.

The principal was actually sitting at his desk a few feet from us, shuffling paper around and, I was pretty sure, listening to every word we said. But, being Japanese, even if he could speak a little English, which I doubted, there were certain things he wouldn't be able to pick up on, like her tone.

Her tone said *this is how they do things! And believe me, brother, I know how you feel. I've been here way longer than you and when you leave I'll still be here, and I didn't get to this position being nobody's fool! So listen to me. Learn from me, and trust me. Don't you dare get uptight with her. It ain't worth it, and in the end you will have only made things worse. She's just being Japanese.*

"You understand?"

"Of course," I said, responding to her tone, and to things that would remain unsaid. "That goes without saying."

"Good," she said. "Well, she mentioned that she had been out of the office Monday and Tuesday this week and so your lesson was kind of done on the fly."

"Yeah, but . . ."

"It's not an issue," she said, cutting off my defense a little sharply. I decided to just relax, then. Whatever will be will be.

"I really enjoyed the class," she added.

"Thanks."

"She also said that she is usually pretty busy, so she doesn't have time to meet with you as often as she'd like . . ."

"Uh, huh," I said, 'cause she'd paused.

". . . And, she'd appreciate it greatly if you would take a greater role in lesson preparation because, with all of her responsibilities over the course of a day, she just doesn't have time to prepare lessons, too."

"She doesn't?"

"That's what she said."

"She's been preparing her own lessons since I've met her."

"She would like *you* to prepare the lessons."

I was about to ask the BOE lady, who happened to love my smile, why, instead of taking it to the Board of Education, essentially my boss' boss' boss, and being that I've sat at my desk since I've met her happily preparing lessons for the other two Japanese English teachers, not to mention helping her tweak her own, why didn't she just tell me that she'd like me to prepare her lessons, as well?

But I knew better than to ask that rhetorical question.

The BOE lady watched me suffering, choking on my unasked question and said, "Well, Mr. Loco, that's it for now. Ganbatte ne (Hang in there)! And, please, don't forget to smile!"

I gave her a big shit-eating dose of this cursed smile of mine and left her talking with the principal. When I went back into the teacher's office, I spotted Yamada-sensei at her desk looking haggard. She glanced up at my approach with that same nervous look she always has. I never paid it any undue attention before because many teachers, hell, most people who I encounter in Japan, have that same nervous look around me. I just figured that it was the default expression in these parts. But now I could see her nervous look for what it really was.

"I think we need to talk," I told her, standing over her with a big plastic smile on my face, showing a mouthful of coffee and tobacco stained choppers. "You got a sec?"

★ ★ ★ ★ ★

When I first started working for *The Company* I was told that they hired teachers for elementary, junior high and high schools and was asked which I preferred. I'd told them anything but an elementary school would be OK. I'd had my fill of preteen kids during my tenure at NEON (an English school franchise in Japan). So, naturally when I received my first assignment it was to cover not one, not two, but five elementary schools. Only temporarily, they'd said, until there was an opening at a high school. My commute to these schools was a hell of a daily hike, but I did it for a few months without complaint. I needed the job.

Little did I know those mostly rich spoiled brats I taught at NEON in Shinjuku were atypical. The kids at these schools out in Yokohama were like a breath of fresh air. They were so much fun that time just flew by. And the syrup on this sundae was my work day would end sometimes as early as noon.

Can't beat that with a baseball bat.

When the High School opening came along, I almost turned it down just to keep those lovely hours with the charming kids at the elementary schools. But the convenience of the high school was too good to refuse. It was two stations from my house and that pretty much mitigated any time disparities. I could sleep an extra hour every morning which meant a great deal with my sleep schedule because I write best at night and often do so until the wee hours. An extra hour was worth its weight in bluefin tuna.

And, man, was I glad I did. This high school was *great*!

I thought.

It wasn't an international school; it was a public school, but there were many exchange students there from all over Asia, and most were English-speaking. And, there were many English-speaking returnees (Japanese who had lived abroad for years) and very high level Japanese English students from all over Yokohama. Their abilities were so high that language classes were held completely in English. I assigned and corrected essays written by students from Indonesia, Singapore, and Australia as well as Japan. I even contemplated starting a writing workshop for those interested in creative writing. The students didn't wear uniforms. They could dress however they liked, as could the teachers. And, the icing on this cake was I was invited to play with the basketball club twice a week and we'd have actual full-on competitive games!

The head of the Foreign Languages Department (they actually taught French, German and Chinese as well at this school) was a woman named Ono-sensei. She was also an English teacher. She was a real sweetheart. She sat beside me and every day we discovered we had more and more in common, and over time developed a rapport I have seldom experienced in Japan. In particular, we shared a love of cinema, especially films by Woody Allen and the Coen Brothers. She could even appreciate Charlie Kaufman. I mean, we *really* hit it off.

I thought.

I helped her plan lessons and together we executed the syllabus she had put together long before I had joined the staff. It was an agenda she'd created with the previous ALT, some bloke from England I'd never met as he'd left the country when he left *The Company*. The agenda actually included a trip to England with the students to spend some time in a high school somewhere north of Manchester. I wouldn't be accompanying the class (thank god) because I had joined the staff after the deadline for down payments. But, Ono couldn't stop talking about how much she was looking forward to getting back to jolly old' England. She'd apparently done a home-stay there when she was a young woman, some 30 years ago, and the impression has been a lasting one, molding her into the professional she is now.

However, despite having been exposed to English as a career for over 30 years, her English still was only at a level where she could communicate and be understood. It was nowhere near the vicinity of fluent and heavily accented with Japanese.

Whenever she'd get to gushing over England, I'd find myself saying to her constantly, "Oh, that's nice." "Oh, you went to the Isle of Wight while you were there? Wow. That's nice." Her accent wasn't British, but she swore it was and I didn't argue. "Oh I can hear it a little . . . wait . . . yeah, yeah, yeah, I can hear it. How nice!"

Anyway, this went on for a few months. Then one day while we were teaching a class, and she was using me as a human CD Player ("just listen carefully to Loco-sensei's reading of the passage") there was an incident.

One of the students, a Japanese one, a returnee who had lived in England with her parents and had recently returned to Japan, asked me if I could repeat a word because she couldn't quite catch it.

"Sure, which word?" I asked.

"Actually I'm not sure what he was trying to say. There were several words I couldn't catch," she said in Japanese to Ono-sensei, like I were merely a CD player.

In Japanese, Ono-sensei responded to the student and included the other students when she said, "Loco-sensei's accent is a little strange and not standard. He's American and from New York so those of you accustomed to the proper English spoken by Oliver-sensei will have to endure. So sorry."

She said this with smiles and nods to her students and at me. I wasn't nodding, but she probably thought I didn't do so because I couldn't understand a word she was saying as opposed to my catching every other word and not appreciating what I heard at all. At the time, my speaking level of Japanese was very low, and since I never had to use it at the school, because everyone seemed to speak English, it wasn't likely to improve while I was working there. So, Ono had assumed I didn't understand Japanese at all.

"I beg your pardon," I said, in front of the class, in English. Ono looked at my face, searching for the smile I usually wore effortlessly, the one that wasn't there anymore. It had been replaced by dismay and a little shock. Maybe even a little of my temper spiked to the surface. Her unprofessionalism was off the charts in my book! "Did you just say my English was not as good as the previous ALT's? Maybe I misunderstood you."

I hoped.

"Well, er, ummm, er, it's your accent, Loco-sensei. The students are having trouble with it. . . I'm so sorry!"

She was turning a deep shade of red at being busted.

I reminded myself that I was not the boss in this room, and quickly tried to cease hostilities and return to my role of underling.

"I'm the one who should be sorry, I cried. "I'll try to speak more standard English if you like."

Then, I started choking on these words and sarcastically added, "I've watched a lot of Monty Python and listened to a lot of The Beatles' songs in my days."

She was still in shock, eyes open wide and mouth breathing, at my having comprehended what she'd said, knowing good and damn well she shouldn't have said anything even approaching it.

But, I'd let it go as I broke into my rendition of "My Fair Loco". The students enjoyed my Eliza-Doolittle gutter cockney accent as well as my Hugh-Grant-Four-Weddings-and-a-Funeral Queen's English impersonation. Both were pretty awful but so different from my "New York", or to hear Ono tell it, "substandard" accent that the kids found it hilarious. I patted myself on the back for skillfully cleaning up the tension I'd caused with humor.

I thought.

Later, in the office, Ono apologized again, this time profusely. Even saying "moshi wake gozaimasen" (a super polite apology) and genuflecting contritely which was the strongest sorry I'd received in all my years in Japan. Of course I accepted it.

"I'm sorry I got upset, " I said.

"Oh no," Ono said. "It's all my fault!"

"But, don't you think more people in the world are exposed to the accents used in America than in England, through music, film, television, books or magazines?"

"I don't know," she said.

"Well, I'm pretty sure that's the case," I said. "So if any English is the standard these days, it's probably spoken in America. You don't think so?

"You're probably right."

"Not that I agree that there is a Standard English," trying to change the tone of the conversation from apologetic to more of a conversational one. "But I think there was a time when the Queen's English was considered the standard. I think today, however, that's just not . . . realistic."

"Hmmmm," she replied, nodding like she'd had a change of heart and been shown the error of her thinking, and from that day until the end of the year, our relationship had one added element, mutual respect.

I thought.

That is, until I heard the result of the questionnaire about ALT quality that had been sent to Japanese English teachers to fill out and return to my company. Mine stated that one of the teachers at the school, no names of course, felt that I was not a good fit for their school. That I did not live up to the standard of English excellence the school had built its reputation on and that that person was afraid I would tarnish it somehow. And thus I was not welcomed to return there the following semester.

I couldn't believe what I was hearing when this information was forwarded to me from *The Company*. They'd put it to me as gently as possible, so as to spare my ego, and added that "sometimes these things happen without the ALT having a clue what was going to go down. That's how it is here sometimes. We'll find you another spot, don't worry. You're still in good standing with us."

And that's how I'd come to work at Mendokusai, and eventually made my way to Syouganai, standing before Yamada-sensei, deciding how to put what I wanted to say to her.

★ ★ ★ ★ ★

"Yes, what would you like to talk about, Loco-sensei?" Yamada-sensei asked, her smile trembling feebly on her face.

"Well . . . do you like to make lessons for our classes?" I asked, making sure my smile was intact.

She flinched and said, in Japanese, "well, kinda, sorta. . .," which I've learned is as strong a "no" as you're gonna get sometimes. But I treated it like a halfhearted yes.

"Well," I said, keeping upbeat. "I really like making lessons! Actually, I *love* it!"

"Really?" she asked a little suspiciously. "I didn't know that."

"You didn't? Haven't you noticed that I make all of Akiyama-sensei's lessons, and Okubo-sensei's, as well?"

"I did notice that," she said, her smile growing just a little brighter, perhaps anticipating where I was going with this conversation.

"And the students really seem to enjoy them. At least I think they do."

"Yes, I heard from both of them that the children really like your lessons," she said, rising from her crypt of illness and despair and looking almost as giddy as a school girl herself.

"Well, here's what I wanted to say: You seem to be very busy quite often. Sometimes I worry that you are working too hard," I said with great gravity, laying it on a little thick, wondering if I should pull back. "I mean . . . I know that you enjoy making your own lessons, but, can I please make a few lessons for you?"

"Well, I . . ." she began, about to no doubt humbly accept.

"You don't have to decide now," I said, cutting her off like I had been expecting a negative response. "Just let me do it for a few weeks, maybe a couple of months, on a probationary basis, you know? And if you don't feel like the students are benefiting or enjoying the change, we can go back to your wonderful lessons. How about it? Will you please give me a chance?"

She stared at me for a tense second and I wondered if I'd poured it on too thick.

"I think that's a great idea!" she said.

"Well, alright!" I cried out, trying to restrain the pressing urge I felt to tell her, 'if you had said or even hinted, even subtly, that you wanted me to make your lessons we would have been where we are now weeks ago, without the involvement of the Board of Education or *The Company*!'

But I bit my tongue, as I was sagely advised to do, and smiled.

Interlude

Chikan Chicanery

LOCO in YOKOHAMA

I could feel the awkward pressure against me, his bodily insistence that I move aside when I was not obstructing his path. Besides, I discerned with a glance that ample space awaited him in the other direction. If this were New York I would've thought he was a pickpocket or nutcase, but this is Yokohama, and the mere fact that he was touching me voluntarily was a red flag in and of itself.

What the hell was he up to?

At the next station the doors slid open and more people filed in. I am accustomed to being surrounded by what has come to be known as the "gaijin perimeter"—a perimeter Japanese tend to place around foreigners in their effort not to come into contact with them—whenever I ride the trains. Sometimes this perimeter is gaping, and sometimes it's pretty tight. The size varies from day to day, but it's generally there. I've learned that people who dare to enter this perimeter sometimes have an agenda.

This guy certainly did.

I've also observed that, once the perimeter is breached by one bold or determined commuter, others will follow suit. It's as if the initial breacher has informed them using some secret Japanese Masonic-like code. "Come on in! The water's warm!"

And, that's just how it went that morning. People filed in, glimpsed me in all my conspicuous foreignness, hesitated—or froze causing a logjam, crashing into and stumbling over one another like something out of a Three Stooges or Charlie Chaplin movie—then, noticing the breacher's rather close proximity to me, decided I must be relatively safe and bounded for any available space even if it brought them within the perimeter.

To my left was a high school girl wearing a traditional uniform with the skirt hiked up rather high, but no higher than can commonly be seen on any given day during any season. She favored one of the kids who had graduated from my junior high school a couple of years ago, but it definitely wasn't her. She was writing a text to someone, her thumb a tiny racing blur.

The space to my right, previously vacant, was now filled by one of the "Women in Black", the uniform for freshmen office workers here.

My rear was occupied by the breacher.

As the passengers boarded, I could feel increased pressure on me. A couple of commuters wanted to get by the breacher to the vacant space on his left, but his hand was gripping the strap over my shoulder like doing so was the only thing that stood between him and prematurely meeting his ancestors face to face. So, the passengers had to squeeze around him.

The red flag became a fire alarm! With not only the option of moving, but the insistence that he do so coming from his fellow nationals, he fought to stay close to *me*? What the hell!

I turned around for the first time to take a good look at this guy. In sync with the turn of my head, he upturned his face and took a closer look at the train's ventilation system. It fascinated him—like he'd never noticed before how intricate yet practical its design was, or at least his expression said as much. But I knew it was just a piss poor effort at chicanery. There was no way he was going to sell me on the idea that he loved ventilation so much that he'd fight crowds the way he had to merely examine them.

What the hell was he up to?

He was your typical "salaryman", 50-ish, wearing a dark suit with striped tie, and a little shabbily groomed with facial stubble and hair that was unusually unkempt, but he looked decent enough. He had a briefcase in his right hand and nothing in the left. Could he be a pickpocket? I couldn't even imagine that if he were he would mark me as a target.

But he was up to something. I just knew it.

I returned to facing forward as the train pulled away from the station. I could feel his breath on my neck. It was a very unusual feeling here—at least for me—to be breathed on. It smelled like this morning's fermented soy beans, miso soup, rice, and fish, and I counted my blessings that I was spared this torture most mornings. That was one of the unsung benefits of the perimeter.

The school girl beside me almost dropped her cell phone suddenly. She caught it, glanced at me kind of coyly, brushed the hair out of her eyes, and went back to thumbing her message. That reminded me that I needed to send a text to my student to confirm our lesson that evening.

Then, abruptly, she jerked slightly, like she'd been pricked with a needle she'd been expecting from a trusted source like her family physician. She sort of half glanced behind her, as if she were checking the shoulder of her jacket for dandruff.

That's when the pieces began to fall into place. The reason for his position behind me, slightly to my left, and his reluctance to be moved from his established beachhead became clear. I had a pretty good idea what he was up to now, or at least I thought I did.

At the next station, a good number of people got off. Some people from my left headed by me for the door to my right. I watched peripherally as the breacher made way for them, actually exiting the car and standing on the platform that I could see through the windows. After the last departing passenger had exited, he let a few newcomers board before him.

Without the breacher occupying the perimeter and attesting to its safety and my civility, the first few people of the new swarm hesitated then fled to available spaces as far from the perimeter as possible. Once he re-boarded and headed back to his position behind and beside me—affirming the harmlessness of the area within the perimeter—the swarm behind him closed in. Again, he grabbed the strap over my shoulder and let the swarm push its way by him, like a man holding a tree branch just before the edge of a cascading waterfall.

That was enough confirmation for me. He was a chikan (groper) definitely.

The high school girl was still thumbing away at her phone, apparently oblivious to the efforts this pervert was making. On the far side of her was another salaryman. Out of the corner of his eye, I could see he was alert and suspicious of what was going on down below. And he was in a much better position to see what was happening, as all he really had to do was look down, and then to intervene. But, he actually turned his head away so that he couldn't see.

Jesus!

As the train sped up, I was being shoved closer to her by the swaying commuters, so that now, involuntarily, I was up against her, too. My left hand, which held my briefcase, was against her thigh. I tried to switch my briefcase to my other hand so as not to be mistaken for the one enjoying this ride too much, but it was tightly wedged against her, as was his. Judging from his height and hers, his hand had to be wedged in the crack of her ass. And with the shortness of her skirt, it was probably wedged under it.

How convenient for him.

I glanced down, but all I could see was her navy blue skirt. Then, when the train jolted a little, I caught a glimpse of her white lacy underwear and a sallow-looking hand on or in them. I couldn't tell which because it was so quick.

I had to make a decision. How much did I want to be a good Samaritan? It had become an issue for me since I'd been living here and treated in a manner that makes me actually pause and question whether I should get involved or let the Romans do as Romans do and mind my own business.

The train braked hard and I thought to use this opportunity to switch my briefcase to my other hand, but another idea just popped into my head.

And I got involved.

Pretending to be thrown off-balance, I thrust my briefcase between the guy and the school girl—knocking his hand away from its position on her hind end, which had to hurt and would certainly leave a mark. Then I grabbed the strap above the school girl and held on as tightly as he had. I could feel his effort to get me to shift back to my previous position so that he could do the same and resume his groping, but I held fast. A few moments later, the train jolted again and I felt a strong, sharp, determined elbow against my ribcage telling me in no uncertain terms, "move motherfucker, this is my catch of the day!"

There was nothing passive about this guy.

The train was pulling into the station at that point so I relinquished my grip on the strap. As it slowed, the elbow that was against my ribs sharply thrust into me, purposely, I suspect, but it could arguably have been an accident. It hurt, though! It hurt like it had been done by someone familiar with how to disable people with a blow. I turned around to face him but, as I did, he realized he hadn't finished studying the ventilation system yet.

Motherfucker!

I took a strap again—urgently, like I'd lost my balance—only this time it was a strap on the other side of him. In doing so, I just missed elbowing him in the back of the head by inches. He'd ducked when I reached across him.

Fuck!

The doors opened and I watched him hustle off the train. I turned to check on the school girl, but she had queued to get off the train through another door. By the time I got to the platform the chikan was nowhere in sight.

★ ★ ★ ★ ★

One of the curses of being unusually observant is that I see these perverts plying their trade maybe two or three times a week here, especially in the summer months. They're a plague on the trains here in Yokohama.

And, if I'm in the vicinity, I usually intervene. Especially if the target is a teenage girl, any of whom could be a current or previous student of mine.

But sometimes, when I'm feeling especially disgusted with the Japanese men on the train who are pretending to be unaware that the girl standing beside them is being flagrantly groped or molested—but simultaneously ultra-aware enough that they've maintained minimum safe distance from me—I'm tempted to leave the Japanese to their own ineffective devices like women-only cars and cameras on the trains.

I'm just saying . . .

4

Bipolar Bear Hug

(Mendokusai Junior High)

Working at two schools two weeks at a time means every other Monday morning I arrive at a school after a two-week absence and walk into the office like I belong there (because I do). But, aside from the English teachers and a few select others, the staff generally need a time-out to adjust to having a foreigner in their midst. Some act as if they're surprised to see me again, like I'm some kind of serial tourist or English day laborer on the hunt. Others take it a step further and start at my appearance as if I were some foreigner who'd fallen off the tour bus and just wandered into their office off the street. It never fails. To these people, I'll always be that special guest Yamada-sensei tried to label me as no matter how long I stay in Japan.

So you can imagine my relief when I reached my desk next to Kawaguchi-sensei's and she said, "Loco-sensei, you look like hell! Didn't you sleep last night?"

I could have kissed her.

Nothing truly says good morning here in Japan like someone saying or doing something decidedly un-Japanese, meaning free of awkwardness, overextended courtesies, and platitudes. It's so humanizing it feels like a hug.

"What do you think?" I replied, shaking my head. "*He* was at it, again!"

I used to blame my roommate for my sleepless appearance sometimes, in lieu of telling the truth, that I was up half the night writing about what I had spent half the day doing. Namely, teaching these amazing kids and struggling not to despise the adults that spawned them.

Then I winked, suggesting that I had some juicy tidbits to share with her later over a cup of coffee at Starbucks or a couple of beers at a bar after work, as she and I would do from time to time.

My roommate at the time, a German cat, Aryan through and through, with those master race traits that most J-girls get all hot and moist over, was not the kind of guy to turn away a pretty face. He reminded me of how I used to be when I first landed here. He used to have a stream of enthusiastic girls flowing in and out of our house at all hours of the night, and he'd do them all, and do them well, with reckless abandon. The thin wall between our rooms was never even a consideration. Or maybe he was trying to impress me, black guys being stereotypically known for sexual prowess and what not. Or perhaps he was some kind of audio exhibitionist who got off on the fact that he knew he might be overheard. I never could get a read on that guy.

Moreover, my being an American, and having been inundated with dark Nazi stereotypes and ridiculous German tropes my entire life, it was hard not to think of the evil Amon Goeth of Schindler's List or those goofy gulag sergeants on Hogan's Heroes when listening to a citizen of Deutschland speak, let alone his grunts and cries of passion when ravaging Japanese groupies.

So, occasionally, I'd give Kawaguchi one of those stories. Sometimes it was on the up-and-up, and sometimes just for entertainment purposes. She loved to hear decadent stories of westerners that confirmed her too-embedded-to-dislodge presumptions about non-Japanese living in Japan. She didn't have many, thank God, but it would be impossible, in my experience, to be Japanese and not have any.

One of these ideas, a humorous one, at least for me, was that foreign guys come here and stay here because they believe Japanese girls are easy and unburdened by so-called western morality. "But, the funny thing is," she told me once or twice when she was being generous with her theories, "what you guys don't know is that these girls are usually outcasts from any semblance of respectable Japanese society." I remember the first time she told me that. I just stared at her, waiting for the punch line, resisting the urge to laugh and say, "*And*? As if . . ."

One thing I've struggled to do but is an extremely useful skill when working in the Japanese workspace (mostly because it's the rare person that's going to address it openly) is to read the atmosphere. Usually the change is so subtle you'd have to be a meteorologist or the sociological equivalent of Sherlock Holmes to deduce it. Sometimes, however, the atmosphere is so thick with disquiet that even someone as culturally removed as me can read it. The atmosphere in the office that morning was tense enough to cut with a dull sword, which subtly hinted something was awry.

"What's going on?" I asked Kawaguchi, nodding at the room. She did her thing when she wants to divulge an office secret, where she looks around, leans in, and speaks in hushed tones.

"One of the first-year students brought a knife to school on Friday, and . . ."

"Who? Let me guess: Matsui-kun? Satou-kun?"

I guess I should have been more surprised, but I wasn't.

"No, no, no. . . it was a girl!"

"Really?" Now that was surprising.

There was only one girl in the entire school I could even imagine doing something like that. She was a first-year student by the name of Mika. I had already pegged Matsui and Satou as future yakuza from the first week of school, but I didn't know what to make of Mika. She wouldn't make the cut as a Yakuza for I imagined one of the prerequisites of joining that fabled criminal enterprise would be some indication of mental stability; at a minimum, sane enough to understand chain of command. Mika had yet to display, at least to my satisfaction, that she even knew the difference between right and wrong, good and bad, even between teacher and entity placed here for her entertainment. She was *out* there. So I had written her off as a totally mental.

"Don't tell me Mika-chan. . ."

"Who else?"

"Did she stab a student?"

"No, no, no . . ."

"She didn't stab a teacher?"

"What? No!" she said, looking astonished at my suspicions, which were apparently beyond the scope of conceivable for her. "Of course she didn't. She just showed it to a student."

"Showed it?"

I was picturing Mika showing a butcher knife to the throat of one of her classmates, laughing hysterically the way she had when she kicked me in the ass the day we first met, establishing, at least for me, that her Happy Meal was shy of fries.

"What the *hell* is your problem?" I'd yelled at her that day, totally uncharacteristic of me. But she didn't know nor did she give a fuck about my characteristics. She'd made a sad face like a clown or a pantomime does and then abruptly burst into wild laughter, jumping around and pointing at me. Then she made like she was going to kick me in the balls, actually looking at them and pointing. So, what did I do? I tried to *gaijin* her ass into submission, something that had a pretty high success rate with some of the unruly kids. I unveiled my "I'm an unpredictable foreigner and I don't play by Japanese rules! *I. will. hurt. you. real. bad.* if you even think about lifting that foot, you crazy little fuck!" glare.

Her foot missed my nuts by inches, actually grazing my zipper.

She didn't even hesitate. If I hadn't leapt back we both would have needed hospitalization.

"Ha, ha, ha, ha, Loco-sensei is an idiot!" She hollered in Japanese. Other students from her home room were watching this with looks of pity and fear on their faces.

Oh my god! What fresh hell is this? I remember thinking.

So, while Matsui and Satou had the run of the other first-year class, Mika ran hers, and apparently she ran the home room teacher, the very prissy chichi foofoo Okawa-sensei, too.

Okawa-sensei was sitting across the aisle from us and looking very distressed indeed.

"Good morning," I whispered in her direction.

She waved and swiftly affixed to her face that same smile she always hits me with, like Miss Japan at the airport waving hello to her cheering supporters upon returning to Tokyo after winning first runner up in the Miss Universe contest— having lost to a black Miss France— mortification smoldering behind her green tea-stained teeth.

I noticed that bitch, Takahashi-sensei, seated next to her, was watching me. Maybe she was wondering if I knew that it was her blade in my back, that she was the one who'd given me those "needs improvement" marks on her review of my performance (fucking with my money) simply because I wouldn't do what she was being paid better than I to do. In fact, something I was told explicitly *not* to do. Namely, discipline her kids. I tossed a grin in her general direction. She smiled and waved, cheerily, in return.

Just one big happy family, we were.

I wondered which one of them had a bigger knife, Mika or Takahashi.

★ ★ ★ ★ ★

Later that day, I called *The Company* and Silky himself answered the phone.

Me: It's Loco over at Syouganai.
Tony: Loco, my man, how are you?
Me: I'd be better if I'd gotten a raise this year.

Tony: I understand how you feel. It's just this economy, you know how it is.
Me: Whatever, man. I didn't call about that, though. I knew you'd give me the party line if I did.
Tony: Well, there are other factors. Do you wanna hear them?
Me: Only if I haven't heard them before. If you're gonna tell me these whimsical ass teachers' assessments of my performance are a factor, you can stow it.
Tony: You know, Loco, sometimes I get the feeling you don't like me very much.
Me: Tony, *my man*, sometimes I get the feeling it's not your job to be liked and it's not my job to like you. But, if it's any consolation, I know, under different circumstances, you're probably a likable guy.
Tony: Ha, ha, ha, you're funny, Loco!
Me: Can't lose our sense of humor in this man's land, now can we?"
Tony: Truer words have never been spoken.
Me: OK, so let me ask you something, Tony.
Tony: Shoot.
Me: A student with, let's just say mental issues, brings a knife to school and . . .
Tony: Is this a hypothetical question?
Me: Of course. Why else would I bother you? A student hypothetically brandishes a knife at . . .
Tony: Brandishes? Whoa! You've got quite a vocabulary there, Loco. Impressive.
Me: . . .
Tony: Sorry. So, did this student hypothetically, ha, ha, brandish this knife at *you*?
Me: No. At a student. But this was after she, hypothetically, put her foot in my ass and tried to smash my family jewels with her second effort . . .
Tony: Oh! I see.
Me: You follow me, right?
Tony: I'm with you. Go ahead.

Me: OK, so, my question is, if that student brandishes a knife at me and I accidentally break her fucking arm disarming her or put her crazy ass through a wall, what would happen to me?
Tony: . . .
Me: You know, hypothetically. . .
Tony: Well, Loco, sir, hypothetically speaking, your job and possibly even your visa status would become hypothetical.
Me: Great.
Tony: And you'll probably get arrested and thrown in jail, too, with these peculiar Japanese laws.
Me: Peculiar? Ha, ha. That's a good word, too. Peculiar. Pretty much sums up a lot of what goes on here.
Tony: That it does. Anyway, Loco, I must be clear about this; harming these children would not be tolerated by *The Company* in any way, shape, or form. But, between us, I just want you to know that *I'd* be behind you 100%!
Me: I can't tell you how reassured that makes me feel, Tony.
Tony: Ha, ha, ha! You're a funny guy! I didn't know that about you. Anyway, hang in there.
Me: Yeah, will do. Gotta go. The chimes are a-chiming. Later.

★ ★ ★ ★ ★

When I was 13 I was enrolled in Jackie Robinson Intermediate School, a public junior high school in Brooklyn. It was my first year of school in the real world.

Until then I had attended a private school so tight-knit that it was basically home-schooling. I had been nurtured in that environment. It was all I knew. My friends were essentially family. Some of the teachers were parents and some of the parents were teachers, and *all* had license to take a belt to my ass if I got out of line, which pretty much insured that I stayed in line. It was a fairly insulated and sheltered world where cultural awareness and the revolutionary spirit were valued and fostered.

It was not the real world.

Jackie Robinson had security guards with walkie-talkies at the doors, and a number of deans, also equipped with said instruments, and probably armed as well, chasing students around the halls. Deans who would gladly place delinquents into the loving clutches of the NYC Police Department. As for the chasees? Some of these guys and gals truly needed to be in custody. Vandalization, assault and battery, molestation, and muggings were not rare, nor was it strange to see a posse outside the entrance laying in wait for some fool who'd fucked some guy's sister or some chick who'd fucked someone's boyfriend, or anyone who had something of value he or she shouldn't have been foolish enough to bring to school, like a new pair of Nikes, gold jewelry, some Cazal eyeglass frames, or a sheepskin coat. He wouldn't be shot or stabbed usually, but by the time it was over he'd probably want to be put out of his misery.

This was the type of school life my mother had sought to protect me from. The world of beat-downs in the cafeteria, blood trails in the stairwells, and minimal learning or miseducation in the classrooms.

This was the real world.

Well, not in Japan. At least, I thought not.

If you were caught with a knife back in old Jackie Robinson, you would definitely find yourself at least suspended, and, depending on the length of the blade, you could wind up, again, in the warm embrace of those boys in blue, notoriously known to serve and protect and break niggers' necks for a living, in the real world.

But, Mika was simply told not to come to school the following day. An order she promptly ignored. Not only did she come to school, but minus her uniform, and wearing a mini skirt that would prompt even seasoned hookers to say, "You *go* girl! Work it! Own it!"

Her mother was phoned, naturally, and showed up that afternoon with Mika's uniform. Later, I was informed by Kawaguchi, on the down low, that when reminded that her daughter was not even supposed to be there that day due to a suspension, the mother replied, "I see. Well, here's her uniform. Sayonara!"

And left.

The next day Mom returned and met with the school's guidance counselor, Katou-san. Katou-san was a returnee and spoke better English than Takahashi and Kawaguchi put together, but didn't teach it. She came to the school once a week (one of five schools she rotated through) and handled whatever issues that might have arisen since her last visit. The first-year students that year kept her pretty busy. Katou and I had grown closer, thanks to her English ability and our shared struggle with these kids, so she'd let me in on what went down in this meeting.

Turned out this was the third school Mika had landed at in as many years for obvious reasons. Her mother was a housewife and, according to Katou, as nutty as the daughter. Katou recommended that Mom get Mika some professional counseling at a facility. To this suggestion, the mother replied something to the effect of "been there, done that! Any other bright ideas, you westernized bitch?" Katou kept her cool and said, "A knife is a very serious thing," to which the mother replied, "She told you she would never do it again, just like she told me. I believe her, don't you?" Katou looked at me with eyes that conveyed *that bitch is out of her fucking mind, and so is her daughter!* But she told me that she simply replied, "Of course I *want* to believe her."

That settled, by the working definition of "settled" in this quadrant of the globe, and Mika was back at school.

★ ★ ★ ★ ★

Greeting time at the start of a class should occur within a few seconds of the end of the Westminster chimes which rang at the start and end of each class. What happens then varies from school to school, and from teacher to teacher and sometimes from class to class, but not much.

At Mendokusai, once all of the kids are seated, the designated student (it changes daily) calls all the students to attention and instructs them to prepare to bow. Then, at that student's command, everyone bows in unison, including the teachers, and says, "Onegai shimasu!" which has a dozen meanings. In this case, from the students' perspective, I presume it means something like, "OK, we're all here now and you've got our undivided attention for the next few seconds. If you wanna hold on to it, you best engage us in a lesson both fun and captivating. Otherwise, God help you!" From Takahashi's though I think it could safely be translated as, "Our Father, who art in heaven. . ."

All seats should be filled by this point, I should add. Absent students weren't rare, but a late student was a rarity. According to the designated area on the blackboard, there were no absent students, but there was one empty seat in the back of the class a solid 30 seconds after the bell. Yes, shit runs like clockwork in Japan usually; and it's enough to make even a westerner like me anal after a while.

And, guess whose seat it was?

Takahashi and I were both eyeing it, as were several students. Then she glanced at me, eyes squinted, lips pursed, and cheeks puffed out. It was a weary look filled with dread and dark thoughts, for a Japanese person, anyway. To me it looked like a petulant child's or a spoiled little girl's face upon being told the reason they couldn't have their way was, "Because I said so!"

"Where is she?" I asked, trying to look like I cared. The only thing I was concerned about was whether she was armed or not.

Takahashi shrugged.

Through the frosted window of the classroom's door, a shadow shaped like a midget sumo wrestler, or maybe a miniaturized silhouette of Alfred Hitchcock appeared. It dawdled there for a moment like it was reminding itself, *stabbing people is bad, stabbing people is bad. . .bad, bad, bad. . .*

I nodded towards the door. Takahashi turned as it slid open and Mika hauled her hefty self into the room, in uniform, leaving the door open in her wake, and schlepped through the aisles to her seat in the back. Surprisingly, the whole class ignored her. Usually, believe it or not, lateness would incur reproof from fellow students, sometimes even hissing and booing it was such a no-no here. But, in Mika's case, it was as if everyone knew that even the slightest sound, movement or eye contact might provoke a regrettable incident. The room was a graveyard. It eerily reminded me of the same kind of "other-ization" I see the adult version of these kids do, in some form or fashion, on a regular basis.

She threw herself into her chair, making as much noise as possible, reached into her desk, pulled out a manga (comic book), held it up before her face and began to read it.

Takahashi sighed aloud and glanced at me.

"Loco sensei, please go ahead and begin the lesson," she whispered, and made her way to the back of the room, like a dead woman walking towards the gas chamber with a priest whispering the last rites in her ear. *"Now, my child, let me hear your confession so that your soul might find ever-lasting peace."*

The students were torn between paying attention to me and sneaking a peek at what they were sure was going to be sensational in the back of the room. Takahashi said something I couldn't hear from the front of the class, but the body language was loud and clear, "*please don't make my life any more difficult than you already have.*"

Mika put the manga down on her desk and aimed those coal black eyes at Takahashi. Her body replied, "*Bitch, if you don't back up off of me, I'm gonna break the promise I made to myself at the door not to jook your sorry ass!*"

Then, Takahashi and Mika both reached for the manga . . .

★ ★ ★ ★ ★

Oh yes, oh yes, oh yes, they both, oh yes, they both, oh yes, they both, reached for the manga, manga, manga, manga . . . (sung to "We Both Reached for the Gun" from the musical *Chicago*).

★ ★ ★ ★ ★

Nope, a tug of war did not ensue.

Mika snatched it from Takahashi's weak and cautious resolve and backhanded her in the gut, shouting "Fuck off, already!"

Takahashi, at that terrific moment, must have had the same thought that raced through my head: If Mika had had that knife in her hand she would be mortally wounded right now. I had to hand it to Takahashi because she stood her ground and kept her cool.

She actually reached for the manga again, crying, "gimme that!"

And the backhand came once again, accompanied by one of my favorite Japanese cuss words, "go to hell, bitch!"

Takahashi somehow blocked the second backhand though, and spewed some of that corrosive Japanese that I could never catch; it kind of sounds like "Hello Kitty" might sound if she were in heat and surrounded by neutered tomcats. They were harsh words, I was sure, 'cause Mika looked about half a heartbeat away from launching into a tantrum. So, Takahashi backed off, and Mika, satisfied that she'd won this battle, returned the manga to its position in front of her face.

Actually, with Mika deep in her manga, and not making efforts to disrupt the class, which was her modus operandi, everything was going very well. The kids were able to practice and use the grammar, and at one point during the class, were having so much fun that I noticed Mika peak from behind her manga to see what she was missing out on. She placed the manga on the desk and actually leaned in to catch a glimpse of the game we were playing in groups.

We made eye contact, Mika and I, and I could see that her temper was still hot, but that it was reserved exclusively for Takahashi-sensei, not her fellow students, and not me.

But, about 2 minutes before the bell rang, Mika reverted to form and started making the Westminster chimes with her mouth very loudly. "Ding, ding, ding ding . . . ding ding ding ding!" she "sang", over and over, until the actual chime began.

As the students were dismissed, Mika came immediately up to Takahashi-sensei, like they had unfinished business that needed settling immediately. She actually came to pick a fight with her. I could see it in her eyes. She just needed a reason.

During the class, Takahashi, a very talented sketch artist, had drawn with a piece of yellow chalk a rendering of Sponge Bob Square Pants. It had been done so accurately and adroitly that the whole class had ooh'd and ahh'd at her handiwork. I noticed that even Mika had looked impressed before she ducked back behind her manga.

Mika picked up the piece of yellow chalk while Takahashi and I were packing up to leave and began to deface the work in crude ways. When Takahashi noticed this she rushed to erase it, then reached to take the chalk from Mika's hand. Mika drew the hand back with uncanny strength, pulling it and Takahashi in like a tractor pulling a weight transfer sled. So Takahashi pulled back a little more aggressively and . . . umph! Sucker punched right in the gut! It was not hard, but hard enough. I saw Takahashi actually pull back from returning the blow, and again I was impressed with her restraint.

Mika laughed, the same way she had when she'd grazed my nuts with her over-sized feet the other day, her pudgy face red and evil.

★ ★ ★ ★ ★

When I got back to the office, I decided that I had better have a clarification session with Kawaguchi-sensei 'cause I wasn't about to endure injury while attempting to teach an armed, bipolar, ADHD-suffering, juvenile delinquent with violent tendencies. And Silky's warning had left me wary, to say the least. I was also determined to help Takahashi who, though I suspected she might be doing something to provoke this violent behavior, I was still kind of on suicide watch with. She might've been a backstabbing bitch, but she didn't deserve to be injured or killed.

While waiting for Kawaguchi to return to the office something occurred to me. Something that stopped me cold.

The feedback I'd received from Silky Tony was from a form given to both Kawaguchi and Takahashi, which meant the knife in my back, in reality, could have been placed there by either of them.

In my heart of hearts I was 99.99999% sure Takahashi was She-Who-Must-Not-Be-Named. But I'd been burned a number of times, and only when I'd let down my guard, disarmed by the general Japanese tendency to appear incapable of such treachery. In fact, I'd learned that, to Japanese, in their hearts, it wasn't really treachery at all. It was quite normal to do things this way. In order to avoid confrontation or any kind of unpleasantness, what I once thought would best be labeled as two-faced back-stabbing bastardry, is everyday fare here. The onus was on me to adjust to this practice.

I felt like I had a pretty well-honed traitor detector *before I came to Japan*. I could tell the difference between a person with whom I could share confidences and a person who'd likely share my confidences with anyone within ear shot. I could intuit authenticity in a person. Not perfectly, of course, but I had a fairly high accuracy rate. Here, however, that detector was about as useful as a Geiger counter inside a nuclear power plant amid a meltdown. Deciding who can be trusted is almost a shot in the dark.

Sometimes when I had "talks" with Kawaguchi, she'd take me into the recording room or the conference room where we'd have virtually soundproof privacy. Yet she'd still speak in hushed tones. All the security precautions used to make me paranoid, like she knew something I didn't know about the walls in that place, like they had eyes, or ears, or both. But that was just her style. She was sneaky, and probably a little paranoid, or what I came to think of as typically Japanese. However, when she returned to the office that day, and I asked her if we could we talk for a sec, with an office full of listening co-workers, she didn't even bother to be sneaky. She sat down in her chair beside mine and smiled. Her eyes twinkled as she read my face.

Me: I'm worried about Takahashi-sensei.
Kawaguchi: Really? Why?
Me: Well, of course you know about Mika assaulting her and Matsui-kun? Forget about it. Not to mention. . .
Kawaguchi: *Assaulting* her? What do you mean?
Me: She didn't tell you?
Kawaguchi: Tell me what?
Me: Ummm . . .

I started smelling something foul. Secrets. Lies within lies. My old traitor detector turned on, all by itself, with a feedback squeal like that CB radio I *borrowed* from Radio Shack when I was a kid. Once I turned it down and tuned it a little, I started picking up a signal. It was a warning coming in. "Breaker-Breaker, Loco, good buddy, back off the hammer! 10-33, I say again, 10-33! Best get in the granny lane! (Slow down, Loco. Danger ahead. Take it slow.)"

I tapped on the brakes and studied Kawaguchi.

Kawaguchi: What???
Me: Um . . . so, er, what do you know?
Kawaguchi: Know about what?
Me: About Mika and Takahashi. Tell me what you know first.

Kawaguchi gave me a benign inquisitive look like she didn't know what to make of my suddenly awkward behavior, probably perceiving that I didn't entirely trust her. But, if she were crestfallen it was her secret because her face confessed nothing. She simply leaned in like she usually did when she was going to lay some heavy shit on me and, in a thick whisper, a little louder than usual, said, "I don't know what happened with Mika, but I bet you it's her fault!"

And she nodded her head across the aisle at Okawa-sensei.

Okawa was the head teacher of the first-year students and the person Takahashi reported to directly. She was a very nice woman, almost always smiling, kind, friendly, and apparently hard-working. Typical. I never liked her much, though. It wasn't her fault, really. It was just that chichi foofoo people have always rubbed me the wrong way, and they generally have this way of condescending to hide their own raging insecurities that's off-putting to say the least. She certainly did. Physically, she was very attractive, though, and shapely for her age, which had to be the late 40s or early 50s. But, the energy she gave off was one of being a disgruntled former beauty queen, or current Mama-san at a hostess bar. And, her voice. Ugh! She made me want to tear my ears off. She sounded the way I imagine Miss Piggy would sound if she were a 50-year old, chain-smoking, heavy-drinking, domestically-abused lounge singer who thought she still had it and nobody had the heart to tell her she didn't, and never really did. It was her abusive ex-husband, Kermit the Frog's, popularity that opened doors for her.

Her smile was waiting for me when I stealthily glanced over there. She wiggled her fingers at me in greeting. Shit! She knew we were talking about her. And Kawaguchi knew that she knew that we were talking about her.

Was Kawaguchi just using me to embarrass Okawa?

I could still hear the crackling of my old detector, trying to find a signal in a typhoon, echoing the warning, "10-33, Loco, 10-33 . . ." all staticky in my head. The last thing I wanted to do was get into the middle of some office politics.

Kawaguchi: The first year students are wild and she cannot control them. None of them can.

She nodded again at the whole first-year students' teacher section. Aside from Takahashi and Okawa, four others were seated there shuffling papers around and looking convincingly busy. Otherwise, the office was very quiet. The only sounds in the universe were the whirl of computer hard drives, the occasional creak of chairs, a persistent buzz from God knows where, probably the fluorescent lights, and the surreptitious sound of Kawaguchi's whispers.

Kawaguchi: But she doesn't say so.
Me: Eeee? What do you mean she doesn't say so? Everybody knows! Matsui and his pal Satou are practically . . .
Kawaguchi: I know, I know, everybody knows, but she hasn't said so. And she hasn't told the principal or the vice principal about the situation. If she doesn't say it's a problem, then it's not a problem!
Me: What??? That doesn't make any sense. I don't get it.
Kawaguchi: She tells the first-year teachers not to speak with the principals, or with us, about the problems in the

classroom with the first-year students. Takahashi told me, but I have to pretend she didn't tell me, because if I don't then Okawa will scold her even more than she does already. Takahashi came to me crying yesterday but I couldn't help her, because of Okawa!

Me: Are you serious? Everyone has to pretend this problem isn't a problem because *she's* decided that it isn't a problem!

Kawaguchi: Yes!

Me: That's insane! What about the principals? They must see everything. They know, of course. There's trouble in their school. Why don't they just jump in and take the initiative? They can see the problem! What the fuck! For chrissakes, students are assaulting teachers!

At this, Kawaguchi went into full surreptitious mode and became her usual sneaky self when she has secrets to tell. She spoke so softly I could hardly hear her.

I thought, *fuck, I can't believe I doubted this woman. She tells me everything and takes great risks to do so*. My detector made a final squawk before it was squelched, like the station where the signal had originated from had been overrun by *zips in the wire*, and destroyed.

Suddenly, I could hear her, clear as a bell. She nodded toward the vice principal's desk.

Kawaguchi: He and she are. . .

And, on the down low, she flashed her pinky and her thumb.

Great. Sex and politics, like curry and rice. Pinky means girlfriend and thumb means boyfriend. I figured both together meant fuck buddies.

I glanced at the front desk where both the vice principal and the principal sat chatting with one another.

Me: Which one?

Kawaguchi: Eeee?

Me: Which one is she (I did the pinky/thumb thingy) with?

Kawaguchi: I don't know . . .

Me: Huh?

Kawaguchi: I don't know. Maybe she's (pinky/thumb thingy) both of them . . .

Me: Uso (Bullshit)!

I knew from that moment that Kawaguchi didn't just dislike Okawa. She hated her!

Kawaguchi: They both know about the problem, deshou? (right?) And they both do nothing, deshou? And they both listen to her lies about how she has the situation under control, deshou? They are both helping her.

Me: Come on, you don't *really* believe she's (pinky/thumb thingy) both of them, do you?

She suddenly burst into a raucous laugh. This was for Okawa's benefit no doubt.

Kawaguchi: No, I guess not. I think she's (pinky/thumb thingy) the principal and he's keeping the vice-principal in check.

Me: So I guess Takahashi is the one really getting (pinky/thumb thingy), *deshou*?

It took her a second to get my meaning. Then, she nodded, grimly, and glanced over at Takahashi, looking all helpless at her desk.

Kawaguchi shook her head and whispered, "It's a damn shame."

★ ★ ★ ★ ★

Later that week, when I arrived to teach what I'd come to call Mika's class, she was standing in the doorway blocking my way.

"Good morning, Mika," I said, eyes on high alert, darting all over her person, scanning her with my Terminator-style threat-assessing algorithm. My eyes locked on something in her hand — *cellulose pulp product derived from wood, commonly known as paper. Not an immediate threat*," a cybernetic voice in my head informed me. I relaxed . . . a little. "How are you?"

Mika had the attention span of a squirrel and I had yet to hear her utter even a single word in English, so I didn't expect an English response. I was just going through the motions.

She wouldn't move. She looked at me through black eyes that I was starting to believe reflected the darkness of her heart. An actual shiver went through me. She reminded me of a Stephen King story that spooked me when I was little, like she could be the child star of the Japanese version of that story: "Children of the Soy Bean".

Behind me, a line of students had formed as they too were waiting to get into the classroom.

Mika looked up at me and suddenly rushed toward me. I stepped back, blocking invisible blows and warding off invisible kicks. She stopped and giggled, as did most of the kids in the hall. I looked around at them all thinking, how was I supposed to know?

I looked back and Mika's arms were thrown wide. She wrapped them around me and hugged me lovingly.

Mika was a big girl and quite strong, and so squeezed me tightly. I could feel her power. She could probably lift me if she had a mind to. My breathing, already effortful from cigar smoking, became even more laborious with every passing moment. Then she let me go like she'd had enough. My back certainly had. She'd tweaked it.

"Loco sensei, this is for you. . ." She reached out and politely, with both hands, handed me the folded piece of paper I'd spied before she realigned my spine. I took it, with both of mine, kinda nod/bowed, unfolded the paper, and read it.

It said, in English, "Happy Valentine's Day, Loco-sensei I Love You!"

It had lots of hearts and manga characters drawn neatly and stylishly all over it, including a Sponge-Bob reminiscent of Takahashi's rendition. The card looked as if it had taken more attention to detail than I had yet to see her give anything except the manga comics she kept in her desk.

I looked up to thank her but her mind had already moved on to other things. She was making her way down the corridor toward the staircase, turned and vanished.

I and several of the students that had been waiting just stood there at the entrance to the classroom, looking at Mika's inspired artwork, scratching our heads.

Valentine's Day was weeks ago.

And, she'd still been in elementary school then.

5
Effluvium
(Syouganai Junior High)

LOCO in YOKOHAMA

At Syouganai, the students were taking their tests, so for a couple of days all I did was write and edit. This is one of the perks of teaching that make it so appealing, the abundance of free time it affords. I imagine that's why many writers have teaching gigs. That, and being around youth day in and day out, has a way of fueling ones imagination and setting a fire under one's procrastinating bum. Surrounded constantly by all that boundless energy, enthusiasm, and promise, as well as watching them from enrollment through commencement, growing and maturing right before your eyes, is like watching hundreds of human hands racing round the timepiece of your life and serves as a daily reminder that time stands still for no one.

Works like a charm, it does.

At Mendokusai I had a school-furnished laptop exclusively for my use sitting on my desk. But, at Syouganai, I didn't. While Akiyama-sensei, who occupied the desk on my left, kept her desk orderly and her belongings where they belonged, my neighbor to the right tended to spread out in my two-week absence, as if he believed I'd never be coming back. So, instead of a computer, I'd come in on Monday mornings to my co-worker's flotsam and his profuse apologies as he bulldozed loads of papers and books, sports drink bottles, and baseball equipment (he was the coach of the baseball team) off of my desk back onto his own unholy mess of a desk. Sometimes my own documents would get mixed in with the bulldozed stuff. Ultimately, these were things I would spend hours looking for only to discover them at the bottom of a stack of shit on his desk.

And peeking out from underneath these leaning towers of clutter rested the laptop he rarely, if ever, used.

I asked him one time if I could use it to prepare some lesson plans and he looked at me like I'd asked him if I could borrow his liver because I was planning to do some heavy drinking with friends that night. So, I never brought it up again. I'd only asked him because the two computers for general use of the staff, which were located in the rear of the office, were in use at the time.

They were used daily by teachers who were not fortunate enough to have a laptop provided to them by the school (meaning temps, substitutes and yours truly), or as a backup should a laptop breakdown. Two relatively archaic machines, one of which was running a Windows version from the late 90s.

Unperturbed, I did quite a bit of quality writing on those machines. Some of my best posts from the early days of my blog, Loco in Yokohama, were written on these venerable devices. Usually I'd be alone at this vintage workstation. Stretched out and lounging comfortably and undistracted, the muse would get so good to me that I'd forget I was at work.

There was one person who could be counted on to snap me out of it, though. Actually snap is too soft a word. He'd bitch slap me out of my rapture.

He was the office computer whiz (every school has at least one) and would come over and do techie stuff in order to maintain those two collector's items. Ozawa-sensei was his name and he was a really nice guy. He was approaching retirement age at full speed, so it was really impressive to me that one of the oldest guys in the office, raised in an age where personal computers were science fiction, had the know-how of a hacker. I'd even brought in my laptop from home one time and he de-bugged it for me and tripled the processing speed.

However, Ozawa's services came with an almost prohibitive price tag. He suffered from chronic halitosis. Thus everyone in his vicinity suffered, as well. A stench not unlike raw sewage assaulted the nostrils every time he exhaled. And it was not the kind that Tic-Tacs, Scope, and Listerine were made for. That would be like putting a mint garnish on a stool sample. Those treatments were merely decorative. I'm not trying to make a joke out of this. I had a childhood friend who suffered similarly and it turned out his condition was the symptom of something much more serious that had gone undiagnosed for years. And Ozawa-sensei, for all his charm and intellect, was a very sickly looking man. His skin had a pasty pallor, so I wouldn't have been surprised to learn his breath was a symptom of one of his organs putrefying as he died a slow odorous death.

He wore a surgical mask, like Japanese allergy and cold sufferers do customarily. Only he wore his everyday. All day. He'd been wearing it when I met him and not a day went by that he didn't. I imagine the mask filtered the smell somewhat but, having never seen him without the mask, I had no basis for comparison. From what I could tell, it mostly just localized it, like slacks do flatulence, forging a perimeter that lead and followed him wherever he'd go like an aerosolized minion. But, since he was pretty old, every trip up and down Syouganai's four flights of stairs left him heaving, huffing, and puffing that miasma of his beyond his locale. Sometimes you could tell where he was in the building, on what floor or in which room he was, or even where he'd been within the past hour, just by following your nose.

It preceded him to the seat beside me that day, as I sat at the terminal hammering away at the keys, but like every other teacher in the office, and probably every other person in his life, I pretended that it wasn't as god-awful as it was. I couldn't tell you what mental calisthenics my Japanese co-workers put themselves through to endure it, but as far as I was concerned, as a foreigner in Japan, you are often beset by comparable annoyances. So it wasn't an incredible feat to think of it as just another unpleasant yet unavoidable feature of the Japanese workplace and living in Japan as a whole.

Ozawa was aware of his condition, I was sure. Perhaps that was why he never removed his mask. But, he was really considerate in other ways as well. When he sat at the terminal beside mine, he sat sideways with his back turned to me, and blew his breath in that direction. But, it was like fanning a fart away.

When he finished his business and returned to his desk, thankfully taking most of his effluvium with him, Yamada sensei, back from yet another mysterious illness, came over and sat in the seat he'd vacated. Her nose twitched and eyes squinted before her mind caught up to her unconscious reaction to the foulness that lingered in the air, well aware of its source. Then her expression normalized so swiftly that I thought I had imagined it.

"Hi," I said to her.

"Hello, Loco-sensei," she said. Though she was smiling, it was so strained she looked as sickly as Ozawa-sensei. She peeked at the screen, saw what I was working on, ascertained that it was not pertinent to my duties here and gave me a look. A look I couldn't read at gunpoint. "Are you busy?"

She had a laptop on her desk, so I knew she'd come to speak to me about something. I turned to give her my undivided.

"Nope. What's up?"

"Welllll . . ." she began and my *"what now"* meter went off. "Do you smoke?"

"Do I *smoke*?"

"Yes. . ."

"Remember, at the Welcome Party, when you asked me what was it that I was smoking? And I said a cigar?"

"Ohhhh, yes!"

"Well, that's what I smoke. Cigars. Why? What's up?"

Where was she going with this?

"Well . . ."

Oh Jesus, spit it out will you?

"Do you smoke in the school?"

All of the teachers who smoke smoked inside the school. There was a tiny little maintenance room *way* off in the back where we'd huddle around a coffee can filled with water and enough ashes and butts to make me consider quitting every time I saw it. But, was this common knowledge to the non-smoking teachers? I wasn't sure, and my meter was still chiming its alarm.

"No. . ." I lied. "I go outside. Why?"

"Oh, no reason . . . only, one of the teachers said you smelled like smoke so . . ."

I didn't ponder for a moment why the teacher would go to Yamada instead of coming to me. Those days were over. I might as well have pondered why Japanese favor chopsticks over silverware, or still install those Japanese-style squat toilets in modern facilities. That's just the way it was, period. So, I just looked at her. She, however, alternated her attention between the aging computer monitor, the quiet office behind her, the fluorescent light above us, the New Balance sneakers on her feet, and occasionally me. This went on for almost 30 seconds!

"Okay . . . well, yep, it's true. I smell like smoke because I, as you know, smoke, and sometimes smokers tend to smell like, you know, smoke," I said, and smiled broadly. "Was there anything else?"

She smiled like she was dying of embarrassment. For a second, I didn't care what she was dying of, I just wished whatever it was would put her out of her misery already. Then I felt bad. It was probably really difficult for her to come to me with, well, whatever the hell she'd come to me to say.

"Well, ummm, anyway, I'm so sorry I disturbed you and . . ."

And she made a move to get up and leave it at that.

"Should I stop smoking?"

"Well . . . no, of course not . . . but . . ."

"I should stop smelling like smoke?" I asked.

Over her shoulder I could see Ozawa-sensei getting up from his desk just then and walking out of the office, taking his stink cloud with him. I wanted to ask her if my breath smelled like pending death would that be acceptable to this shy and mysterious teacher with the sensitive olfactory receptors?

Yamada smiled that same smile she had a few weeks back when we'd had that talk after she'd spoken with the BOE Lady behind my back. The way you might smile when you know that death is inevitable so you might as well go into that dark night bravely. Maybe there was something in my voice, or in my eyes, or even in the air for all I knew, some foul invisible emanation that made her mull over her own mortality.

"I'm so sorry Loco-sensei," she said, and skedaddled.

★ ★ ★ ★ ★

I arrived at the school the next morning and I almost sprinted to the two dilapidated computers, my little office within the office. Since the kids were still testing and I had no classes scheduled, my plan was to complete yet another blog post in my series, "Hi! My Name is Loco and I am a Racist". I had started it the previous day after my weird little talk with Yamada, and was very happy with where it was going. I had saved what I'd written on my handy USB memory stick, backed that up by emailing it to myself, and gone home.

Before I left home for work that morning, I'd filled my pockets (pants and jacket) with all the essentials: lighter (actually three lighters 'cause I always lose them or they die when I need them most), wallet, keys, cell phone, change, "Black and Mild" cigars, and . . . shit where was my memory stick?

This happened occasionally and I'd usually find it thirty minutes into a fruitless search, strangely right in the place where I'd left it and where I'd searched first, like some poltergeist was fucking with me.

I strip searched my room for a solid ten minutes. That's all the time I had, though. I had a bus to catch and if I missed it I'd have to run to get to work on time. The search produced nothing except that lighter I'd been looking for off and on for a week.

On this stick I had a back up of all of my lesson plans (just in case one of these senior-moment-having machines broke down on me) as well as other materials I use for teaching. I also keep notes for essays and stories that I've begun but have yet to complete. I back the memory stick up periodically on my PC at home and the PCs at both my schools, but not as regularly as I should, and unfortunately, not the previous day.

I tried to recall if I'd left the stick at the office. I'm usually pretty careful with that though, because some of my writing is not exactly the kind of stuff my co-workers would gush over. Quite the contrary. And I presumed nothing about any of them anymore. Especially when it came to who knew English and who didn't. I'd been thrown for a loop by a co-worker I'd known for years as uni-ligual'd suddenly breaking into English better than the English teacher's enough times to know that you never fucking know. They are all professional educators meaning they are all schooled and some are very well schooled.

But, I wasn't too worried, just a little.

So, when I'd arrived at the school at 8:15, 15 minutes earlier than usual, I'd done so to give myself time to find the stick before any of the other teachers did and before the morning meeting began. I gave the computer area a once over, unconsciously trying not to alert anyone to my search. But, I came up with nada. So, I opened Windows explorer figuring I'd just download the file from the email I'd backed it up to, but I got an error message informing me that the school's internet service was down.

Shit.

"Akiyama-sensei," I whispered loudly. She was seated at her desk not too far away. "What's up with the internet?"

"Eeeee?" she shrieked, and glanced at the big board behind the vice-principal's desk, where there was a bunch of kanji I could read surrounded by twice as much I couldn't. Then she turned back to me. "Oh, the board says it's down today due to testing. Sorry."

Fuck me.

Now how the hell was I going to work on the piece I'd started?

I gave the area one last hard target search for the memory stick. I was peering behind the monitor when I smelled Ozawa-sensei's approach. Judging from its potency, he was already close. I thought to turn and make a run for my desk, but I hesitated too long.

"Lose something?" Apparently, he had been watching me do my search.

"Not really," I said, and hesitated before continuing. "I think I might have left my memory stick here yesterday."

I'd said this in Japanese. He knew no English.

"Where??? Over here???"

Uh- oh!

I heard the catch in his voice and I'd seen this phenomenon before. It was the reason I'd tried to keep my search low-profile and hesitated to tell him about it. I silently cursed myself, but now that the deed was done, I just had to ride it out.

Ozawa-sensei got down on his hands and knees and practically crawled under the computer desk.

"Maybe it fell under here," he said, his voice slightly muffled through his mask.

"Please, no, there's no need for you to . . .," I was saying in Japanese, and being ignored, when he popped up from under the desk with dust bunnies in his thinning hair and on his well-worn suit, and a memory stick in his hand. It was one of those gray memory sticks that are available to teachers and are in abundant supply in the supply cabinet.

"Found it! Is this it?"

"I'm afraid not. My stick is black."

"Black, eh?" he asked, and gave me a scolding look that would probably leave four out of five students shamefaced and contrite. I wondered if he expected the same of me.

Yamada-sensei must have spied what was going on and came over to offer her assistance.

Any time I'd speak to a teacher other than an English teacher, she felt this need to come over and translate everything being said. She was just being nice, I knew, but it really got annoying sometimes, especially when I'd be holding my own and understood pretty much everything the teacher was saying. Moreover, it sent the message to the other teachers that speaking to me is something that could be done with less instances of confusion if she were present, effectively handicapping me in the eyes of others, and inclined them to avoid interacting with me when she wasn't around.

Not unlike a very friendly, but client-less Seeing Eye dog that has taken to walking ahead of you everywhere you go and steering you clear of obstacles, simply because you wear dark sunglasses which the dog associates with blindness. You're not quite sure how to tell it "fuck off, you miserable mutt! I ain't blind," because the one time you tried it started whelping like a pup, and made you feel like a petty person. What's wrong with you that you can't even find it in your heart to let a friendly dog feel useful, you chide yourself, as you walk around smelling its ass all day.

I tried to tell her to cut it out once, but as I began to tell her, to put it to her as gently as possible, that while I appreciated her unsolicited assistance, and her efforts to be a mediator between the Japanese world and the outside world I represented, I wished she wouldn't, she actually started looking somewhere between astonished and that panicky look she'd had when I'd pulled her coat on her bullshit previously.

So I, begrudgingly, let it drop.

And she, persistently, kept it up.

Ozawa welcomed her assistance, of course.

"Ah, good morning, Yamada-sensei! We have a problem here," he said in the only language he spoke. "It seems Loco-sensei was a bit careless with his memory stick and may have forgotten it in this area yesterday when he left the office."

"Oh, I see!" she said to Ozawa. Then to me, in English, "Did you, ummm, misplace your memory stick?"

I looked at the two of them for a hot moment during which I considered saying *I just remembered . . . I've never owned a memory stick in my entire life! My bad. Sorry to have troubled you guys*, and walking away.

"I might have," I said, instead. "The last time I saw it, I think I was over here."

She turned back to Ozawa who was waiting, a little impatiently, for her interpretation. It was almost meeting time.

"He says maybe he did, but he's not sure."

"I see," Ozawa said thoughtfully. "Well, I'll mention it in the morning meeting and see if any of the other teachers have seen it."

Oh God, no!

But, that plane had left the terminal and, short of a terrorist threat, there was no delaying its takeoff. The chime was a-chiming and the other teachers were already standing.

The principal and the vice-principal were at the front desk watching the three of us at the computer station. We all hustled to our respective seats. The VP let a pregnant moment of silent reprimand pass before he said, "Good Morning!"

And everyone bowed and replied almost in unison, "Good Morning," and we took our seats.

The morning meeting is a pretty formal affair, particularly so at Syouganai. And it's fairly strict. During the meeting, all the issues of the day that affect all teachers are discussed in brief. Then the meeting breaks up into three meetings, one for each grade. The scheduler opens the general meeting by making all of the official announcements. Then he opens the floor to remarks or announcements from anyone who cares to make any.

I sat there hoping against certainty that he wouldn't say anything so when I heard the scheduler say "Any other business?" and I heard Ozawa say "Hai!" I just closed my eyes.

"Loco-sensei has misplaced his memory stick," Ozawa said in formal Japanese. "He'd been using it in the computer area yesterday. It is not a regulation memory stick used by us teachers. It is his personal stick, and it's black. Does anyone have any information as to its whereabouts?"

I spray-painted a shameful smile on my face, lifted my head and looked around at all the concerned faces looking back at me. No one had seen it.

"Well, if anyone should come across it, please forward it to Loco-sensei. He is a little distressed over it so, please, let's help him out, shall we? That is all."

Some other teachers spoke, but I wasn't listening anymore. Once the meeting had concluded, several teachers stopped by my desk.

"I'm so sorry to hear about your memory stick Loco-sensei. I hope you find it."

"Thank you Suzuki-sensei. Thank you so much," I replied with the appropriate amount of appreciation and concern on my face, or at least I think I did. I just tried to make the face I'd seen Japanese people make in this situation, a situation where you are responsible for causing people to break with the routine of their lives to do something for your benefit.

Some teachers saw this as an opportunity to show how much they really liked me. Apparently, they had been too *shy* over the course of the past few months working in the same office as I to ever say so, but now that they had the perfect opening, some who hadn't really said anything but the most compulsory stuff were now espousing words of encouragement.

"Keep your head up, Loco-sensei," said Sakura-sensei. I'd actually thought she was a little off or something. She worked with the Special

Ed kids but during her free periods she'd sit at her desk mumbling to herself, so I thought the Yokohama Board of Education had gotten really progressive and started hiring under the premise that "it takes one to know one", or, in this case, to teach a dozen.

"It'll surface. They always do. Don't worry!" cried Yamate-sensei through a mask of empathetic anguish.

Even Akiyama came over.

"Oh Loco-sensei, you po' thang. There, there," she soothed, patting my hand consolingly, repressed laughter contorting her face and threatening to explode through her eye sockets.

"Fuck off!" I hissed, and she burst into laughter.

This went on all morning. Even the principal and VP had got in on the act.

★ ★ ★ ★ ★

Later that day, I came back from my lunch, coffee, and smoke break to find several memory sticks on my desk, none of which were mine.

And beside them lay a golden watch.

I took a quick glance around 'cause I'd suddenly had this sneaking suspicion that I was being watched or even videotaped. After a moment, I chalked that compulsion up to paranoia. Someone must have been doing something at my desk and accidentally left it there. I figured they'd return for it sooner or later. That thought plus the residuals of the paranoia I'd felt prompted me not to touch it or even look at it again.

Yamada-sensei and I were to teach a lesson together later that week so I went over to chat with her about it. Ever since she'd made a federal case about it with the BOE lady, I'd been proactively and almost aggressively going out of my way to make sure that the impression she'd had of me being unhelpful was eviscerated.

While we were chatting, another teacher, Mori-sensei, came over and interrupted us, or rather, he interrupted *me*. There was no urgency in his demeanor. Nothing to indicate that his interruption was justified. It was as if he presumed any conversation of which I were a part couldn't possibly be of any importance to either party, nor worthy of the courtesies afforded instinctively to two Japanese engaged thusly.

LOCO in YOKOHAMA

Moreover, it seemed to me, that any business that took place in the Japanese language, among Japanese people, superseded any business that happened in English. And since I was the only one in the office prone to holding conversations in English, that meant I was superseded by anyone, be it staff or student. I could be in a conversation with anyone, but if a Japanese person interrupted sometimes it would be like if we hadn't been having a conversation at all. Mid-sentence, hell, mid-word sometimes, whatever business I had would be preempted by any matter, be it important or not. Just another quirk you have to kneel down and suck on or wind up making a federal case out of here in Yokohama.

"Yamada-sensei, I beg your pardon but do you see that watch on Loco-sensei's desk?" he asked Yamada like I wasn't standing right there comprehending every word. "Does it belong to him? A student found it on the third floor staircase."

Yamada was well aware of my Japanese level. We'd had a number of conversations in Japanese. But you wouldn't have known that from her behavior. It was as if she'd never heard me utter a single solitary word in her mother tongue and I had even gone so far as to admonish her that if she had any respect for me, and for the English language, not to use Japanese when speaking to me whenever possible.

Also typical Japanese quirkiness or, as Silky Tony so politically put it, peculiar behavior.

"Oh really?" she said, and glanced at me like I were a mute and she'd forgotten her sign language handbook at home. Then she walked over to my desk, picked up the watch and brought it to me. "Is this your watch?"

"No," I said to her.

She turned to Mori. "I'm sorry, but he says it isn't his."

Mori scratched his chin, pantomiming perplexity.

"I'm sorry. It was the student that thought it was his. She said that it has his smell."

Then he giggled and snorted.

"You don't say," Yamada said, in Japanese, of course, giggling and snorting herself, but covering her mouth in a fashion as to suggest she was embarrassed by finding his statement amusing. Then she turned back to me. "Is it yours?"

"No."

She turned back to Mori again and said, "I'm sorry but did the student say it smelled like him?"

"That's what she said. I, myself, am not aware of any smell, but children have very keen senses."

Oh, God, not with the smells again.

As I watched Mori trying to refrain from laughing at the comedy routine feel of this conversation, I recalled that he was one of the teachers I had hassled about English once.

Like most teachers, he greeted me every morning, but while he'd "Ohayou gozaimasu" everyone else in the office, he'd always make a point of greeting me in English. Sometimes he'd even go so far as to greet me in Japanese, then apologize like he'd made some great social faux pas, and say, "I mean, Good Morning," with an apologetic pat on the back like he was afraid I might take offense at his use of Japanese, or that there was an off-chance I might be under the impression that "ohayou gozaimasu" meant "go home gaijin!"

"That's true," Yamada said to Ozawa, then turned to me again. "So, it isn't your watch?"

"No, it isn't my watch, and that's the third time you asked me." I rolled up my sleeve and pointed to the G-Shock on my wrist. "*This* is my watch." Then, I pointed to the watch in her hand. "That is *not* my watch."

Then I turned to Mori and said, in Japanese, "It ain't my watch."

"I'm sorry, Loco-sensei but a student says that it has your smell," Yamada said, and broke into a fit of giggles again.

"May I?" Yamada handed it to me and I gave it a whiff. It did smell like smoke, cigarette smoke, though, not my cigar smoke. But no doubt it was a smoker's watch. There were about, I don't know, 10 of us in the office—*including* Mori-sensei himself, it occurred to me at that moment. "Smells like cigarettes. You smoke, right? Is it yours?"

"Eeeee??" Mori-san shrieked. "Of course not!"

"Are you *sure*?"

It took him a second but he finally realized I was messing with him.

"I'm sorry, Loco-sensei," Mori-sensei laughed as I handed him the watch. He gave it another quick once over and mumbled something in that incomprehensible Japanese that men speak through locked jaws sometimes. Yamada giggled yet again.

"What?"

"He says . . . umm. . . he says that it's not . . . real? That it's . . . fake. It's a fake."

"A knock-off?"

"Yes, like the ones we can buy in Chinatown."

"I see," I said.

"May I please have a look at it?" came Ozawa-sensei's voice from his desk where he'd probably been listening to the whole conversation.

His breath reached us first. If Mori and Yamada smelled it they were in the wrong profession. They ought to be in film. They could give Pat Morita and Lucy Liu a run for their money. I took a couple of steps back. Not only did his breath cling to him, if you were in his presence too long, it tended to cling to you, as well. One time, after a prolonged conversation with him, I could smell him on me even on the commute home, and suspected that others could, too (though it was hard to distinguish from typical Japanese evasive behavior). I wanted to burn my clothes that evening.

"Why, of course," Mori said, and handed the watch to Ozawa.

"It belongs to one of my students," he said with a frown. "A Chinese student."

Both Mori & Yamada said "We should have known!" at the same time.

"I can handle this!"

Mori & Yamada thanked him and he walked away, his breath lingering like exhaust from a bus leaving the station.

"So, it belongs to a Chinese student?" I said, fishing for something. Perhaps an answer to how it ended up on my desk. Or perhaps just some acknowledgment from them that they'd taken time away from my life that I'd never get back with this foolishness.

But, then again, I'd done the same, I realized. Judging from the stack of memory sticks on my desk, maybe half of the office had joined the search party.

"Eeeee? You understood?" Yamada cried, utter surprise on her face. "Wow! Your Japanese is really good!"

I grinned, and walked away without a word.

That night when I got home, I found the memory stick on my desk next to my computer where I always kept it.

Fucking poltergeist, I swear!

6
Are You African?
(Mendokusai Junior High)

As part of the lesson, Kawaguchi-sensei asked me which languages I could speak, probably assuming I would answer English only. In fact, the simplest answer would have been English only. I mean, as far as fluency is concerned, it *is* the only language I speak.

However, from kindergarten through 8th grade, I was heavily exposed to Swahili (an African language spoken in Kenya, Tanzania and other East African countries) and between high school and University another six years were spent gnawing on and yawning at the French language.

So, in the spirit of teaching the students that there were more than two viable languages in the world, I answered, "of course, English, but also a little French, Japanese, and Swahili."

"Are you African?" one student asked.

"Er . . . no," I said, after a brief hesitation during which my mind was flash-flooded by thoughts and questions.

"Did you ever live in Africa?" another student asked.

"No . . . well, not really." Another flash flood . . .

★ ★ ★ ★ ★

I understood the reason the students had asked these questions. It was simple deductive reasoning. If you speak an African language, you must be African or have lived there at some point. Otherwise what's the use? However, they didn't ask me if I were French or British, though I speak languages originating from those European countries, as well. Of course I wasn't French or British. My complexion didn't mesh well with their image of people originating from those countries. And any fool could see I was not Japanese. But, I am black. So I, for all they knew, could very well be African. Yes, it was very simple deductive reasoning.

I try not to think for my kids or assume anything about what they know or don't know. Why? Well, they constantly surprise me. Sometimes they know the most obscure stuff. Like their having heard of Swahili, for example, was a surprise. And other times they have no clue about stuff I think any educated kid of any age in any country in our day and age would know, like what the Bible is, or that Hawaii is a part of America.

Did they know that Africa, like Asia, was a continent of many countries with diverse languages, cultures and histories, or that there were black French people and black British people, or that there were even Africans of Caucasian, Asian and Indian descent, I wondered. From what I could tell from quizzing them on occasion, and by the skimpy manner in which the world was being presented to them in their social studies and history classes, compounded with the negligence and/or oblivious indifference evident in the media, and so forth, I had my doubts.

But one thing I was certain of was that they knew that there were black African people. Why? Well, for one, the walls in the hallways of the school informed them of that.

Whenever a black face went up on the wall, invariably, it was one of those dusty-faced, smiling, or crying, hovel-, shanty-, or hut-dwelling, half-naked (or haphazardly clad) Africans living in destitution in the AIDS-plagued, Malaria-ridden, untamed jungle of some nameless, warring tribal nation south of the Sahara, and the brave, compassionate Japanese volunteer and representatives of the altruistic and well-funded Japanese charities who've left the first-world comforts and sovereign safety of Japan to assist them in their time of dire need.

And those presumed charity cases living under those unimaginable conditions (in Japanese imaginations) and I had something in common, didn't we?

I'd told them at the start of the semester that I was American, a New Yorker through and through, but the anomaly of being able to speak a landlocked African language gave my students a "What the hell! I thought he said he was an American" moment.

Were their minds able to grapple with questions like, "Why would anyone who wasn't from Africa, and didn't plan to live in Africa, study an African language?" And was it within my purview as an English teacher to challenge their thinking on such topics? Was it my place to teach them something they couldn't possibly learn from that propaganda smeared on the walls of the school? Or would I be crossing some line? There were so many questions that begged for answers.

Like I said, a flash flood.

★ ★ ★ ★ ★

"So, why do you know Swahili?" one of the more inquisitive students inquired.

"I studied it in elementary school," I replied, trying to think of a way to put it where they would be satisfied, if only momentarily, so we could continue the English lesson. "I had to study it, the way you have to study English."

My simplified response didn't do much good. There were still looks of confusion on the students' faces. Even Kawaguchi looked stumped.

"Do all . . . um . . . elementary school students have to study Swahili?" she asked incredulously.

"No, not all."

"Do people in New York speak Swahili?" another student asked.

They were really struggling with this one.

"No," I said. "I went to a very special school!"

I wanted to say more but I just knew that was out of the question. My time at each of my two schools was very limited. Pretty soon these third-year students would be taking tests to enter the high schools of their choice, so time was of the essence.

"So, anyway, let's continue with — "

"Why don't you tell us about your school?" Kawaguchi asked. Then she asked the class, in Japanese, did they want to hear about Loco-sensei's very special elementary school. There was a roar of approval.

Kawaguchi glanced over at me and smiled, gestured towards the class like a model on a 70s game show presenting a showcase of prizes, and said, "Loco-sensei, if you please."

I looked out at 40 or so eager familiar faces. I knew all of them by appearance and even a good number of them by name. I played basketball after school at least once a week with some of the guys and girls. I even ran into them on the streets more often than I liked, Yokohama being that close-knit a city. But for some reason, I felt nervous suddenly. I hadn't planned this.

Periodically I'd propagandize their lessons, insert information that would make them think about much more than the grammar point du jour. I had never even fantasized that I'd have the chance to lecture, and so had never considered how or even what I would say if the opportunity to go off-script ever presented itself.

"I can't explain everything in Japanese, nor simple English, and they — "

"Don't worry, I'll translate," Kawaguchi said.

So I manned up, took a deep breath, and proceeded to do what I wasn't being paid to do and taught a little about the black struggle in the US, giving them highlights of why and how I came to learn Swahili.

★ ★ ★ ★ ★

I started my explanation by telling them about my mother, how she was as progressive as black mothers got back when I was child, and was determined that my early education begin outside of the NYC public school system.

"Why?" Kawaguchi asked, as much for her benefit as for the kids'. I was sure that in her translation she was simplifying my explanation so that it was digestible for young Japanese minds, so I spoke fluently and naturally as if she and I were alone and having a conversation in a cafe. I even looked at her as I spoke as much as I did the class, explaining that my mother and many black educators believed that public schools were poisoning black souls with propaganda, most of which was flat-out lies about the superiority of Europeans and their descendants in America, or half-truths so diluted with deceit as to make the truth seem preposterous.

But that, in the 1970s, this small private family school in Central Brooklyn set out on a mission to instill in the young black minds in attendance a sense of African cultural awareness and history. Their concept was simple and direct. If you wanted black children to grow up with a sense of pride, self-love, and respect for themselves and others, then you had better indoctrinate them with some knowledge of themselves that didn't begin with savagery and slavery and end with the poverty, illiteracy, drug addiction, crime, and all of the other social ills they could look out of the window and witness.

That intensive proper education was necessary in order to diffuse the bomb that the public schools and the media had planted in young black minds, a Molotov cocktail of deception that informs them that they are the descendants of barbaric, cannibalistic, blood-soaked idol worshiping savages running butt-naked in the deep dark jungles of Africa and that if it weren't for the civilizing efforts of their white forefathers, they would still be doing so. A detonation of self-abnegation and self-hate that would destroy all traces of anything worth preserving if left unaddressed.

LOCO in YOKOHAMA

I told her that my mother and my school were very serious about correcting the image issue, and giving children like me an image of beauty that was not white, an image of power that was not white, an image of success that was not white. Otherwise, black children would grow up associating beauty, power, and success with being white. The women will want straight hair and lighter skin, and the men will feel powerless without a gun or a wallet overflowing with cash and enough flash to prove they weren't the losers they were designed and thought to be.

I paused and scanned the faces of my students to see how Kawaguchi's almost simultaneous translation of my words was going-over. They seemed mesmerized, eyes trapped somewhere between attentive and glazed, like they were hearing about life on Mars being told by a Martian. I feared I'd gone too far and lost them, especially since I knew most of what I'd said was very far removed from anything most of them had ever heard about . . . well . . . anything, particularly about black people. With no mentions of basketball or hip-hop (their go-to topics whenever they'd question me about America), I hadn't given them a foundation of familiarity to build upon. Even Kawaguchi had a perturbed look on her face, so I hesitated to continue.

"Anyway —" I said, feeling like I squandered an excellent opportunity to open true channels of cultural communication by being too direct.

One student asked Kawaguchi a question in Japanese, but all I could catch was a couple of words, one of which was "Swahili". Several other students seemed to approve of the question, or had questions of their own, and soon the room was a-buzz with crosstalk, most of which I couldn't catch.

"What's going on?"

"Well, they want to know more," Kawaguchi said, glancing at the clock over our heads. "Me too! We have time."

"Oh. . ." I said, and smiled. "Well, what was her question?"

"She wanted to know why Swahili? There are many languages spoken in Africa, right?"

That question surprised the shit outta me.

I looked at the girl who had asked it. A girl named Miki. All of 15 or 16, as they all were, this being a third-year class, but her age wasn't what made the question surprising. It was just that it suggested unsuspected depth of thought, particularly for a Japanese teen. I must've had a goofy expression on my face 'cause many of the kids started laughing the way they do when I shuck and jive with them.

I really didn't know the answer. Maybe I had known at one time, but it wasn't coming to me at that moment.

"Probably because it was the easiest to learn," I said to Miki, off-the-cuff, in Japanese. After I said it, it felt like the truth, though.

Then I turned to Kawaguchi and told her that exposure to this African language was part of the indoctrination I received. It was not that Swahili was so important, or would even prove useful for an African-American with no plans of relocating to East Africa to know, but that this exposure had a more profound and weighty objective. That language is more than merely the power to communicate, but has been used to empower and subjugate countless times over the course of history, not to mention the role language plays in ones ability to think critically, and to establish a linguistic and cultural foothold on the path of history.

Kawaguchi nodded at this as she conveyed it to the kids. I knew her English comprehension level was much higher than her speaking ability, but the fact that she had only asked me two or three times for clarification of a word or idiom was really impressive.

I turned back to the kids and told them that while the public schools were force feeding European languages, culture, and history to essentially African minds, my elementary school sought to remedy this atrocity by limiting overexposure and replacing it with awareness and knowledge of black contributions to the progress of humanity. So, I grew up knowing more about George Washington *Carver* than I knew about George Washington, more about Kwanzaa than Christmas, more about Angola and Senegal than about France or Germany, more about John Coltrane and Thelonius Monk than about Mozart or Beethoven. And, of course, Swahili over a plethora of languages of European descent.

★ ★ ★ ★ ★

The bell began to chime just as I was finishing.

One student blurted out, "How do you say 'goodbye' in Swahili?"

"Tutaonana," I said, the answer coming easily. 'Tutaonana watoto.' It means, 'See you later, kids.'

I'm teaching Japanese kids how to speak Swahili, in Japanese!

LOCO in YOKOHAMA

Teaching the African language my teachers taught me when I was a kid, watching these Japanese children play with forming the foreign words, gave me the extraordinary awareness of having come full-circle, of having fulfilled something I hadn't even been aware I'd been trying to fulfill. And even though my journey had lead me to Asia, and a good number of my experiences here have been dehumanizing, albeit unintentionally in most cases, and left me with a sense of being fragmented, this new sensation, this epiphany of sorts, made me feel more complete and integrated as a human than I had in all my years here in Japan. Perhaps, and not to overstate it, but in all my years on earth! Moreover, I knew, intuitively, but with absolute certainty, that I wouldn't have been able to fully appreciate this de-fragmentation of energy if I hadn't gone through the sensibility shredder that life in Japan has been, and if I hadn't been pushed to the brink of faithlessness and utter apathy.

I stood there looking over the students, most of whom were chatting about what they'd just learned or had moved on to other topics, feeling an enormous gratitude. Then someone tapped me on the shoulder.

"Nice job," Kawaguchi said, with a nod/bow.

"Thanks."

"Loco-sensei?" came a voice from behind me. I turned and it was one of the students, Miki. She was one of my favorites. Always attentive and enthusiastic. She was the one who'd asked why my school had taught us Swahili among all the available African languages.

"Yes, Miki-chan?"

"I want to learn Swahili, too!" she said in English, giggling.

"Me too," her sidekick said, practically bouncing in her enthusiasm. I glanced over the faces of several other students that had hung around and they all seemed to be on the same page.

"Really, now," I said, knowing damn good and well that I wasn't qualified to teach Swahili. "Why?"

A couple of them scratched their heads, but Miki-chan didn't.

She said, "I want to go to Africa!" And before I could get off my favorite question, she answered it by adding, "I want to be a doctor to help African children."

Clearly, the wallpaper in the hallways with the desperate, indigent Africans had had an effect on her. Was this the desired effect, I wondered.

"Me too," bouncing little Me-too-chan chimed.

Judging from the faces of the others, they would sooner become MIB or LIB (the freshman office workers of Japan who wear black suits to work every day) than don a white lab coat and diagnose the deathly ill or hand out condoms to reckless oversexed natives living in the middle of a sweltering mosquito-infested jungle, or whatever ill images of Africa they had bouncing around in their skulls.

"Well, I'm sorry, but I've forgotten most of my Swahili," I said in Japanese. "I can teach you a few words and phrases though."

Their faces all lit up.

That's when I noticed Terrence.

★ ★ ★ ★ ★

Terrence wasn't an English enthusiast so I was surprised to see his face among them. He'd usually take to the hallways and horseplay with his cronies. But, something about the lesson must have sparked his interest. I shouldn't have been surprised though.

Terrence wasn't the only so-called haa-fu (what Japanese call people mixed with some other ethnicity or race) in Mendokusai, but he was the only black one among the third-year students.

His father was Kenyan and his mother Japanese but, as far as who he was, how he carried himself, and how he interacted with the world, he wasn't half-anything. He was all Japanese. It had taken me several months to get that through my thick skull, but eventually it got through.

Terrence was tall, lanky, and fairly dark-skinned with a curly Afro. He had a scratchy husky voice and was going through adolescent changes, but I imagined at the far side of that vocal maturation would be a Barry White baritone that'll drive the girls wild.

Terrence and I had the strangest relationship I'd ever had with a student and, trust me, that's saying a lot.

Our relationship began my, and his, first day of class back in 2007. I had just begun my tenure at Mendokusai junior high and he had just arrived, fresh from the local elementary school along with more than half of his classmates. Thus most of the students already knew or knew of one another while I knew nobody, students nor faculty. Kawaguchi introduced me to the class while I scanned this sea of young, nervous, excited Japanese faces. That's when I came upon an island in this sea,

Terrence's black face. He was just as nervous, just as excited, and just as Japanese in every respect aside from his color and features.

My shock was conspicuous.

The class turned to see what had given me the jolt, and saw Terrence. Some shrugged with indifference, as if to say, 'whatchagonnado'. Some smiled with comprehension, like this was well-traversed territory. He gets that a lot, they seemed to say. Terrence rolled with it. No more or less embarrassed than any student would be if put on the spot on the first day of class. And that was when I realized, abruptly, what I had done. I had done to him what has been done to me ever since my arrival here in Japan, I'd singled him out as different.

I tore my eyes off of him and ordered myself not to set them on him again in any significant manner or in any way different from the way I set my eyes on any of his presumably full-blooded Japanese classmates for the rest of his days in the school.

But, because of his blackness and my delusional pleasure at being around someone who I thought could vaguely identify with me, I had immediately taken a liking to him, which made it all the more difficult to treat him like everyone else despite my efforts.

And I seemed to be having the same effect on some of the other students, particularly Terrence's friends. They tried to push us together at every opportunity. If I asked any of them a question, whether in English or Japanese, and Terrence happened to be in the vicinity, they'd turn to him as if to say, hey T, any idea what this guy's rambling about? They'd probably never seen him interact with another black person so they were probably curious as to what would happen. Would Terrence suddenly shed this veneer of Japanese-ness that he'd been masquerading since they'd met him and become the gaijin he appeared to be, the one that surely lurked within him?

To be honest, after meeting him a couple of times on his own, and seeing how Japanese he appeared to be, I'd secretly hoped the same thing!

The first time I ran into him alone, I'd said to him almost instinctively, "Hey! What's up, Terrence?"

"Ah! Loco-sensei, ohayou gozaimasu," he replied, nod-bowed, smiled coyly, and tried to keep it moving. It was typical behavior among most of the Japanese boys I'd ever run into outside of the school, especially the shy ones. But, coming from Terrence, it felt cold and dismissive, somehow.

I caught up with him. I can be pretty persistent once I get an idea in my head.

"So, Terrence, how do you like the school?"

He donned a smile that cried, "If I weren't Japanese, obliged to be appear polite, I would runaway full-speed from you right now!"

I'd see that face a thousand times a day. It meant, among other things, he didn't know English.

I stood there feeling silly.

I'd only met one other black person in Japan that didn't know English. It had happened several years earlier. There'd been this girl, haa-fu from all appearances, standing on the train platform near me. She was so beautiful I wanted to propose to her right then and there.

I told myself I don't deserve to live if I didn't at least try to talk to her.

"Hey, how are you?" I asked, and she looked at me the same way Terrence did. She told me, in Japanese, that she didn't speak English at all, but I had filed that away as she was just trying to avoid being picked up. She'd probably been getting harassed by foreigners left and right, she was so fine.

"Do you speak English?" I asked Terrence, in Japanese.

"Sorry I don't." There was no guile, no shame. Of what use is English to me? I could almost hear him say.

"Do you speak any other language besides Japanese?"

"Sorry, I don't."

As I walked beside him towards the school that morning, a thousand questions raced through my mind, but I felt uncomfortable asking any of them. It was none of my business.

But curiosity trumped decorum and rudely I pried.

"Are you African?" I asked.

In Japan, I've learned not so much that a non-Japanese is a non-Japanese, despite what many non-Japanese here have said about the natives (that they don't distinguish between races, which is nonsense), but that black is black, and white is white, etc,. And though Japanese claim to be able to distinguish between Korean and Japanese, (something I struggle with to this day) I've yet to meet a Japanese person who could distinguish between a mainland African and people of the African Diaspora, or French and Irish, or Russian and Sicilian.

Though there are many variations of "black" in Africa, and in America as well, rarely have I been unable to ascertain, at a glance, whether a person was from my quadrant of the globe or from a nation in the the motherland. I might mistake a Caribbean person, especially Haitian or Cuban, for African, but rarely an American. Facial structure is usually how I can make this determination, and Terrence's screamed straight from the motherland, via Asia, as clearly his features were diluted by his Japanese heritage.

"No, I'm not African," he replied, shuddering a bit.

I was surprised at the response.

"Where are your parents from?" I asked, and immediately regretted it. I could vaguely hear the echo of a thousand 100% Japanese people asking him similar questions. But, with the obedience of the culture he had been nurtured in, he told me that his father was Kenyan and his mother Japanese. He smiled again, uncomfortably, offering more than a subtle hint that I should drop this line of questioning if I have any sense of propriety about me.

I did. So, I dropped it.

I would find out later in the school year from my co-workers that Terrence's father had gone back to Kenya while he was an infant, so he was being raised by his Japanese mother and, shockingly, a Japanese step-father.

From that point on I rarely paid him any undue attention. I often go out of my way to interact with the students as much as possible for, in addition to making my work life more enjoyable, I told myself I was acting in a humanitarian capacity. The more kids that interacted with me and others who had chosen to spend their lives in this field, and experienced that foreigners, and in my case black men, were no more a threat than anyone else, the more likely that the future of relations here would be impacted positively and the foolishness I endured would occur less often.

But, unfortunately, when I interacted with Terrence, I felt it prudent to be unfairly cautious.

I surmised I could not treat Terrence as I treated the other students. Maybe it was one of the side effects of my having lived in Japan for so long. From what I'd learned of the haa-fu experience and from what I'd experienced as a foreigner and black man living in Japan, and from what I remembered of my adolescence, I presumed his life in Japan must've been and would continue to be an ordeal.

And though I was very curious to know how he coped, and would love to have offered him any support that I could provide, I kept my two-cents in my pocket for his sake. It was hard enough for a teen to fit in. Even for a teen in a school in NYC fitting in could be a dangerous balancing act. Even for 100% "pure-blooded" Japanese teens, I'd noticed, it could get really tricky. So I knew I had better back off, and let him make his way the best way he knew how. Besides, chances were, having been born and raised in this culture, he had a much better handle on the situation than I could ever have.

But, when I saw his face among the kids clamoring to chat with me the day of my impromptu lecture, I figured he had to be curious about the language spoken in his father's homeland. It gave me a tinge of a feeling I wasn't particularly proud of. It wasn't pity, but it lingered in that same Pandora's Box of useless dehumanizing feelings that were better left locked away.

Why? Because Terrence, as he'd informed me that day when I tried to pry into his business, was no more African than I was.

★ ★ ★ ★ ★

In that Pandora's box were some painful memories of when I was a kid back in Brooklyn, younger even than Terrence. Back then, my friends would tease me.

"Are you African?" They'd ask.

"Hell no!"

"So why the fuck do you, and your whole family, dress like that?"

Yes, indeed, evidence to the contrary.

On a regular basis, I'd be decked out in a dashiki and a kufi while my friends in public school wore whatever the hell they wanted to wear to school. I even had an African name, Baye. A name that my friends, with little or no effort or imagination, could turn into the most degrading jokes.

What I never got around to telling my friends was that during my first week of school my teacher told us that we must all choose an African name from a book of names, and for the remainder of our school lives, we would be known by that name.

"Why," I'd asked.

Even at that age, I had an inquisitive mind and wasn't afraid to make inquiries.

I was told that my name was a "slave" name and that the true names of the Africans brought to America in chains had been discarded like refuse and replaced arbitrarily by rather random meaningless names, befitting dogs in most cases, and their owner's surnames became their own.

Little did I know how significant that moment would be. Not only would that name follow me home that day, but it would follow me into my life after school, and even until this day, it remains the name I am known by. Even friends I've had for over thirty years do not know my "slave" name.

Why did I respond with, "Hell no!" to my friends? Well, that's a little more complicated.

Though, at the time, I was being taught to love and honor my African ancestry, I didn't exactly live in a vacuum. I watched *a lot* of TV, and movies, too. The images of Africa I received in school, of a land rich with ancient and advanced civilizations and natural resources, of kings and queens, of great empires and universities, were countered by the bombardment of negative images. It was those that influenced the minds of the people I had to interact with outside of the cultural sanctuary of my school.

And, unfortunately, I was influenced by these people and images, as well.

Of course, as a child, you don't question these images. Seeing is believing for the most part. I just figured that Africa was big enough for both, the savage cannibalistic tribes on TV and the advanced civilizations of my textbooks. Naturally, I wanted to be associated with the positive images, the flowing robes of princes and the kufi-wearing scholars, but unfortunately most of my friends outside of school had no exposure to the positive images, only the negative ones. So I was subject to being called names like African "booty-scratcher", "spear-chucker", and "monkey-chaser", by my own black brethren.

Like Terrence, among those that were essentially my own kind, I was often viewed as abnormal.

Naturally, I blamed my school. This led me to resent the education I was receiving, and even resent the Africa I was being forced to hold in such high esteem. And I would not have even an inkling of the enormous gift I'd been given by my school until my first foray into the public school system as a teenager, where I would see firsthand what little I had been missing out on for all those years. Little by little, I would realize the enormity of the task my teachers had taken on.

Even now, I am still learning.

This resentment even expanded to include African people after a while. Some of my initial interactions with actual Africans left much to be desired.

Back in NY I used to get the feeling that most, if not all, African-Americans were beneath contempt in the eyes of many African visitors and immigrants for a variety of reasons, including but not limited to our legally living in the so-called land of Milk and Honey and not finding a way to milk it dry. Their perspective was akin to Antonio Montana's in "Scarface" who said, "If I had come here (to America) 10 years ago, I'd be a millionaire by now. I'd have my own house, my own car, my own boat . . ."

In Japan, however, the Africans, be they Nigerian or Ghanaian, Sudanese or Botswanan, were really the only "friendly" black people. Usually, if I encountered an African-American he'd give me a look like I owed him money, or cower like he owed me money. Or, they'd pretend they didn't see me. I got it, though. I avoided other foreigners, too, sometimes. Perhaps it was a side effect of living in a culture in which the natives could best be described as evasive. There's a sort of unconscious assimilation where you find yourself imitating the behavior of the greater society, even though you don't necessarily approve of the behavior. Perhaps, too, it was due to a bit of that self-hate my school had tried to secure my soul against.

Africans, however, invariably approach me with, at minimum, a warm greeting, and often try to strike up a conversation. They seemed to be impervious to all of the Japanese behavior around them.

I suspected it was because they too came from mostly racially homogeneous countries and, having been spared all the rarefied trappings of a diversified city like New York, held no illusions about their place here in Japan. The Africans I'd spoken with, mostly Nigerians and

Ghanaians, appeared to have no racial sensitivity, no significant qualm with anything that went down here aside from those that hindered their business ventures. And, in most cases, they'd found ways to deal with those hindrances. The 1000 daily paper-cut-type slights that troubled me seemed to fly well under their radar.

I envied them.

Sometimes.

Other times I'd be certain that kind of thinking would do me more harm than good. Just a little too pragmatic and hopeless for my taste. But, the handful of Africans that I have interacted with in Japan do not represent the thinking of an entire continent. To me, this is common sense. If it weren't for the school I attended as a child, as well as my experiences growing up in NY, I might have been able to lump all Africans into one and label them. But, you see, I have an aversion to that kind of thing. I try to deal with each person as they come.

Easier said than done.

I brought all of this to my interactions, or lack thereof, with little Terrence. My lifetime of experience dealing with other races, cultures and nationalities, with all its complexity and confusion, influenced my behavior. No wonder I felt so cautious. Last thing I wanted to do was corrupt his mind or burden him with issues that I haven't even sorted out yet.

And this illustrated one of the reasons I think this experience of living in another culture has been ultimately beneficial for me. It constantly gives me opportunities to really see what I'm made of, this equation called identity. And, what the world is made of, this constant search for affirmation, for cultural uniqueness and distinctions.

Sometimes what I see is not pretty. Sometimes its beauty is overwhelming. Sometimes a simple question like, "are you African?" can open a door and send me to a place in my heart I may not have ventured otherwise; a place where the designation "African" has about as much meaning as the designation "American". None whatsoever.

I'm American as much as I'm African as much as I'm Japanese . . .

What I really wish I could have told my students when they asked me if I were African, before the thought was washed away by the flash flooding in my mind, before I thought of the racial aggrandizing I was subject to as a child, and the Ludovico-type conditioning I'd been subject to as a New Yorker so as to enable me to co-exist with other cultures and people relatively drama-free, before I unearthed all of the feelings, good and bad, about people I have encountered from the African continent, and contemplated all of the racial and cultural prejudice that paralyzes progress and our true evolution as a species . . . I wish I could have told them and shown them, unequivocally, that the question of whether I was African or not was, for all intents and purposes, irrelevant.

But, I suspect, I'm not quite there, yet.

★ ★ ★ ★ ★

By the time I got back to the teacher's office, Kawaguchi was already there and speaking to several of our co-workers, and judging by their reactions to my reentering the office, apparently I was the topic of discussion. It made me feel a little queasy. Of all the quirks I've had to find a way to accept in order to live here with some semblance of a peace of mind, being talked about by Japanese people, either behind my back or in my presence, their presumption being, since I'm not Japanese, I can't understand what is being said, like adults might do around an infant, is one I've yet to learn how to stomach. But, since Kawaguchi was at its center, I felt pretty confident it was in good taste and I'd be let in on the topic eventually.

There was no guarantee that I would like what was discussed, though.

I forced a smile at all the faces smiling and nodding at me as I headed for my desk.

I was about to sit down when I heard Kawaguchi mention me by name, followed by a pretty forceful, "Ne!" It was immediately followed by several cries of approval and agreement from the people who had been listening to her hold forth.

Yes, tar and feathers will teach him a lesson, I thought, and laughed to myself.

I wondered if it had anything to do with the impromptu lesson I'd just given to Kawaguchi's class.

When their little huddle broke up, Kawaguchi came and sat at her desk, and said nothing. She just organized her materials for the next class, with this self-satisfied grin on her face.

"You gonna tell me?"

"Tell you what?" she said, innocently.
"Y'all were talking about me, right?"
"Oh, that? Don't worry, it was nothing."
"Really?"
"Really!" she said. "Have you got any plans for the weekend?"
And she left it at that.

A couple of months later during one of my stints at Mendokusai, I walked into the office and I knew that something was up. I greeted everyone as usual. Takahashi and Chichi Foofoo, the principal and vice-principal, that cute office clerk and the even cuter nurse. Everybody had a different look in their eyes, a different timbre to their voices. I have a high sensitivity to vibe. But I couldn't make heads or tails of whether this was a good one or a bad one. It felt like that vibe you might get when everyone knows something that you don't know. Something that will have a direct impact on you. But, since I've been in Japan, and due to the exclusive nature of Japanese people when it comes to interacting with foreigners, I have that feeling almost every day, and that has dulled my read of that vibe. Even when it feels particularly strong, like it did that day, I still blow it off as crossed signals here in Japan because, more often than back in the states, that's exactly the case.

The morning meeting was proceeding as usual, and as usual, I paid it no attention as I prepared for my first period class. I did however notice that, though Kawaguchi's handbag and cell phone were on her desk, she was not at it. Just as I was starting to wonder where she might be, the door to the office slid open.

This was out of the ordinary and drew my and everyone's attention. During the morning meeting, the doors are strictly kept shut and a teacher is posted at either door to ensure they stay that way for the duration of the meeting. Often sensitive issues are discussed and, if a student were to walk in during that discussion, it could cause the faculty some embarrassment.

Nevertheless, in walked Kawaguchi and two third-year students whom I recognized. One was Terrence, and the other was Miki-chan. She smiled at me and gave me a little wave as she passed by my desk. As they made their way to the head of the office I noticed the two students were holding something that looked like a movie poster.

This kind of thing happened every so often. New students transferring to the school mid-semester would come and formally introduce themselves to the staff. Or sometimes students would be invited to the morning meeting to receive awards or to give speeches or to thank so-and-so-sensei for helping them win this or that sports tournament, etc.

I wondered what the occasion was.

Once prompted by Kawaguchi, Terrence started speaking, of course in Japanese. He spoke for about a minute in a very low voice like he suffered from disabling shyness, but everyone seemed to hear him clearly so maybe it was just my language deficiencies. And as he spoke, I felt myself being drawn closer to the poster they were holding. I could only catch some of what he'd said but what I did catch stopped me cold.

He was talking about Kenya, the country of his father, which he had never seen and knew very little about.

". . . I will go to Kenya one day to meet my African family. Though I am Japanese, I am also African, too. I know everything about my Japanese family. I want to know more about my Kenyan family. After Loco-sensei's class, I asked my mother about my father. She told me that he'd gotten sick and passed away when I was still very young. But I have many uncles and aunts and cousins in Kenya, she told me. I want to meet them all."

And now that I had an unobstructed view of what these kids had put together, my heart skipped a beat. As he talked a bit about what he'd learned from his mother, I was stupefied by the work they'd done. It was actually a rather large poster of Africa, every country filled in with the country's name and the languages spoken there (in Japanese katakana characters, but better than nothing). Some even had photos, structures and faces, black faces. And they weren't sick or starving, deprived, depraved or disenfranchised. There were artists in South Africa, a group of engineers in Mozambique, some fascinating architecture in Botswana, and oil refinery workers in Nigeria. There were police officers in Uganda and merchants in Zimbabwe, architects in Angola, and a young student in Tanzania. There were marathoners in Kenya and fishermen in Gambia, etc.

". . . and Loco-sensei!" When I heard my name again it snatched my attention from their amazing project. Terrence had turned my way, as did every head in the office. "Thank you, so much. You gave me the courage to pursue my secret dream and find my treasure."

Then he bowed deeply. I sorta bowed in response, with what I'm sure was a dumbfounded look on my face.

Then, Miki began to speak.

"Habari ya asubuhi, Mwalimu!" she shouted.

Everyone watched her in stunned silence and I had to pick my jaw up off the floor!

It meant good morning in Swahili, but I hadn't taught Miki that. The girl had done her homework. Her pronunciation was different than mine, though. Sounded pretty native, in fact, like some of the Africans who'd visited my school when I was a child.

"That means 'good morning, teachers,'" she said in Japanese. "With my parents' help, I have found a website which teaches Swahili. I'm learning it from a junior high school student in Tanzania."

She pointed to the photo of the student attached to Tanzania on the poster.

"Her name is Femi. She is 15 years old and lives in Dar es Salaam. She tells me many things about her life in Africa. She wants to be a doctor so she can help people live healthy lives. She wants to visit Japan someday, so I'm also teaching her Japanese. I am so happy that I've made a Tanzanian friend. Thanks to Kawaguchi-sensei. She suggested that our class get to know more about Africa, and we have. This was a group project!"

I glanced over at Kawaguchi-sensei and she winked at me and smiled.

Then Miki turned to me and said, "And also, Loco-sensei! Asante Sana (thank you, in Swahili), arigatou gozaimasu (thank you, in Japanese)!" Then, she switched to English and added, "Thank you for teaching us about African-Americans. I hope we can speak in Swahili together. Tafadhali (please, in Swahili)."

I nodded to her, and choked back tears.

Then Miki and Terrence both bowed simultaneously at the staff and Kawaguchi ushered them out of the office. The meeting was called to a close and I stood there in a shower of praise from the puzzled faces of my co-workers. It was a good morning.

★ ★ ★ ★ ★

Later that day, I saw a mob of students standing in the hallway on the third floor near the water fountains, staring at the wall very intently. I was expecting to see graffiti or perhaps some kind of obscenity, their attention was so locked in, their expressions so enthralled. But, I was wrong. It was the poster Kawaguchi's class had made, mounted there on the wall, where one of those "Japanese Helping Pitiful Africans" posters used to be.

Interlude

You Ain't Gotta Explain Shit To me

LOCO in YOKOHAMA

I got on the train one morning and found myself standing next to one of my buddies from *The Company*. He was wearing earphones and hadn't noticed me so I nudged him. He didn't respond. I nudged him a little harder. He pulled his earphones out of his ears and turned on me like he was about to let me have it. Luckily he looked at me first.

Buddy: Hey! Mannnnnnn, I was about to. . .You don't even know.
Me: Sorry about that.
Buddy: Nah, my bad. it's just that some mornings I just wanna —
Me: You ain't gotta explain shit to me!
Buddy: (He laughed, *hard*!) Yeah, I guess not. A few weeks ago some Japanese guy was pushing on me almost the same way. I turned around, grabbed his wrist and told him in perfect Japanese "You asshole! If you do that shit again I'm gonna shove your hand up your ass!" I guess my Japanese scared the shit outta him.
Me: Yeah, and being about 6'7 and built like brick shit house didn't hurt either, I bet.
Buddy: (He laughed some more.) Somebody ought to write a sit-com about life here for us vertically-unchallenged folks, riding these damn cattle cars and teaching these bad ass kids.
Me: I'm on it!
Buddy: What? You're a writer?
Me: I dabble. Mostly I write about my kids and co-workers at the gig.
Buddy: You must have some of those little fuckers that love to tell teachers to go to hell.
Me: I do indeed.
Buddy: I learned most of my bad Japanese from them.
Me: Me too.
Buddy: One time I got mad at my wife and said "shine omae!" (Go to hell!) She actually slapped the shit out of me!
Me: Wow!
Buddy: That's some incredibly harsh shit to say to a Japanese woman. I mean back in the States, women would just roll with it, right? They'd be like, "and?"

Me: Yep. But not here, unless you set it up early that you have a bad case of potty mouth. I always do that now. It doesn't always work, but sometimes I can get away with saying some outrageous shit.

Buddy: Ha, ha, you're crazy. We should hang out some time. Damn, I forgot your name!

Me: It's Loco.

7

One Moment Please

(Syouganai Junior High)

LOCO in YOKOHAMA

The day I met Okubo-sensei my first impression of her turned out to be spot on.

It was at a very auspicious event, the annual Get-Your-Ripe-Gaijin farmer's market held right here in Yokohama the first week of April. It ought to be held on April fool's day, but it was actually taken very seriously. Perhaps calling it a farmer's market is overstating it a bit, though, because while some of the foreigners were fresh from the farm, the majority of us were far from fresh. It was more like the Westminster Dog Show. No, that would be unfair, to Westminster, that is.

But calling it the Yokohama Sideshow would not be.

So, let the sideshow begin. Hurry, hurry! Step right on in!

★ ★ ★ ★ ★

Marvel as 100-some odd foreigners are marched onto a stage before an auditorium audience of twice as many Japanese teachers for the sole purpose of . . .

Actually I'm still not sure why.

All I know is we're called to cut our spring vacations one day short every year to participate in something the powers that be have deemed important.

Stand in awe as these 100 or so foreigners as diverse as your typical MTV fare— basically vanilla with a dash of ethnic sprinkles for flavor— dressed in varying levels of professional attire, ignore persistent shushing from *The Company's* reps, these highfalutin guys and gals with the power to end teaching careers in Japan with a single swipe of their mighty iPads.

See the head honcho among them dispense glares that would give most children, and even some weakly constituted adults, bad dreams. She does this every few moments and the area becomes as hushed as a prison mess hall when a particularly sadistic warden makes an appearance, a silence that lasts until the moment she turns her back to deal with other business. Then the roar returns with a vengeance, as with every passing second our, meaning my, patience with this annual ritual wanes.

Then, after we wait a most taxing 1800 or so seconds, give a take a second or two, in the hallway outside the auditorium, where we can hear the closing remarks of the Japanese speaker introducing us, you're sure to gaze open-mouthed as we are marched onto the stage. The more attentive of you notice that the front row of this procession, where I am, dangerously teeters on the edge of the stage meant to hold maybe a maximum of 50 people. And your breath bates at the knowledge that an accidental nudge from the rear, or even a mild breeze, can send any one of us plunging into Japanese laps.

And the more discerning of you can't help notice my acrophobia-suffering ass inching backwards.

At the close of the show, each foreigner's name is called, one by one, by the Master of Ceremonies, at which point we climb down from the stage to join our Japanese benefactors seated and waving to get our attention.

★ ★ ★ ★ ★

I climbed down from the stage and walked over to where a 50-something woman, seated beside a familiar face, was waving to get my attention. The face I knew belonged to Takahashi, returning for a second tour of duty at Mendokusai. It was nice to see her, though I had expected to see my buddy Kawaguch, the more senior of the two.

"Hey you!" I said, in greeting. "Here we go again!"

Takahashi was still able to smile then, having not met Matsui or Mika-chan yet.

"I'm feeling very excited," she said. I liked her optimism, though it was probably just lip service 'cause of all the strange ears in the vicinity. We both had been warned that the incoming first-year students were going to be a trying lot. "I have a feeling it's gonna be a great year!"

"I hope you're right," I said and turned to the other woman, standing there with a grin only a grandchild could love on her face.

"This is Okubo-sensei," Takahashi said, her face hardly concealing how awkward she felt at that moment. I wondered why. It wasn't like she'd never introduced me to someone before. "She is the head teacher at Syouganai Junior high."

I threw on the charm. I've learned my smile is currency, especially here, so I whipped out a fat bankroll on her.

"It's a pleasure to meet you, Okubo-sensei!" I said. "I've heard so many great things about Syouganai and I'm really looking forward to working with you!"

LOCO in YOKOHAMA

Okubo smiled and waited for me to finish my unctuous greeting then glanced over at Takahashi with a look on her phizog that didn't so much say, "Would you mind translating what he just said?" or "Can you make heads or tails of what this guy is going on about," as it queried, "Why can't we be Venus instead of Earth? I'm thinking about buying a new car, did I tell you? You have unusually big breasts for Japanese. Are the mushrooms still on sale this week at Tokyu supermarket?"

And then she spoke.

Although every other word was English, and her pronunciation was astoundingly accurate, it was altogether unintelligible, even to me, a seasoned Japanese-English receptacle. This wasn't the first time I'd met an English teacher who couldn't speak English worth a damn. It was, however, the first time I'd met anyone who butchered it the way Okubo did, reflective of, at best, a total lack of syntax and structure, and, at worst, acute dain bramage. But I tried to roll with it as best I could.

After a moment of struggling to appear engaged during this onslaught, I gave up and switched to Japanese.

I re-introduced myself in Japanese to this Japanese teacher who'd been teaching English for over two decades, yet couldn't make a single simple sentence and, despite her deficiencies, had somehow been tasked as head English teacher at Syouganai junior high. But my use of Japanese enigmatically prompted her to translate my Japanese questions into incomprehensible English in an apparently unconscious compulsion to confirm I understood the words coming out of my own mouth. This compounded her own confusion because then she wasn't sure, or rather she was pretty damn certain I didn't understand a goddamn thing she was saying. Even when I'd switched back to English, she painfully attempted do the same thing to *my* English, only then she'd add a little chuckle after every word, apparently acknowledging, and embarrassed or amused by the irony of her position.

The reason for Takahashi's peculiar smile I now understood. She jumped in and explained to Okubo that my Japanese was good. Okubo smiled, nodded (as if she understood what Takahashi had said), and resumed her deconstruction and ultimate destruction of everything she said and everything I said, unabated by Takahashi's sporadic interventions.

Okubo would partially restore my faith in first impressions here in Japan, for she remained true to it the entire time I knew her.

BAYE McNEIL

★ ★ ★ ★ ★

It was still early in the semester when team-teaching with Okubo-sensei started to really bother me.

Not that I was so hung up on or silly enough to believe that any semblance of a quality English program existed in Japanese public schools. I wasn't. I had figured out even before my first year of teaching in public schools that the main culprit for the seemingly insurmountable challenge English has become to Japanese was the proliferation of katakana. Katakana, the system Japanese use to write and pronounce words of foreign origin, in my estimation, is culpable for both the Japanese inability to hear English and to speak it in most cases. It's an inoculation given to children that does more damage than the ailment it was created to address, and eventually this damage becomes irreparable because in order to learn English, they'll inevitably be tasked with un-learning katakana first. Outside of Japan, this is entirely doable, but for those who don't plan to live abroad, and will spend the remainder of their days in an environment where a word like "McDonald's" has six syllables instead of three, and English vowels are limited to one pronunciation, fuhgedaboutit.

So, no, I wasn't hung up on anything teaching-related. It was just that, well, it was difficult to stand by idly while the Japanese English teacher undermined and/or dismantled everything, no matter how minute, I tried to establish with the class. I didn't have high expectations. I didn't expect my students to walk away from their three years under my sway with the ability to converse in English. I really didn't.

I did, however, have a job to do. And, I took it as seriously as I felt I needed to.

I endeavored to make my classes fun and I designed my tasks to engage those students who were not completely averse to engagement. Even those students who had absolutely no interest in pursuing English beyond Junior High School knew that, if you came to Loco's class and you gave a little effort, you could have fun, with English, and you might very well walk away having learned some English almost effortlessly.

At least, this was how it was when I had run of the class. But, unfortunately, this was not always the case.

After my first few times team-teaching with Okubo, I unilaterally decided, in the best interest of the class, and my own sanity, I had better take over her class. The kids were falling asleep. Hell, even I was falling asleep, standing up. Something had to be done. Moreover, she liked to use me as her English voice box. She'd hand me the textbook, full of the strangest English ever set to print, replete with enough sweeping generalizations and stereotypes to make even the staunchest Japan apologists cringe, and force me to read this Japlish Jabberwocky aloud to the students. And then, tortuously, have them repeat it. This I would have to repeat for each of the eight classes, sometimes as many as five in a day.

I'd heard about this phenomenon, but had been blessed thus far not to work with any Japanese teachers who favored this method of under-utilizing native English-speaking teachers. But, my luck had run out. By the end of the day, I'd want to empty a full clip of Cop-Killers into Okubo.

Part of the problem was, like Yamada-sensei, she too had been making her own lessons before I came along. While Yamada's issue had been she was afraid to speak up, Okubo seemed incapable of speaking up, so I got all proactive and, without prompting from her, went ahead and made a lesson. Then, through my buddy Akiyama, I made the case to Okubo that it was in her best interest to let me make all the lessons, so she could have more time to handle her awesome administrative workload. This was necessary to save face, you see. She knew her classes sucked, you see. But, she was also the boss, Akiyama's and mine.

You see.

She readily agreed.

But, alas, it was not enough. She was a boss, and not the type to sit on the sidelines with her mouth shut. I guess I couldn't blame her, really. She knew no other way and change is rarely easy for anyone. Though my proactive-ness meant I never had to play the role of her human CD player again, her compulsion to interrupt my lessons with her foolishness didn't subside.

This inexplicable need to translate everything that emerged from my mouth into English gibberish or Japanese, which Akiyama had informed me on the down-low was often gibberish as well, was unfortunately not her only idiosyncrasy. I noticed yet another annoying tendency. Whenever I'd say something she didn't quite understand, which happened a great deal more often than it ought to, she had this habit of saying, "One moment, please," in well-practiced English, and then totally changing the subject and proceeding as if whatever I had said had not even warranted a response.

This is how it played out . . .

I gave the class a listening task. First, I explained the task, in English, using very few words that these second-year students weren't expected to know, and as many visual aids and sight cues as possible. The idea was to get the kids used to listening to instructions being given in proper English. But, in a class where only English is spoken, of what use was *she*, Okubo must have been thinking. And, she remedied that by jumping in and translating everything I said into Japanese. She must have felt gratified as the mildly confused faces of the students, accustomed to her style of English teaching where English is used maybe, generously, 10% of the class, became only slightly less confused.

I held my tongue as we started the listening task, a simple skit I wrote to illustrate the natural usage of the grammar point. The kids got it. I knew this because when I checked their understanding, hands were flying up! But, just to be on the safe side, and to give the students a chance to prove their comprehension, and something I did to help me with my Japanese comprehension I must confess, I got the students to translate chosen lines from the skit into Japanese.

At least, that's what I tried to do.

Okubo jumped in again and suggested that the skit was "muzukashii desu ne (difficult, isn't it)?" using that consensus-seeking tone I can't stand sometimes, and the group instinct took over. Half of the class decided that what they *thought* they understood they might not have understood as well as they thought.

I wanted to kill the bitch.

She proceeded to translate the skit, line by line, into Japanese. And, the students, even the ones who had understood the skit before her translation, nodded that 'naru hodo (oh, I see)' nod they do when they want to show they get something that they hadn't gotten before.

The ultimate result of this foolishness, I knew from experience, would be they'd stop listening to my English explanations altogether and start waiting for Okubo's translation every time.

I wasn't raised to acquiesce to the aged simply because they're older, as many Japanese are, so it was all I could do not to confront her in front of the class. But I held my tongue. Later in the class, though, while the kids were doing a reading exercise, I whispered to her, "If you translate everything I say into Japanese, the students will never listen to my English. They'll just wait for your translation."

She smiled, nodded, seemingly in agreement, and replied, "One moment, please . . ."

★ ★ ★ ★ ★

When you start at a new school, the first-year students are the only students that might not have experienced a foreigner teaching them English. You may very well be the first non-Japanese person they have interacted with in their entire short lives. This won't be the case with second and third-year students, however, nor with the teachers. They will have worked with or been taught by your predecessor.

In my case, it was a gentleman by the name of John.

John had been teaching at Syouganai for three years before my arrival. The students knew him well, and so did the faculty. And, he'd left an imprint on everyone, both good and bad.

This was an imprint that so far had, unfortunately, hindered me as often as it had helped me. The next day, team-teaching with Okubo, there were instances of both.

One of the things you must do as an ALT is adjust to the teaching style of every teacher you team-teach with. I'd usually spend the first couple of weeks studying their style and trying to see how I could best fit in. Or, in Okubo's case, how she would like me to fit in. She'd been teaching English the better part of a quarter of a century, so she had her way of doing things and it was unlikely I or anyone else would be able to inspire much change in her.

But, from the very beginning of class that day, there was a glimmer of hope.

Many Japanese English teachers like to start the class with an English song. Okubo used music, too. . .I learned that day. If I had known that previously, I would have tried to recommend a song to her. It turned out that that wasn't necessary.

"Today," she said to the class, in Japanese of course, "we are joined by John-sensei, and he will . . ."

One student shouted out, "You mean, Loco-sensei, don't you?"

Okubo laughed to herself, in that crazy way she does after every other word she utters. "I'm sorry. Of course I mean . . ."

"Don't you even know his name?" another student yelled out.

Okubo laughed again, a flustered cackle.

"John was white, he's black!" the first yeller yelled.

"John-sensei was Canadian, Loco-sensei's American!" the second added.

"John was boring as shit, Loco is cool!" another chimed in.

The whole class laughed. I bit my lip to hold mine in.

"OK, OK," Okubo-sensei sang. "Let's do the song, now. Open your notebooks to the song's lyrics."

I cringed in anticipation of one of those irksome staples Japanese teachers use. She whipped out a CD and, to my utter surprise, from the boom box's speakers emerged, reggae?

Oh my god! It was Jimmy Cliff doing his rendition of "I Can See Clearly Now".

Okubo realized with a glance at my empty hands that not only hadn't she told me about the song but that she hadn't provided me with the sheet the students and she already had.

I told her not to worry about it.

She smiled and nodded as she reached for her bag.

The kids liked the song and everyone sang as well as they could. But, Okubo spent half the song strip-searching her bag of materials for a copy of the lyrics for me.

As if . . .

I told her again, in English, in Japanese, and in a combination of them both, that I didn't need one, that the song was very famous, covered by a dozen artists, and I knew the words by heart. But, due to the affliction she suffered from, the sounds emerging from my mouth were discarded like junk mail, or like Anti-Virus software does cookies.

"One moment please," she said.

Three-quarters of the way through the song she found a sheet with the lyrics and handed it to me like she'd found the contact lenses I'd misplaced, the ones I was blind without. She was looking at me, beaming with pride, a gleam in her eye that said "no thanks required, just doing my part to improve relations between our species."

I just stared back at her, sans the detestation I felt, and sang, ". . . *I can see all the obstacles in my way* . . ."

After the class, Jimmy Cliff's voice still humming in my heart, I asked her, in every language at my disposal, how she had selected that song; a song that was as far from the standard musical menu as J-pop is from listenable.

"One moment please."

A full 15 minutes later I got my answer. That is, after we got back to the office and once I had asked Akiyama-sensei to ask her for me. Akiyama had begrudgingly become my go-between, and, for all intents and purposes, the unofficial Head Teacher, especially as it pertained to communications between Okubo and me. I felt bad about that, but what was I to do?

"She said the previous ALT, John-sensei, had chosen it," Akiyama said, looking mind-boggled, as any conversation with Okubo had a tendency to do to the other party.

Well, John might have been *boring as shit*, but at least he had good taste in music.

★ ★ ★ ★ ★

"His Excellency" came from one of the best public high schools in Kanagawa prefecture. He was just visiting, the principal explained the next day at the morning meeting in a rather prolonged intro replete with some very flowery Japanese in which the man's entire resume was offered up as proof of his status as a man among men.

He stepped forward to introduce himself, bathed in the afterglow of the words of praise that had just been poured over him by the most powerful man in the school. He was a tall, sharply-dressed, bespectacled fellow, and spoke Japanese very carefully like someone trying desperately not to be misunderstood, or someone speaking to the mentally-challenged.

"Is he Japanese?" I whispered to Akiyama, once his intro was done.

"Hush!" she said, in reverence, over the extended applause, elbowing me playfully.

Yeah, she'd noticed, too.

"Of course he is!" she said after a moment or so, once the clamor had subsided.

"Why the hell does he talk like that then?"

Akiyama started to say something, then stopped, then started again, then stopped again.

"What?"

"I don't know how to say it in English," she confessed.

"Say it in Japanese, then."

"Kare wa erai hito (he is an erai hito)," she whispered, her two eyes scanning the room sharply for raised eyebrows or any clue that she was being heard. She had everyone in the office visually covered.

"Erai hito?" I mouthed back. I'd heard the word "erai" before. Sometimes my co-workers would say "erai" to me, especially when they'd catch me studying or deep in concentration writing a story, or something like that. In that case, I learned it meant someone who distinguished himself by how hard he worked at something. I assumed Akiyama's usage was along the same lines, but only for a second. I'd learned my lesson about assuming anything in Japan the hard way. So, I pulled out my dictionary.

It informed me that an "erai hito" was like a big-shot.

Was it being used the same way we would use "big-shot" in America, I wondered. I then glanced over at the visiting erai hito, chatting with the principal and vice principal. His pride at being a teacher at one of the most exclusive public schools in the area shined through. He had a swagger, as much as I'd seen from a Japanese person, redolent of Ichiro Suzuki or a yakuza boss. He was speaking up to them, using the appropriate honorifics and all, while at the same time looking down on them. Probably 'cause they were kissing his ass so. A regular osoji-matsuri (flattery fest).

Yeah, I knew what erai hito meant.

Akiyama had watched all of this, reading my face as I read the definition and checked out Erai-sama. When I smiled kind of snidely, she knew I got it.

"How do you say it in English?" she asked.

"We have different ways. You can say "big shot" or "VIP". VIP is much nicer than big-shot, though."

"He's a big shot, right?"

"Don't hate on the man," I said jokingly to Akiyama, and started fingering my cellphone. "You know you wish you had his job!"

"How did you know *that*?"

"Huh . . ." I said, distracted by some message on my Twitter page. "Know what?"

I looked up, and Akiyama was staring at me, bedazzled. She looked like I'd told her fortune.

"Did I tell you that?"

"Tell me what?" She looked kind of scared, actually.

"That I wanted to teach at that same school sooooo bad," she cried. "And I still do!"

"Maybe, you did, " I said. But I didn't think so, I was just messing with her. "Why?"

"I don't remember telling you. "

"I was just joking, Yoko," I said. "Don't worry! You don't look envious or anything."

She relaxed a little. She liked when I call her by her first name. Her eyes were still somewhere between suspicious and relieved.

"Apparently he's an English teacher," I told her to change the subject. "And, he's gonna be visiting my first period class with Okubo. This oughta be good. I'll let you know if he's an asshole."

Finally, she lightened up and laughed.

For first period, Okubo-sensei and I were teaching third-year students with. When I arrived at the classroom, guess who was standing in the back? He was looking very full of himself, smug as a tenured Yale professor visiting a prestigious high school full of ambitious American students that wanted nothing more than to be in his good graces and someday attend Yale.

The students seemed to pick up on his vibe, too. When there'd been visitors previously, the students would glance back at them quite often, but with His Excellency the kids hardly did so, as if they were embarrassed to be under his scrutiny.

Okubo's introduction didn't help any.

"Today, class, we have a very, *very* special visitor. Direct from his lofty position as head of the foreign language department at the number one high school in Kanagawa prefecture—" and she said some crazy long ass name I couldn't catch, but all the kids knew it well— "please join me in welcoming the illustrious, the exquisite, the sublime Mister Big Stuff!"

Applause rang out as all heads turned his way now.

The majority of the students gawked 'cause they were just aching to attend this school they'd heard so much about. How impressive would that be! This was the kind of school that would make them the pride of their families for generations to come, that almost guaranteed that Keio, Waseda, or even Tokyo University—the crème de la crème of Japanese schools— would give them the time of day. The remainder of the students, however, couldn't care less about which high school they went to, if they went at all. They just wanted to see what a big shot educator looked like. But, they gave him their undivided attention nonetheless because . . . well . . . from Okubo's over-the-top introduction they must have gathered that anything less would have been tantamount to scholastic sacrilege, punishable by lashes in the school garden, or worse.

Mr. Big Stuff swaggered to the front of the class, sopping up the spotlight like a biscuit does gravy. He stood before the mostly rapt teenagers, seizing the moment of silence by the teats, and with the skill of a seasoned politician or a reverend at his pulpit, he milked it, creamed it and churned it into butter.

And then he began to speak.

I was already filling in my mental report card for Akiyama.

I just knew his English was gonna be atrocious.

★ ★ ★ ★ ★

"Hello, students! My name is Mr. Big Stuff," he said in English.

"Eeeeto," began Okubo-sensei, clearing her scratchy throat. "Kochira-sama no namae wa, Misuta Bii-gu Sta-fu desu (This honorable gentleman's name is Mr. Big Stuff)!"

He glanced sideways at her. Actually, he cut his eyes and slashed her throat open with them. I'd rarely seen such open hostility from a Japanese man. It was kinda shocking.

"I will teach you one thing today," he said, raising a finger, finding his smile, casting its warm glow on the student body. "I want to —"

"Misuta Bii-gu Sta-fu sama wa, anata-tachi ni—" Okubo began, translating every word, and giggling nervously after every other syllable.

"I'm sorry, you're Mrs. Okubu, right?" he asked, softly, turning to her.

"Sumimasen, anata wa Okubo-san, deshou ka (I'm sorry, Mrs. Okubo, right)?" she said to the students, lost in translation, still doing what her brain told her was necessary to justify her being there at all.

Some of the students, realizing what was happening, started giggling.

"Okubo-sensei," I called to her in a stage whisper. "He's talking to you!"

"Sorry, Loco-sensei," she said, giggling stupidly, and then screwing up her face like I'd interrupted her thought process. "One moment please."

Mr. Big Stuff was still eyeing Okubo. Clearly he comprehended the situation, if that bewildered look on his face was any indication. He looked like someone watching a person he'd known for years to be sound of mind and body suddenly having an epileptic seizure. She was still grinning like an imbecile at the class, waiting for the next line to translate.

I sidled closer to her and tapped her on the shoulder.

She turned on me like I'd stepped out of another dimension. Then laughed, embarrassed, as if to say, 'oh, it's just you Loco-sensei.'

"He's trying to get your attention," I said in very slow and careful Japanese, reminiscent of how Mr. Big Stuff had spoken to the whole faculty in the morning meeting, knowing damn well she still wouldn't understand me. At least that had been the status quo to date. I caught his half-smile out of the side of my eye. I gestured in Mr. Big Stuff's direction and she turned around to face him.

Under his breath, he said to her in Japanese, "If you don't mind, could I speak to the students without your translation? I know you mean well but it kind of defeats the purpose of my little lesson if you translate my words, don't you agree?"

She turned purple, and giggled hysterically as she bowed and backed off, saying to the class, in Japanese, "The magnanimous Mr. Big Stuff will teach you a short lesson now."

He looked at her with an astonished look on his face a little longer than decorum dictated he should. I just knew what he was thinking: 'This bitch is crazy!'

Erai hito or not, he'd garnered himself some cool points on my report card. Quite a few.

The students were watching this exchange, bemused and embarrassed for Okubo. But, like me, they too had gotten used to her antics so it came as no surprise.

"OK, so," and he proceeded to test their listening with a little story about his three daughters. Most of them understood even without Okubo's translation. It was no surprise to Mr. Big Stuff and I, but Okubo, it just didn't seem to register with her. She stood off to the side grinning and nodding her head, entertained by something therein.

His English benefited from having lived abroad, but, he'd probably been back in Japan quite sometime because he'd reacquired or retained some of the typical issues Japanese have when they've only studied English in Japan. He dropped or confused several articles and prepositions and a good number of his words he pronounced Japanese style. But, overall he was pretty damn decent and spoke English with the confidence of someone whose verbal skill has been praised and positively reinforced. That added an air of fluency to it that I liked, too. Confidence is a rare quality here when it comes to English. I constantly try to impress upon my adult students that confidence is key to communicating and that if they spoke with even a little pluck, people would often overlook whatever grammatical deficiencies they had and focus on the message.

When he was done, the students applauded. So did I. He basked in it.

He'd only taken up a couple of minutes with his unannounced mini-lesson but I decided to skip the warm-up game and jump straight to my lesson plan to make up for the time lost. I began by telling the students about my summer plans. This was a listening task which the kids handled with ease, primed as they were to actually listen in English.

Thanks to Mr. Big Stuff.

He stood in the back of the room taking notes, looking every bit the consummate professional. Occasionally he'd nod approvingly at my technique. I don't know why, but it made me feel great!

During the peer work portion of the lesson, I walked around the classroom checking that the students were using English and understood the lesson. I was really working my way around to where he was standing, though. Every time I stopped to help a group of students, I'd look up and his eyes would be locked on me. His smile was ingratiating.

Finally, I got around to him.

"Hi! My name is Loco," I said, extending a hand. He took it.

"Nice to meet you, Loco-sensei!"

"Nice to meet you, too."

You have wonderful skill with students!"

"You think so? Thanks!"

"Yes, you are great, and kids seem to like you so."

"Well, they're great kids," I said, a little embarrassed by the praise.

"How long have you been on Japan?" he asked, errors flowing casually and confidently from his mouth.

"About 7 years now."

"Wow! You must be fluent in Japanese until now!"

"No, my Japanese is OK. Not as good as your English, though!"

"Oh, no, no, no, my English is poor!"

"Did you study English in the US?" I asked, watching his face.

"Well, yes," he said, showing nervousness for the first time. "I live in the States for two years!"

"Really?" I asked, hiding the distaste I feel every time I hear anyone un-American, particularly Japanese, call America 'The States'. I don't know why. It just feels like they're trying to be too familiar. "Where?"

"I lived in Tennessee. I was a junior high school student in there."

"Tennessee!" I snapped. It was the last place I expected to hear.

"Yes," he sighed, like it had been a shameful confession.

"Well, at least you don't have a Tennessee accent," I laughed. "People might mistake you for an Elvis impersonator."

And, I sung a bar of "Love Me Tender" in my best Elvis voice. He laughed hard.

"I went to Graceland while I live there!" he said, through his laughter. "It was beautiful place. Elvis was so great!"

I looked up and several of the students were gawking at us. They rarely get to see an actual English conversation.

Later, when I met up with Akiyama in the teachers' office, she asked, "So, how is he?"

"Who? Mr. Big Stuff?" I asked, smiling. "Well, not what you'd expect from an erai hito. He was actually pretty down to earth!"

"*Down to earth*?" she said, looking confused. "Ummmm, one moment please."

We both fell out laughing.

I owe Mr. Big Shot a debt of gratitude, though. He'd set Okubo straight. Somehow his admonishment had actually gotten through that fog in her mind because, from that day on, Okubo never translated my English into Japanese again.

8
Protocol
(Mendokusai Junior High)

I learned a new word, "uzai"! And like most of the things I've learned here in Japan, I learned it the hard way; from my favorite thirteen-year-old terrorist: Matsui-kun.

During the class (in which nothing was learned and by the looks of things, soon, nothing will be attempted to be taught either), Matsui-Kun suddenly stood up on his chair and hollered, "Babaa, I mean, Takahashi-sensei! Can I go outside?"

The class laughed at his faux-Freudian slip. "Babaa", used the way he used it, means an "old hag" or "old bitch". Takahashi was fuming, and again, that glutton for punishment in me I call a heart went out to her. I mean, it seemed she was getting very little if any support from the other teachers and every time I returned to the school, the students and classes kept getting exponentially worse.

"Let's take our seats everyone," she said, calmly.

Matsui ignored her. It was a balmy 65 degrees outside, so Matsui decided to take a stroll on the terrace overlooking the exercise field and gymnasium. He slid the glass door open and went outside. Satou-kun was quick to rise and join him. Takahashi pretended not to see any of this and urged me to ignore it as well. While Matsui began shouting down at second-year students out on the field, cheering them on as they played soccer, I tried to get through the game of the day, "the buzz game".

The buzz game is a game in which all the children in the class stand up, and starting with the student in the front row on the left or right side of the class, begin to count from one. Any number that has a three or is divisible by three should not be said. Instead you must say, "Buzz" while keeping the rhythm by clapping after each number; for example, it's "one", clap, "two", clap, buzz, clap, "four", clap, "five", clap, "buzz", etc. It gets pretty tricky in the higher numbers, English being a second language for 99% of the kids, but the kids usually get into it.

Even Matsui-kun.

So when he heard the clapping, he rejoined the class, Satou in tow. He proceeded to mount his chair, as usual. Then he took it to next level, and climbed perilously atop his desk. Up there he began clapping and counting off all the numbers as loud as he could. Each student should only say their number or "buzz" so he was distracting the students who were trying to concentrate on the game, his goal no doubt! All the students watched him up there, unchallenged by the so-called authority, and like that touching scene at the end of "Dead Poets Society", some of them started mounting their desks, too.

I glanced at Takahashi. She had her cheeks puffed up in a pantomimic expression of anger, but her eyes were misty, and I could see it was all she could do not to start crying in front of the students or run screaming out of the room. I looked up at Matsui. For a menace, he really was the cutest kid in the school. He had a ridiculously disarming smile and he knew it, and he wielded it like magic wand. He weighed less than my knapsack and I couldn't help but imagine that, if I were to have a son with a Japanese woman in Japan, I would want him to have the courage and individuality of this little mofo. He was such a rarity.

"Loco-sensei, that old bitch Takahashi is noisy, ain't she?" he asked in Japanese.

While a good quarter of the other students halfheartedly clapped and tried to keep up the motions of playing the buzz game and of being in an institution of learning where they might expect to learn something, a solid seven or eight students were now standing atop their desks chatting and throwing things at each other like this was the most natural thing to do. The only quiet people in the class were Takahashi and I. So I wondered why Matsui called her noisy.

"She isn't noisy. You're the noisy one!"

"You got it wrong!" he snapped back, his Japanese traveling at a terrific clip. "Not noisy. She's "*uzai!*"

All the students laughed. I loathed these awkward moments of vulnerability. I had so many holes in my Japanese that it was child's play for the kids to crawl into the holes and play with my head. That's why I tried to avoid using it as much as possible, but the kids were always trying to communicate and they simply couldn't in English.

"What does Uzai mean?"

"Uzai is uzai!"

Everybody laughed.

"When do you use it?"

"I use it when I get irritated! And that old bitch makes me sick!"

I wanted to support him because, like most children, his ability to judge character was spot on. He could perceive her for what she really was, someone of dubious respectability. But that wasn't my job at the moment and I had to consider other things, like the power this "babaa" had over me with her friggin' pen. The power to stress up my life. The power to sic Silky Tony and *The Company* on me. I had to intervene on her behalf somehow, so assuming a stern demeanor, donning my *daddy don't take no mess* mask, I said to Matsui in English, accompanied by hand gestures, "Alright, Sparky, come on down from there."

The other students were clearly taking their cue from Matsui. If he acquiesced, they'd all acquiesce. If he got down, they'd all get down.

Matsui looked at me with that heavenly smile of his, cocked his said to the side, took a cursory glance at Takahashi Babaa (her new name in my mind), folded his arms, and said, "No!"

I must've looked pretty fucking silly standing there with "no" dripping from the frozen smile on my face.

I'd lived here in Japan a number of years by then. And, in all that time, I could count on one hand the number of times someone Japanese, male or female, had said directly to me, in response to a question, request, suggestion, or in this case, a command, "no!" In the US, I would say it was about the equivalent of a child hawking up a big thick curdling glob of phlegm and firing it right in your face, someone else's child. A child you couldn't break in half over your knee.

It actually took me a moment to even process it because I'd become so unaccustomed to hearing the word "no" in all its glory. I mean, it really is an awesome word. I know the current zeitgeist says that "yes" is a much stronger force for good in the world and all, but "no" ain't no slouch. "No" is the quintessential word of rebellion and revolution, concepts I was taught, at an even younger age than Matsui, were the only methods for achieving meaningful change.

Again I had to refrain from applauding him.

Fortunately, the bell rang and he just got down of his own accord, looking at me through smiling eyes as if to say 'this was fun, wasn't it?'

Takahashi Babaa-sensei was halfway out of the classroom before the Westminster Chimes were even completed.

★ ★ ★ ★ ★

When I was about 10, and still attending the private school I discussed earlier, there was a protocol for everything, from how to ask for permission to go to the bathroom, to how to say prayers in Swahili before meals, to how to pledge allegiance to Black Power and the struggle for black nationhood.

For example, the protocol for answering questions went something like this: the math teacher would pose a question like, "What is the product of 5 and 5?" (And, yeah, he would word the question in such a way so as to trip you up). He would then call on a student to answer the question (God have mercy on those who couldn't) and that student would have to, according to the protocol, hop up from his seat, stand at attention, and say, "Hapa! ("here", in Swahili) I appreciate what's been said, and if I understand correctly, the product is 25."

Yeah, it was a mouthful for a seven-year old.

In Japanese junior high schools there are protocols, as well.

Case in point: The teacher's office in the school is considered holy ground, and the teachers are the clergy. At least the teachers feel so, and would like the students to respect that notion. So, there is a protocol students must follow in order to enter or speak with a teacher; a humbling one, of course. And on the anal retentiveness or slackness of the teachers does this ground's holiness wholly depend. To this end, when a student comes to the office to speak with a teacher, they must follow, to a "T", the following protocol: They must first knock, beg forgiveness for having disturbed the honorable teachers within, announce themselves by name, year and class, and, then, even if the teacher they want to speak with is standing before them or is in clear view, they must ask whether or not that teacher is currently in the office. And, then they must wait for an official response.

It goes something like this: "Please forgive my intrusion. I am Hideki Kawasaki of the First-year Class two. Would you be so kind as to tell me whether Ms. Takahashi is in the office?"

In response to the student, a teacher would reply either that Takahashi wasn't in, or if she were there she'd go to the door to speak with the student. Once his business was completed, the student would then take his leave, but not before saying, "Please forgive me for having disturbed you."

This is a mouthful for Japanese students, as well. So, until they get it right, some teachers will stand at the door with the student having them repeat it over and over. This is done to the first-year students in an effort to keep them in check and show them who was running the show around here. But by the time the kids are third-year students, they know very well who runs the show—they do. By then, the protocol would be rote, so they'd inject their own personalities into it. They might downgrade "would you be so kind as to tell me whether Ms. So and So is in the office" to "is Ms. So and SO here" or even the Japanese equivalent of, "yo, So and So, you up in this piece, or what?" if they were one of the knuckleheads. But every student followed this protocol, if only a modified version of.

However, nobody did it like Matsui-kun.

In the 10-minute break between classes, the kids usually horse around, read manga, play cards, or just stand around the old-fashioned kerosene stove heaters in the classrooms trying to stay warm (there was no central heating in junior high schools) in the winter like it was a camp fire. Sometimes the girls would even sing songs. Or, on muggy summer days, they'd try to stay within the oscillation field of the one of the two electric fans in every classroom.

However, there were two students from every class whose responsibility it was to come to the teacher's office and assist the teacher of the following period with whatever supplies they may need carried. For English class, we often used a boom box, so the two students would carry the teacher's bag with our lesson materials in it and the boom box up to the classroom. This duty supposedly rotated around the class, but it always seemed to be the same students as far as I could tell.

But the next day after the "no" phlegm-hurtling incident, this duty must have rotated around to Matsui and Satou.

I was sitting at my desk trying to not look like I was writing a book about life in Japan, when from the doorway a high-pitched voice, at the highest possible volume, screamed: "Please forgive my intrusion!"

Some teachers actually jumped out of their seats like a gun had gone off, while others gave their necks whiplash turning to look at the door. I was accustomed to this yelling, and so were the first-year teachers sitting over in their section near the door, Takahashi among them. But, the other teachers were totally alarmed, which tickled Matsui senseless. He started laughing in the doorway.

When he noticed me he screamed, "Yo! Loco-sensei! What's up? Takahashi is an annoying bitch, ain't she?" Then, there was this collective gasp of shock from the office that sounded something like "Gaaaaaaan!" as he casually sauntered onto sacred ground, Satou shadowing him.

I just shook my head, trying not to smile.

"Where is that bitch, anyway?" Ain't she here?" Then he turned where he knew she was sitting and hollered, "Never mind, I found her! Listen here, lady! Hurry the hell up, will ya?"

How much of a deviation was this from the norm? Well, comparing the two of them to the trench coat mafia on that horrific day at Columbine high school would only be overstating it a little.

The teachers, these high priest and priestesses, sat in various stages of stupefied in their now desecrated sanctuary. At the head of the office, the principal and vice principal, who'd witnessed this sacrilege, glanced at one another, in a brief moment of indecision over who should be the one to handle this situation. I actually thought I caught the VP cock his eyebrow, but it may have been a tick. Nevertheless, it was the principal who rose and came from behind the front desk.

All eyes were glued to him, even Matsui's.

This was to be a moment.

He walked towards Matsui. Matsui stiffened as the principal approached him. I almost thought I saw something in his eyes that might have been intimidation, but it was only there for a micro-second, and I think it had more to do with the principal's height (he was actually taller than me, at about 185 cm) than any threat he actually posed.

"Are you OK?" the principal asked, in a way that conveyed the question, "What the hell is your problem?"

"I'm just fine and dandy!" Matsui responded in Japanese he'd use to address a classmate and not an adult, and with a tone that was more at "I don't have problems, Mr. Man. I *sling* problems! You looking to score? You came to the right place! I'm your boy!"

All of this as Satou-kun came creeping into the scene, sliding up beside Matsui as if he'd sensed trouble brewing and if something was going to go down and someone was going to get hurt, he wasn't about to let Matsui be the first. He'd make a great secret service agent if Matsui were Prime Minister.

The principal noticed the arrival of Satou-kun sidling up next to Matsui, too, and he really didn't know what to make of it.

But I did.

In NY, we'd call that shit gangsta. Straight gangsta!

LOCO in YOKOHAMA

He reminded me of "Bob the Goon" in Tim Burton's Batman. The Joker was a ruthless sociopath, but his number one henchman, Bob the Goon, was the man who got shit done, and was ever-ready to bust a cap in someone's ass at his boss' behest. In one scene in the movie, The Joker had unexpectedly had a gun drawn on him by a crooked cop. But, in a flash that would impress even Sergio Leone, Bob the Goon's gun appeared over the Joker's shoulder, cocked and aimed at the would-be assailant's head!

I couldn't help but notice the principal had actually taken an involuntary half-a-step backwards.

Takahashi was standing there like she had been hoping and praying that the principal would do something on her behalf, maybe expel the boy, or at least scold him for blatantly disregarding the protocol in the office; it was something no other student in the school, other than the mentally-challenged cases in the special class, had ever done. If not aggressively discouraged, it could certainly undermine discipline and bring chaos.

But, he didn't.

In fact, the principal turned to Takahashi and, without words or even body language, conveyed, 'You heard him, get a move on, Missy! And get this little menace outta my office. Can't you see he's embarrassing me in front of my staff?'

It was all in his eyes.

Matsui's and the principal's eyes met one last time as he gave the principal a cheeky little manga wink, as if to say "ain't nobody bad like me, right?" Then he spun on his heels and made his way over to Takahashi's desk. Then, as if to amplify and aggravate what the principal had said to Takahashi with his eyes, Matsui snapped, "Move it, bitch!" as he snatched up Takahashi's tote bag full of teaching materials.

Then he headed for the door to the office. At the door he spun back around, like he'd forgotten something, and screamed at a deafening decibel, "Sorry to have disturbed you guys!"

Then he exited the office, without as much as a glance back.

Satou crept out behind him covering his rear, lugging Takahashi's boom box on his shoulder like some throwback to Brooklyn in the 80s, sauntering agilely in reverse, eyes sharp and nimble, face as deadpan as a hit-man.

He never said a word.

Interlude

You Had Me at Sumimasen

LOCO in YOKOHAMA

I was on the Toyoko Line, headed home to Yokohama, enjoying the extra space I'm often afforded by my fainthearted fellow commuters. The car was full but the seat beside mine was empty. I noticed, but on any given day the amount of attention I pay this phenomenon varies from "too much" to "as little as possible".

This was one of those "as little as possible" days.

I had my iPad on my lap and was reading (and responding) to some of the comments I'd gotten on a blog series I was working on.

I looked up to see that the train had pulled into Jiyugaoka station. The person sitting on the opposite side of the empty space beside me got up, collected himself and got off the train along with a good number of the other passengers. As the boarding passengers filed in, I told myself not to pay them any mind. I hate that spat-on feeling I get when I see Japanese people, clearly eager to sit down, spot the empty seat near me, and actually make an instinctual move toward it. Then, once their eyes scrape over me, abruptly alter their trajectory and scurry away. Almost as much as I hate the magnetism this behavior possesses, that of a 20-car pile up on the highway, with bloodied corpses hanging out of shattered windshields. I have to consciously force myself not to watch.

I closed my eyes, nodded my head downward towards my iPad, and re-opened them, only to read a comment on the post, some sycophantic japanophile drivel about how I was to blame for the behavior I was avoiding watching at that moment, due to my being a loud, obnoxious, extroverted by nature and living in a country where the introverts have the power.

I took a deep breath, and before I could exhale, I noticed two tiny legs standing before me. I looked up to see a mother and daughter that had boarded the train. The mother glanced at me, then at the seat. Then she pointed and aimed her daughter towards it, frankly shocking the shit outta me.

The youngster, all of four or five, resisted her mother's nudge, and cried, "Kowai," eyes brimming with fear. She grabbed and clung to her mother's leg for dear life, eyes transfixed on me.

Her mother was genuinely dumbfounded by her daughter's reaction, and would have exploded, and taken half of Tokyo with her, if embarrassment was made of nitroglycerin.

There was something else there in her eyes and expression, though. Something I couldn't get a read on.

Generally when this kind of thing happens, if I'm acknowledged at all, the parent will adopt a mien that suggests she or he was thinking, "thank god he's a foreigner and has no idea what my child said." It's almost cute. Like they believe this fear is some well-kept secret, like the body language of the child doesn't scream the meaning of the word.

At least I tell myself it's almost cute.

I braced for the next move. How will Mama address this? Reinforce the fear? Ignore it, as if it's to be expected and nothing can be done about it? These are the two most popular options, and I expected nothing less.

I tried to turn away, but the rubbernecker in me seized control of my neck, and commanded, *"You loud, obnoxious, extrovert, take it like a man!"*

But, this woman did nothing of the sort.

Instead, *she* took the seat beside me and her daughter took the seat on the other side of her.

She glanced my way, smiled warmly, and said, "Sumimasen" as if to say "Sorry about that. Kids, whatchagonnado."

I shook my head and waved it off, with a sympathetic and indulgent, "iie" to say, "don't sweat it, Love. I work with kids every day and they say and do the damnedest things."

I'm sure I was smiling at that point, but my mind couldn't immediately wrap around what had just transpired.

As per usual, I slid away from her as far as I could, which was about half an inch or so. I do this instinctively whenever Japanese people sit down beside me. I've found that this gesture tends to alleviate some of their discomfort, and there is almost always discomfort. I'm not talking about physical discomfort. Generally, there is sufficient space for a person to sit beside me without having to squeeze in. Besides, I really don't care about anyone's physical comfort. It was, without fail, the last free seat on a crowded train upon which nobody is supposed to be truly comfortable. And to expect to be comfortable, particularly here in Yokohama, would, to my reckoning, be irrational. No, I'm talking about mental discomfort; a general inability to sit still and relax evidenced by persistent shifting, fidgeting, repeated sideways glancing, inching away, sometimes even scratching.

She must have noticed me sliding away, because she looked at me sideways, then down at the little sliver of seat that appeared between us as a result of my scooching over, and kind of smiled and bowed.

I just grinned.

I returned my attention to the foolishness I was reading on the iPad.

Every so often, I noticed peripherally, a tiny head poking out from the other side of mom. It was the little girl. Whenever I would turn my head her way she'd duck back behind her mother, in that peek-a-boo way children do. Her face was still sour, though, like she hadn't made up her mind whether I was *"kowai-*worthy" or not, and was wondering what the hell was her mom thinking trying to seat her beside me.

Around the third or fourth time she peek-a-boo'd me, I waited with my face in her direction for her to re-emerge. When she did, I turned away and waited for her to duck her head back behind her mother. Then, I turned her way again and waited. When she re-emerged this time, before I turned away, I caught a glimpse of a smile on her face.

Then, I noticed we were pulling into my station, so I packed up my iPad and stood to disembark. As I made my way for the door, I turned one last time.

The little girl was looking at me. Her fear was gone, replaced by what could have been glee. She waved at me and said, "bye-bye."

I waved back, glancing at her mother and this time I *could* read the expression on her face. It was gratitude!

I knew exactly how she felt 'cause I felt the same.

9
The Makings of Mrs. Betty
(Syouganai Junior High)

Yamada-sensei had been absent on and off ever since the day I confronted her about calling me "Loco" in front of the class and telling the students to do the same. Each time she'd been absent, she'd had an excuse. Either it was her own health problem or the health of someone near and dear to her.

Then, one day, she suddenly put in for an extended leave of absence for reasons and a duration none of us were made privy to. She was entitled to her privacy, after all.

I felt responsible. Kinda. I mean, I did kinda come on strong and let my true feelings go for a joy ride. Sometimes I went months without letting anything get under my skin. I'd simply shut down mentally and emotionally and let the everyday nonsense glide by like it was happening to someone else. The downside of this coping strategy was, when I did let loose, there was a chance the agitator might catch it for all those folks I'd let slide. People like the guy on the train that took his wallet out of his back pocket and held it securely in his hand once he noticed me behind him, or the staff girl in the McDonald's who—after I had already placed my order, in Japanese, as I had been for half a decade—turned over the Japanese menu to reveal the English version on the underside. She did this while wearing a smile so wholesome and angelic that it wouldn't be out of place in a convent and appeared to be operating under the oblivious belief that she had done me a great service. Either of them could have caught it, but I refrained and kept that shit inside because I knew that, at least at work, I had this temporary sanctuary from the foolishness—an air pocket in the painfully slow pillow-soft suffocation I suffered while mingling among the masses.

And, although unintentionally, Yamada had taken to ritualistically desecrating my sanctuary.

Only three teachers, as far as I knew, were directly impacted by her declining attendance. There was me, but I was torn between celebrating it and lamenting it. Then there was Akiyama who, in Yamada's absence, shouldered the bulk of Yamada's teaching responsibilities. That is, she did until a few weeks of this had passed— and this is one of the reasons I loved her. She'd got fed up and called a meeting with the principal and VP during which she told them, in no uncertain terms—it was hard to believe she was from the land of uncertain terms—that she was not going to teach any more of Yamada's classes and that it was beyond unfair for them to expect her to carry this burden. The principal and his vice tried to get her to back down, but Akiyama—her voice clearly heard through the principal's closed office door—emerged from the skirmish victorious.

The next week, the third teacher affected by Yamada's absenteeism arrived. She was a substitute teacher brought in to pick up the slack and make all our lives a little easier. She would do much more than that, though. Her name was Betty. At least that's what I called her because she reminded me of an incongruent cross between the affable Betty White and the cantankerous Bette Davis.

On her first day, she arrived at about lunch time.

I was sitting at my desk, chowing down on some fish from the hot lunch boxes we got delivered daily, when a shadow fell across my meal. I looked up to find Akiyama standing over me.

"Yes, my dear," I said, chopsticks in hand, a clump of the tastiest rice in creation trapped between their tips.

"The new substitute teacher has arrived."

"Cool!" I said, and returned to my lunch. But Akiyama didn't budge.

"Yes, what can I do for you, dearest?"

"She's waiting in the conference room."

"Uh-huh."

"She doesn't get around well."

"Can it wait a few minutes?" I asked, nodding at my food.

"Well..." she sang, which meant "of course not".

I put the lid back on my lunch box and followed Akiyama to the conference room.

From the doorway, I saw her for the first time—an old Japanese woman, alone—just sitting there, reading a magazine. My first impression was that she looked like "not getting around well" should be among the least of her concerns, not to mention getting up every morning and carrying herself to a junior high school with some of the craziest kids in Yokohama. In fact, by appearances, of greater concern should have been her next breath or heartbeat. But I reminded myself that this was Japan, a land where the life expectancy made America's seem medieval by comparison.

Her hair was white and wispy with what looked like violet highlights. I could see the age spots on her scalp through it. Her glasses were thick with an antique frame and a thin gold chain that looped around her wrinkled neck, librarian style. The windowless room had a different smell than its usual L'air du Syouganai—a confluence of stale air, ancient carpeting and wood polish. Instead, it had the sweet homeopathic pungency of pain ointments, astringents, and denture adhesives, laced lightly, but unmistakably, with a perfume a woman of class might dig, like Yardley Lavender.

She still hadn't noticed us.

"Hello?"

She looked up from the magazine she was reading and, as soon as she saw me, lit up like we were old friends reunited after a long separation.

"Well, there you are!" she sang in English, fairly naturally. "You must be this Mr. Loco I'm hearing so much about!"

She started to stand, but it took some preparation. She placed the magazine on the conference table, laid both hands flat upon it, and slowly pushed herself up, a grimace detectable behind her grin. I closed the distance between us so she wouldn't have to walk. She stuck out her hand and I took it. It felt brittle and a little cloying, but somehow strong and confident. . .and weird.

It took me a moment to realize that hers was the first Japanese woman's hand I'd shaken in all my years in Japan.

"So, shall I call you "Mr. Loco", or "Loco-sensei?" she asked.

I liked her immediately. Akiyama and I shared a glance and I could see she liked Betty, too.

"Loco is fine."

"Well, Loco it is. My name is Betty."

"Mrs. Betty. Nice to meet you!"

"Oh no, just "Betty" is fine!"

She was older than my grandmother would be if she were still around, over-indulging on Colt 45 malt liquor and chain-smoking Pall Malls, so I knew there was no way I was going to drop the "Mrs."

"My, my, my, so you're an American, right?" she asked.

I wondered what Akiyama told her about me.

"Yes, from New York."

"New York!" Then she said something in Japanese that I couldn't catch, but Akiyama smiled. From what I gathered about her character, I just knew she was saying the Japanese equivalent of stuff like, "as I live and breathe", and "I do declare". I don't know how I knew, but I knew it.

181

"Well, I'm an old woman, as you can see. I've been teaching in Yokohama for over 40 years."

"Wow!" leaped out of my mouth. "Only English?"

I was seeking an explanation for her above average ability.

"Oh, yes!"

"Well, welcome to Syouganai!" I said, cordially. "I look forward to teaching with you."

"You have very good manners, young man!" she said, not so much surprised as beguiled.

"Thank you," I replied.

"Unlike this *Yamada* person, what a bitch!"

I wasn't sure I had heard her correctly. I glanced at Akiyama. She had turned a little red in the face. Then Mrs. Betty said something in Japanese that I couldn't quite catch again. Rather, she hissed something. Akiyama replied in Japanese, nodding her head in agreement. I figured she was speaking in euphemisms, some country dialect or old-school slang. I imagined she said something like, "Well, Betty's here now, so don't y'all fret none."

I don't know why I saw her character as American and distinctly Southern. She just reminded me of the great grandmothers I've known—those sacred cows of the black community who could do and say whatever they wanted without even thinking about it much. They were the ones who could, and would, step into the middle of a gang fight, slap fire out the gang leaders and tell them to 'cut out this foolishness, and take y'all asses home fo' I take off my belt!'

And they'd do it, without remark.

The next day I would find out how right my first impression was.

★ ★ ★ ★ ★

On our first day of teaching together, Mrs. Betty stood to the side of the class and let me take charge since they knew me already.

"Good Morning, class!"

"Good morning, Loco-sensei!" the students replied in unison.

"How are you today?"

"Fine, thank you. And Yooo*uuuuu*?"

I giggled. It was a running gag, this corruption of the "you."

"Fine, thanks."

I turned to Mrs. Betty. She was the very portrait of gentility, poised as a porcelain statuette, demure and dainty.

"This is a new English teacher here at Syouganai. Her name is Mrs. Betty. Please greet her!"

The class turned to look at this old woman who looked like she had two feet in the grave and was clutching on to the edge of the six foot hole, hanging on for dear life with her fingernails. At least, her body looked that way.

Her eyes, which were sharp, cunning, and black, told another story.

"Good Morning, Betty-sensei!"

"Ah, good morning children. How are you?"

"Fine thank you, and you*uuuu*?"

She replied in Japanese, her tongue lashing out like a whip.

I don't know why I couldn't understand this woman's Japanese. Women are actually the easiest to understand. Most of my interactions and closest relationships since I'd been in Japan had been with women. It was usually the men I couldn't comprehend at all. They'd often speak through their teeth, like their mouths were wired shut, and they'd have the nerve to mumble on top of that.

The kids stirred in their seats, clearly perturbed by whatever Mrs. Betty had said.

"Ready, go!"

"Fine, thank you, and you?"

Ah, she'd scolded them for their distortion of "you," I surmised, and my imagination told me she'd said, "I don't know what kind of foolishness y'all are used to, but that game's over! Betty's here now! So, we're gonna speak English the way it's meant to be spoken, y'all got me? Good! Now let's try that again!"

"That's better!" she said. "I'm fine, thank you, dears."

Then she nodded to me and offered me the floor.

The serious faces of the students lightened a bit as I took the lead. I usually do a warm-up game before a lesson. Something to get them excited and thinking in English. They were still learning English numbers so I went with the buzz game. The kids love it.

"Okay, let's play the buzz game. Everyone stand up!"

There were always one or two students that couldn't be bothered, and Akiyama would spend a few minutes twisting their arms to join—generally without success—while I got going with the game. This day was no different. Two students remained seated. I gave them a look, to no avail. These first-year kids had figured out that they could pretty much do whatever they wanted. What, with some of their upperclassmen running around the halls out of uniform, with spiked blond hair, and talking on their cell phones—which was supposedly strictly forbidden—it was no surprise that they reached that conclusion. They just knew that the school exercised tolerance, and if that kind of stuff could be tolerated, then their simple refusal to play a silly counting game would surely be tolerated.

And, usually, they would be right.

Mrs. Betty, with her ivory walking stick, slowly made her way to the closest student who'd decided to go against the grain. A boy named Taro-kun who was gaining a reputation around the school for being his own man.

It was difficult for me to watch her handling of Taro while monitoring the game and keeping it fun. And with all the clapping and counting going on, it was impossible to hear the Japanese I probably wouldn't have understood anyway. What was clear from the glimpses of body language I caught was that he resisted her initial urging, but changed his tune quickly at her second assertion.

Very quickly.

What the hell!

The other rebellious student—Taro's buddy—having seen Taro get up and start clapping, probably figured if she'd gotten Taro to do what no other teacher had been able to, then his chances of one-upmanship were slim, so he stood up without waiting for Mrs. Betty, who had been en route.

She hobbled back to the front of the class looking like Yoda after he'd opened up a can of whup-ass on some clones.

After the game, I told Mrs. Betty that Taro never joined in the game anymore and asked her how she had gotten him to play this time. I glanced over at him and caught him glaring at Mrs. Betty, giving her the stink-eye.

"Oh, I just asked him nicely. He's really a good boy."

I didn't believe her for a second.

Back in the office, I told Akiyama what had happened with Mrs. Betty and Taro and her eyes like to have popped out of her head.

"He played the buzz game?"

"Yep."

She turned to Mrs. Betty, sitting across from us, and asked her how she'd done it.

"Can't let them walk all over you," she said in barely recognizable Japanese. The rest she said in Betty-go (her language). I just watched Akiyama's face absorbing this tale with fascination. Then she burst out laughing and half the office stopped what they doing, most of them laughing as well, or letting out a stunned, "Eeeeeeee," revealing that they'd all been tuned in.

In moments like these, I get pissed with myself for having settled for fairly proficient Japanese.

"What!" I snapped at Akiyama once Mrs. Betty was done.

Akiyama looked at me like she'd forgotten I was there.

"Oh! Ummm, yeah, she was telling us. . .Wow, it's hard to explain. . . she was telling us about the old days in Yokohama. When teachers could hit the students." And, she started laughing, again.

"What else?"

"She said she told Taro about how she used to hit disobedient students like him in the head with her cane, and send them home with lumps and bruises." She started laughing again. "And she told him that her memory goes bad sometimes and she forgets what year it is."

Ah, well, that explained it. I glanced over at Mrs. Betty, as she apparently anticipated I would. Her eyes were waiting for mine. She flashed a crooked smile and a shot me a quick wink.

★ ★ ★ ★ ★

Later that week, I got to know this remarkable woman a bit better. From jump, and for the second time in a long time, Akiyama being the first, I trusted my intuition and opened myself up. Maybe it was due to her age or the way she carried herself, or the fact that, like the first Japanese woman to win my heart, Aiko, she seemed to embody all that I find admirable and boundless about the human spirit. My trust was the least I could extend to show my appreciation for that gift.

And my heart was hot on its heels.

Akiyama, Mrs. Betty, and I all had a break at the same time, a rarity, so we were sitting in the office chatting. Akiyama and I were trying to uncover the makings of Mrs. Betty. It was not that she was all that mysterious, but just that we had been pretty busy that week so time did not allow for much Q & A. But, our schedules had afforded us a little free time that day.

"So, Mrs. Betty, have you ever been to the U.S.?" Akiyama had asked.

When Mrs. Betty spoke, she did so in a sometimes elegant and sometimes raunchy mixture of Japanese and English. Always. It was not that her English was poor. It wasn't. I wasn't exactly sure why she did, but I figured she was a bit modest about her linguistic ability.

"Yes, I have," she replied.

"You've been to New York, I bet," I said.

"Oh yes! I drove from the West Coast to the East Coast once. Yes, indeed, all the way to New York!"

"What?" I snapped, shocked. It was one of those things, on a long list of things, I'd always promised myself I'd do, yet have yet to get around to doing. "Wow!"

"Dear child, Mrs. Betty has gone *everywhere*. I'm one of those nut cases you hear about who spend their retirement sticking their wrinkled faces in every nook and cranny of God's green earth."

"How long did it take?"

"About three or four weeks, I reckon. I'd gone with a girlfriend of mine. What was that child's name? Patricia, yes, it was Patricia. She was a sweet girl. We were friends at university and I summered with her family for a few years after we graduated. They lived outside Portland, up in Oregon. Beautiful country. I loved it up there. Still go there sometimes. Anyway, she'd invited me to go with her. At first I'd told her no. I was scared to death! Just two women driving across that big country . . . and me not even American."

"When was this?"

"Dear me, it must've been, well, I think Richard Nixon was your president, then. I remember 'cause there was a big scandal."

"Watergate?"

"That's right! Watergate. Patricia's mother loved him something fierce though. She had a picture of him on the wall right in the living room over the sofa. He was a scary-looking man, if you ask me. Well, anyway, she kept pushing and begging me and eventually I said 'what the hell'."

She proceeded to tell us about all the places she'd visited along the way: Las Vegas—where she'd seen Elvis perform, the Grand Canyon, Monument Valley, Mount Rushmore, etc. The list went on and on.

As she weaved her tale of her road trip across the American landscape, she filled it in with little anecdotes about the adventures these two women had had along the way. And, though she never said it in so many words—and though Akiyama hadn't caught the allusions—references to "rendezvous" and "spending time", I was pretty sure she'd implied they'd gotten laid, as well.

"Yes, that was my first adventure out on my own. I caught the bug after that. I was always traveling. In fact, I met my husband while doing so. We just happened to be in Mexico, two Japanese people on a tour of Mexico City and the Aztec pyramids.

"He was, God bless his soul, a scientist, and loved to explore. We fell in love immediately. How can you not love a man that loves traveling, learning new things and expanding his mind, right?

"He died about ten years back. Dear, sweet man."

She sat there with a sad smile on her face reminiscing about her husband, and missing him simultaneously.

"But," she said, with this great idea lighting up her whole face, "Do you like hot springs, Mr. Loco?"

"I love them," I said. "Why?"

"Well, me and my husband bought a summer home in Izu, with an onsen."

"*A private hot springs* in your summer home?" I confirmed stupidly, distracted by the image that had popped in my head of such a place.

"Yes. We used to rent it out, but, that after he passed it just got to be too much trouble for me. I couldn't be fussing over that paperwork. My children and grandchildren use it from time to time, though. Would the two of you like to come to Izu for the weekend and spend some time with an old woman? It's kept pretty clean and it's a short walk from the beach."

I don't know if I was gawking by outward appearances, but mentally, I was.

Maybe she thought she had to sell it harder 'cause she added, "And, I might be old, but I can still barbecue like nobody's business! You can even bring a friend if you like."

Izu Peninsula is one of the most beautiful spots in Japan's Kanto region. I'd gone there a couple of times, but usually in the winter. It can get pretty damn pricey in the summer time. She didn't have to twist my arm.

Akiyama and I looked at each other and smiled. Oh, yes, we were definitely going!

10

Is Loco-sensei a Nee-Gah, Too?

(Mendokusai Junior High)

There was a cute little haa-fu, all of 13 years old, among my first-year students. She was half-African-American, half-Japanese, and went by the name of Risa. She spoke both English and Japanese fluently. She was tall and had light brown skin, with what my mother would call *good* hair—long and curly straight like a professional hair weave, only natural. Her eyes were an alluring mix of Asian and African-American. One day she was going to have to carry a baseball bat to keep the boys at bay, and an industrial-sized can of mace in her purse for the pervs!

She was born in Yokohama, and after having lived in Mississippi for several years, her family returned to Japan. She then, mid-semester, was enrolled at Mendokusai and, by all appearances, was adjusting to life back in Japan and at the school fairly well.

That is, until that day.

There was another English speaker, a returnee, in the same class. He, however, was 100% Japanese, but his family had lived in Saudi Arabia for several years and he'd attended an international school there, so his English was fairly fluent, as well. His name was Hideki.

I learned that day that, beneath my radar, a bit of a rivalry had sprung up between the two.

I had noticed from our first meeting that Risa was a bit outspoken compared to her Japanese classmates, and not shy about her English ability whatsoever. This was remarkable because most of the English-speaking students at my schools would only speak to me in English when their friends were not around or totally buried the ability for fear of appearing outstanding or even being ostracized. But Risa seemed to be unaware of these consequences and displayed conspicuous pride in her own bilingual-ness. Hideki, however, though he was not as shy as most of his classmates, was much less outspoken than Risa.

Recently, according to Risa, he had taken to teasing and criticizing her. And apparently it had gotten to a point where she felt compelled to bring it to my attention. She caught me in the hallway during the rest period just before English class was to begin, and said, "Mr. Loco, Hideki says I have an accent."

"Really?" I hadn't noticed. "Let me hear you talk."

"What do you want me to say?"

"What does your father do?"

"He's uh petty offisuh in duh Navy. He's been in duh Navy since befo' I was bohn. He's from Mississippi an' you kinda reminds me uh him."

"Well, Risa, I think Hideki might be right. You do have an accent. It's a Southern accent, kinda like my mother's. But, big deal! He's got an accent, too. His sounds British. I have an accent, too. Everyone has *some* kind of accent."

"He said my accent was a *black* accent."

Now, how the hell would he know that?

"What do you think he means by that?" I asked, curious about how this was affecting her. Outwardly, she wasn't giving me much to work with, looking just as perky as always.

"I dunno, but he said it was "black" and the way he said it made it sound like a bad thing. Is a black accent bad?"

"There's no such thing. And if there were, it wouldn't be a bad thing, so don't pay him any mind."

Whenever she and I have a conversation, all the Japanese eyes in the vicinity are riveted and ears are glued. It was so rare for them to see two native English speakers go at it live, especially if one just also happened to be their classmate, as well. I worried about how this might impact her school life with her being able to communicate with the teacher better than anyone in the school, and all the Japanese English teachers put together, so I'd try to keep our interactions to a minimum. Risa, though, jumped at every opportunity to flash her skill.

As she continued reporting her conversation with Hideki to me, I started picking up on something in the tone of her voice. Though she presented all of this with nonchalance and a giddiness that I could only attribute to her youth, I knew that what Hideki said had upset her.

So, now this situation was on my radar.

And, now that it was, I could see clearly what was happening.

I'd ask a question and, if it wasn't too difficult, several hands would rise, but if it was difficult, only two would, Hideki's and Risa's. All of the answers were simple for both of them so I avoided calling on them as often as possible. It felt fair, but as far as they were concerned, they had as much right to answer the questions as their mono-lingual'd classmates. Hideki seemed to grasp what I was up to though and refrained from raising his hand every time. But, Risa was oblivious. She continued to raise her hand as often as possible, obliging me to call on her from time to time. Moreover, she'd even raise her hand to ask questions or volunteer remarks, which she'd happily translate into Japanese for her linguistically-challenged classmates—something that other bilingual students I've taught would rarely, if ever, do.

Yep, I could see what was going on. It was older than the spiked club. It was probably what prompted the use of it as a murder weapon in addition to hunting and protection from beasts in the first place—good ole' fashioned jealousy.

I decided I had better do something to dial it down, but I wasn't exactly sure what. I figured I'd speak with the staff at *The Company*, or maybe Silky Tony himself, at the next monthly meeting to see if they had any suggestions because I suspected my Japanese co-workers would be just as clueless as to how to resolve this equitably as I was. I mean, it was such a rarity. In all the years I'd been teaching in public schools, there had been a couple dozen or so English-speakers. But, by and large, somehow, whether through experience or intuition, most knew to downplay their ability as much as possible.

That which might be cool and impress friends can also be intimidating for those lacking the ability—not to mention make you stand out in a place where being outstanding is often shunned.

Then, the following day, Risa, with a girlfriend in tow, ran up on me in the hallway, still her giddy and ostentatious self.

"Hi, Mr. Loco," she sang.

"Hi Risa-chan, what's up?"

"Well, it's kind of funny," she said, playing with a kinky curl in her hair. "But not, you know?"

"What is?"

"Hideki called me a nee-gu-ro."

"A *what*?" I snapped.

"It's bad, right?" she said, nodding to herself. "I thought so."

"Well, er, what, what did he say *exactly*? Maybe you were mistaken."

"I don't think so," she said, pensively. "He said I was nee-gu-ro."

"Is that all he said?"

"He also called me a *nee-gah*, but I know that's bad. I wasn't sure about Nee-gu-ro, though."

"Ummm, I see," I said as calmly as possible. My stomach was twisted in knots, though. "Did you tell your homeroom teacher?"

"No, I just wanted to tell you because I knew you'd understand."

"Actually, I—"

"I says to him, I says, 'Is *Loco-sensei* a nee-gah, too?' Right? And he—"

"What?"

"—didn't say anything. He just . . ."

"Wait a minute—slow down. Let me get this straight. Hideki called you a negro *and* a nigger?"

Risa nodded her head.

"Thank you for telling me, Risa," I said, keeping my cool. "And, don't worry. You did the right thing. Go ahead to your class now. And if he says anything like this again to you let me know, OK?"

"OK," she sang, and she and her buddy, who probably didn't understand a word of the conversation but was attentive throughout, just skipped away. You'd think she'd just told me something inconsequential like she'd aced an exam.

Kids. . .

I stood there for a moment thinking about what my next move should be, feeling a little bewildered that I was even in this situation. I mean, every time I'd hear things of this nature involving my kids I'd be similarly nonplussed. One time, one of my third-year students, a girl, was caught on the roof giving some of the guys blow jobs. I couldn't imagine any of my kids doing this on either end of the blow job. If you knew my kids, their innocence, their naiveté, their utter openness and friendliness, you would be shocked, too. But, I had to remind myself that, first, these were teenagers. Experimenting, challenging authority, and breaking rules is what they do. It sure as hell was what I did when I was their age, and, second, Hideki was not raised in the same environment as the other students. Who knew what he'd learned at international schools in the Middle East?

I decided to report this to Risa's homeroom teacher. When I told him, and explained to him what a "nigger" was and how it was used in other countries—he'd actually never heard the word—he was more shocked than me, and appropriately angry. Apparently he'd gotten my gist about its usage when I compared it to the use of *burakumin* (Japanese outcasts discriminated against for centuries) as an insult. He, in turn, as I looked on, reported it to the head teacher of the first-year students, who was also appropriately furious. He then brought it to the vice-principal's attention, who was more enraged than I thought he was possible of getting, confirming he'd been given the proper explanation in this impromptu game of dengon-gemu (Telephone). A huddle was held in the center of the office in which the three of them, along with a fourth teacher, decided Hideki's fate.

The huddle, which consisted of a whole lot of gesticulation and breath-sucking, resulted in a clarification session with Risa and the re-telling and confirming of the story several times. By day's end—I was told the next day—Hideki found himself on the business end of some harsh scolding by his homeroom teacher, during which Hideki defended his racist remarks by saying, "It's her fault! She is always showing off her English," claiming that doing so made him feel inferior. He explained that, at one point, he and Risa had had their hands up at the same time to answer a question—and though I had called on him to answer it—following his answer, Risa had made some kind of remark in English regarding his response that he couldn't catch, and that made him upset because he felt as if she were trying to best him.

I tried to recall the particular moment and it came back to me in living color. I was telling the class about my own junior high school life and explaining the similarities and differences between junior high schools in NY and the ones here in Yokohama. I told them that, in NY on graduation day, we wear a cap and gown while the Japanese tend to wear their school uniform for commencement. I passed around a pic of me on graduation day from my junior high school to illustrate and they got a real kick outta seeing Loco at their age.

As a similarity, I mentioned that we, too, had to be at school by 8:30 am. However, if you wanted to have breakfast, you needed to arrive by 8:00 am and breakfast would be made available to you by the school.

Hideki had raised his hand and mentioned that, in Dubai, he had to be at school by 7:30. His voice was barely audible, but his pride in having a different experience than his entire class was evident on his face. And, at that point, Risa's hand had shot up and she, once I had looked her way—but I hadn't called on her—added that, at her school in Mississippi, classes started at 8:00 am and there was also breakfast available. She had some other remarks related to something I had discussed previously in the lesson, about graduation, which the Japanese teacher had found more remarkable than I had. Risa picked up on that curious energy from the Japanese teacher and expounded while magnanimously translating it into Japanese for her classmates, and they responded appropriately with "oohs" and "aahs".

If I had been tuned into Hideki at that moment, I might have noticed that he hadn't been impressed by Risa's self-aggrandizing "generosity". I might have even detected, through the emotions playing out on his face, the jealousy seething within, and that decisive moment when he resolved to exact revenge on little resplendent Risa. And I might have even caught a glimpse of what the thought—or feeling—of saying "*negro*" or "*nigger*" does to a child of 13 who understands what he's saying, knows it's something that he shouldn't say, and says it regardless because he's intent on inflicting pain on another.

But, to be honest, I was glad I hadn't notice. I have trouble enough sleeping.

Interlude

On Reading, Writing and Alchemy

I was running 20 minutes late for work, but it was a beautiful Tuesday morning, so I didn't even bother to rush. It was one of those days where, rather than check your watch every few yards, you stop to sniff at flowers and notice that the shade of blue the sky is today is actually a shade you rarely see; it was the kind of day that songwriters write sappy, catchy tunes like *Beautiful Sunday* about. In fact, I'd been whistling that song until I crossed the threshold of Syouganai. That's about when Takahashi-sensei ran up to me excitedly and yelled, "*Oh my God*, Loco-sensei! What happened?"

I stopped whistling.

"*Communion with the good earth*" feeling, gone.

"Well," I said, and realized I wasn't prepared to explain why I was late. "I was, I mean, the train was . . ."

"I don't care about that," she snapped. "I mean your hand!"

I looked down at it like it was someone else's hand that had been bandaged tight enough to obstruct circulation and immobilize it. How I had managed to ignore the throbbing ache is a mystery.

"This?" I held it up.

"Yes, of course!"

"Oh! I broke my pinkie playing basketball on Sunday."

"Really? That's terrible. Are you okay?"

"It still hurts a little."

★ ★ ★ ★ ★

What I didn't say was that, on Sunday, after having watched Kobe Bryant open up a whole keg of whoop-ass on the Orlando Magic the previous day, I was feeling overly enthusiastic and tried to represent not only all the playgrounds in Brooklyn, but in the entire friggin' USA. And I was puttin' in work until rapidly ascending pinkie met rapidly descending ball head-on, on a rebound attempt.

Guess who got the better of the clash?

Of all the dumb-ass shit to get injured on, a friggin' rebound.

Absurdly, I'd thought I was invincible. I'd never broken anything before. Most of my friends had been on crutches or had had casts plastered on their arms and various other injuries. One of my friends even had to shit in a bag attached to his waist for weeks after being stabbed in the guts, but, me—nothing. I had started to believe that I was invincible and that only tiny accidents could befall me.

Well, so much for that fantasy.

Monday was a holiday so I'd gone to a hospital that afternoon and told them that I needed to see a doctor, showing them the finger my fellow weekend warriors had put in a makeshift splint. I'd told the staff in Japanese, "I think it's jammed."

"I see. Well, we don't handle these kinds of cases here."

"You don't?" I asked, puzzled. It was a medical hospital, specializing in sports injuries. They even had an emergency room. So, I added, "it might even be broken."

You know, just to add a little drama to it, maybe conjure up a little sympathy.

"Ah, so sorry."

I recognized the expression on her face. Yep, no doubt about it; it was the *Great Wall of Japan*. I'd met this wall before, many times. It's tall and solid and ancient and apologetic and polite as all get-out. I could stand there beating my head up against it for an eternity in a foreign language I haven't mastered or I could keep it moving. After all, Japanese hospitals have been known to turn away people in much worse conditions than mine. The only reason I like the hospitals is because most of them accept credit cards. My health insurance required payment up front—to be reimbursed at some later date—and I didn't walk around with loads of cash on me. It was one of my NY habits I'd yet to break despite all my years in one of the safest countries in the world.

"Well, where should I go?" I asked, capitulating before the wall's impenetrability.

They directed me to a clinic conveniently not far away.

The clinic accepted me, and after filling out a single form, I was hustled before an English speaking doctor.

Lucky me.

"How can I help you?" he asked with all the confidence and self-assurance of the competent. I immediately felt at ease in his care. It was a stark contrast to the way I felt after he removed my slapdash splint and took a glance at my pinkie.

"Hmmm," he said in what has to be the international language of doctors. He looked like he wanted to test it by manipulation and I withdrew. He smiled at me and said, "Let's get some x-rays, shall we?"

They shot my finger from different angles and then told me to wait in the hallway a few minutes. It felt like an eternity. I just knew it wasn't a finger jam. All day I had been feeling my bone shifting queerly beneath my skin.

"Loco-san," the nurse called out.

What's the verdict? Is my summer fucked?

I walked back into the doctor's office where my X-rays were displayed on a wall-mounted light box, and there it was in black and white, indisputable evidence that my invulnerability was a hoax; there was a crack between the joint and knuckle.

Upon seeing the fragility of my mortality, I felt a little freaked out. I hid it, though, which is very unlike me.

★ ★ ★ ★ ★

I thought about the previous day when I had left the gym with my finger haphazardly immobilized. I was walking to the coffee shop to meet my private student, my digit throbbing with every pump of my heart. I had decided that I would not panic. I would just finish out the day. I had three private students scheduled after my basketball practice and I wasn't about to cancel any of them. I needed the money—if for no other reason than to pay for the doctor's visit I'd decided to make the following day.

I had about an hour to kill, so along the way I stopped at a book store.

"Do you have any English books?"

"Not really, just a few upstairs."

I went upstairs and, yep, she was right. There was one tiny rotary of English books, which was one tiny rotary more than I had expected to find. They had a bunch of classics, all the Harry Potter books, and the two Obama books. I'd read their whole selection already, but I needed something to distract me. I gave the rotary one more twirl and a book practically jumped off the shelf at me. Somehow my twirl had dislodged it. I instinctively reached out to catch it with my bad hand and my three free fingers caught it.

The name of the book was *The Alchemist*.

What can I tell you? I really hate books like this! It's one of those international bestsellers that people read and then recommend to anyone and everyone they know. It's one of those allegorical, philosophical, spiritual, mind-numbing, oversimplified, *if-only-the-guy-who-writes-fortune-cookies-would-write-a-book* type books. I don't know what made me buy it. I read the back cover. Hoopla, hoopla, hoopla. What did I expect? But, I needed something to distract me from my pending mortality—if the bone rattling under my skin that I was trying not to think about was any indication of the verdict I would face the following day. So I bought it, went to the cafe where I was to meet my student, ordered some coffee, lit up a Black & Mild, and started reading it.

You know what? Let me go back a little further . . .

★ ★ ★ ★ ★

When I was back in NY, working as a salesman at a respectable company making—after bonuses—respectable donuts, I dreamed of being a writer. And, at that time, a friend of mine lent me a book called *The Fountainhead*. Yes, yes, yes, it was Ayn Rand and her endless rambling and sermonizing about the nobility of man's individual creativity and the scourge of the parasitic second-handers running the world into the ground.

Yep, she rocked my boat!

With Howard Roark as a role model—wasn't nobody going to pimp Loco anymore—I wrote my first novel and quit that job that paid well, but ultimately was taking me nowhere at hyper-speed. And with that, I had reclaimed my life.

Yes, with a bit of "beginner's luck", the creative forces of the universe had conspired to put me on the path to achieving my dreams.

Who knew that path would lead me to Japan, to a clinic in Yokohama where a doctor would be hovering over film of my fractured pinkie, with a verdict that would change my life on the tip of his tongue, while a paperback copy of *The Alchemist* burned a hole in my back pocket.

Huh? Who knew?

★ ★ ★ ★ ★

LOCO in YOKOHAMA

Like most people, I love a good story, so I read a lot. And, though I love to read new books, if I fall in love with a book, I always read it again. I've even repurchased books I've already read if my copy was lost or loaned out to parties long forgotten—a writer and publisher's wet dream I am. I do this mostly to see if the story has stood the test of time. Have I outgrown it? Or, it me? Have I changed since the last reading? And, if so, how? Has the story, or at least its meaning for me, changed? Some books help me understand the art of telling a story or the craft of writing better. Other books help me mark my growth as a human being.

I have a list of books that are like good friends to me—books that speak to me, comfort me, instruct me or simply entertain me. Most books, I read just once. Even if I think it is an exceptional read, once is enough. Sometimes I read a book two or three times before retiring it. However, I've read all of the following books at least four times and, at most ten, and they *still* do it for me: *Their Eyes Were Watching God, The Catcher in the Rye, Beloved, Shogun, Bonfire of the Vanities, Bright Lights, Big City, The Fire Next Time, Dune, The Killer in Me, The Friends, Without Remorse, The Vampire Lestat, Jurassic Park, The Godfather, Me Talk Pretty One Day* and, yes, *The Fountainhead*. Actually, during my last read of *The Fountainhead*, I skipped over 200 pages, and that was a red flag. It didn't augur well for future reads.

I was sitting in Doutor's, a café chain, reading *The Alchemist* when I had the thought, "*long time, no see.*" It had been a while since I read a book that made me feel that way so quickly. A whole lot of dead trees. But from the first few pages, the book had started a conversation with me like we'd been best friends kicking it in a previous life and had been interrupted only to pick up where we'd left off here in my current life, almost without missing a beat.

The loud screech of a chair against the floor tore my attention from the book. I looked up to see a rather attractive woman. She was sitting not far from me, and I could see, as she made no effort to hide it, that she had been staring at me. She grinned, and in her grin it was obvious that something about me had impressed her so much that she'd lost all sense of the propriety I'd come to expect from Japanese women.

However, and this was very unlike me as well, I couldn't care less. I returned to my conversation with my papery friend, who was catching me up on his adventures in Spain, Morocco, and across The Sahara.

The main character, Santiago, had left Spain to follow his dream of finding treasure near the pyramids of Egypt. I told him that I, too, had left my home in Brooklyn in search of something, but I wasn't sure what. He told me about an alchemist he'd met along the way who taught him how to understand the language of the world. I told him about Aiko and how she'd impacted my life and helped me understand many things about the world and about myself.

"She sounds like an alchemist to me," he'd said.

"Actually, I think she was the treasure I didn't know I had come to Japan to find," I said without even thinking.

He told me that, when he arrived at the pyramids, he was mugged and beaten by bandits. I told him about the loss of Aiko and the battering my self-worth has taken here in Japan. He told me that, after the beating, he learned- from one of the bandits no less, the true location of his treasure.

I scratched my head.

"I'm not sure what I'm learning here among these bandits," I told him, meaning the Japanese. Then, my iPhone alarm beeped. It was time to teach.

★ ★ ★ ★ ★

"Well, it's fractured," the doctor said. "But not seriously."

My eyes were transfixed on the X-ray. A fine was line cut diagonally across the first metacarpal, a bone chip dangling on the edge of the crack. I caught the doctor looking at my eyes, and again he smiled.

"It's a little crooked," he said, and it was. It bent to the left. "But, if you don't mind a little deformity—"

"*Deformity?*"

"—it'll heal in six weeks or so."

"*Six* weeks?" My first thought was "*Damn, there goes my summer. But I can get a lot of writing done so . . . wait a minute! Oh shit! Will I be able to type?*"

Maybe he misread the concern on my face because he added, "But, if you want it to be straight again, perhaps you will need an operation." He slowly took my pinky in hand and showed me with a gentle touch. "We'll cut along here, insert a metal rod, and, in 6 months or so, it'll be like new."

"*Six months!*"

I felt my tear ducts welling up. I never knew how important writing was to me until that very moment.

Then, without any invitation, "Santiago" started whispering in my ear, *"Sometimes there's just no way to hold back the river."*

"You're the doc, Doc," I sighed in surrender. "I'll do whatever you suggest."

He looked at me, through me, actually. He had the kind of eyes that have been there, seen it, and written a thesis about it.

I felt his two hands caressing my swollen pinkie and it felt very calming, like some kind of ancient secret physical therapy. As I looked down, I saw him grip it just so, and suddenly yank and straighten it. I screamed out in agony. But the doctor wasn't moved. He kept pulling and twisting adroitly for a few seconds longer. I couldn't watch. I looked up at the nurse, who stood by with a handful of gauze and other materials necessary for immobilizing my finger. Apparently she'd known or had anticipated what the doctor would do. Upon seeing this, I relaxed, and though the pain hadn't subsided a lick, I felt relieved to be in the hands of professionals.

"Well, it's straight now," the doctor said, deadpan, like nothing out of the ordinary had just occurred; like I hadn't scared the shit out of all of the patients waiting just outside his door. "So you may not need that operation after all."

He wore the same knowing smile while he and the nurse worked on setting my finger. Once they were done he added, "Come back next week and I'll take another look."

There was joy there in his face—not a sadistic joy, but the joy of not only knowing what he was doing, and being able to do it well, but in knowing that he had discerned his path in life, followed it, and now he was living his dream. I don't get this feeling from doctors very often. In fact, it's rare. Most of the doctors I'd visited back in NY seemed to be distracted, like I was keeping them from more important matters, or aloof and cloaked in professional distance.

I looked down at my finger then at the X-ray of its cracked crooked skeleton then back at it, with one prescient thought in my mind. *This is a sign.*

Santiago had spoken to me a great deal of signs at that cafe the day before.

"Signs," he'd said, "are like messages from the Creator."

"I know," I said. Santiago has a tendency to get a little didactic at times; redundant too, to be honest. But, so do I. It's one of the many things we had in common. "I've believed in signs my whole life. You know that!"

"I know you *think* you have," he said. "But, your belief ends at acknowledgment way too often, and your resolve to finish things you begin is weak at best. You don't have faith in the Creator or yourself."

He'd said it quite harshly, too, spanking me with his words and speaking to me in a way I'd only let a friend or family member speak to me. Actually, I don't even let family get away with that crap anymore.

But, he was right.

★ ★ ★ ★ ★

"Are you OK?" my student had asked me. I was still smarting from the pimp-slapping that Santiago had given me just moments ago.

I shook it off and apologized to her. "It's just this book. It's . . . I don't know."

I often wind up getting personal with my private students, but I generally avoid getting *too* personal. She was one of the exceptions, though. We never used textbooks anymore. Our lessons had evolved into something akin to a paid friendship.

"Ee?" she'd said like she couldn't quite follow what I'd said. "A book?"

I wanted to tell her that it was fucking with me the way books fuck with me sometimes. That it had gotten in my head, deep in my head, and was pushing buttons and turning dials and flipping switches. But instead I asked her, "Have you ever read a book that feels so familiar that you think the writer was thinking about your life when he wrote it?"

She looked confused. I tried to think of a way to ask the question more simply.

"No," she said, shaking her head. "I mean, what happened to your hand?"

"You mean this?" I asked, holding up my damaged digit.

"Of course. What happened?"

I told her. She said, "Oh my God! Basketball is dangerous! You must be careful."

I didn't say I'd been playing basketball since I was a kid without serious injury. I didn't say I planned to return to playing the moment I recovered, and hopefully with the same level of confidence and disregard for the possibility of injury that I've always had.

"Thanks, I will," is what I said.

"Are you sure you're OK," she asked, searching my face.

"Do you know what 'alchemy' is in Japanese?"

"Ah-ru-ke mi? No." She whipped out her electronic dictionary and handed it to me, not even attempting to phonetically spell it, which was what she would usually do.

For "alchemist", the dictionary offered a string of complicated kanji. I couldn't read it. I just knew it was something about gold. "How do you say this?"

"Renkinjutsushi," she struggled to say. "Maybe. I've never seen that word."

I repeated it, trying to memorize it for some reason. "What does it mean?"

"I'm not sure . . . an artist or scientist maybe. He makes gold."

"OK," I said, wondering if there were alchemists in Asia in ancient times. If there were, they'd probably be Chinese. Those guys go way back like the Egyptians and other African civilizations. They would have tried to unlock the secrets of the universe for sure. J.K. Rowling touched on it in her first Harry Potter book. It was about "the sorcerer's stone" and "the elixir of life", as was *The Alchemist*. One of my favorite cult films, Hudson Hawk, hypothesized, for comical purposes, that Da Vinci was not only an artist, but was, among other things, an alchemist and had built a machine that could make gold.

"Do you want to make gold?" she asked, half-smirking, and probably half-wondering if I was off my rocker.

"What is gold, anyway?" I asked. I wanted to explore my thoughts with someone and my student had been a willing companion for going on two years now. Sometimes I even feel guilty taking cash for our lessons.

"A valuable, shiny metal. You make jewelry with it and stuff like that." She pointed at my gold bracelet, dangling over my makeshift splint. I had inherited it from my father when he passed away from cancer several years ago. "It's beautiful!"

I looked at it carefully, as carefully as I had the day that I first received it. That day, it seemed to radiate on my wrist, warm to the touch—like it had a life of its own. I had the lock welded shut. I never remove it, and since I'd been in Japan, I didn't really even think about it. It's 18 carats, heavy, and, like she'd said, valuable—and the only threat to its separation from me had been the lousy lock it used to have. And I'd fixed that permanently. Now, it was like a family heirloom I planned to give to my offspring one day.

When I no longer needed it.

I used to wear a two-finger ring with my five-percenter name, *"Unique"*, written in cursive—a diamond embedded in the "i". I had planned to give that to my heirs, as well. But, I was strapped for cash one day so I had pawned it and never looked back.

It had served a purpose, my purpose.

The idea of making gold from valueless metal, of making something precious from nothing, resonated inside of me. And it made a sound, and that sound was as beautiful as gold. It was the sound of my purpose, and had been since I could remember.

"Writing is like making gold," I just blurted out, watching my bracelet catch the light, sparkling like a brilliant idea. Then, catching a glimpse of my fucked-up finger, despair creeping up on me like a ninja in the shadows, I wondered how long it would take before I could—

"How's your blog?" my student asked, interrupting my gloomy thought.

She was a writer, too. She was an office lady by day, but wrote inspired haiku poetry in her free time. I tried to help her translate them into English sometimes, but I could never give them the panache they had in Japanese.

"It's OK."

"I had some free time yesterday and I read some of it. *10 ways how not to go loco in Japan,* or something like that."

"Yeah," I said, surprised, looking up from my hand. I was very selective with which students I gave my blog address to. I'd given it to her on a hunch. "What did you think?"

"I think number 11 should be, write."

I smiled.

I was still smiling when I arrived late to work two days later.

11
Manzai of the Onani Brothers
(Mendokusai Junior High)

I had two third-year students who, over the course of three years, had made it their prime directive to shock and awe me, and their escapades escalated with each passing year. Just try to imagine Jackie Gleason and Art Carney of "The Honeymooners" fame, then picture them together as junior high school students in the 21st century. Now make them Japanese. The resulting picture would probably resemble Yuuji-kun and Kintarou-kun. Yuuji was kind of chubby, but with the pep and agility of an athlete. Kintarou was the straight man who could set anyone up for a prank with the skill of a seasoned pantomime.

I knew from the first time I met them, back when they were first-year students, that they would be inseparable and a handful. I'd learned from their classmates that they had been a popular duo since elementary school, so, for the two of them, junior high school meant some new audience members—classmates coming from other elementary schools—and fresh teachers to impress with their stagecraft. And they were up to the task. Both just happened to have IQs that were off the charts, so not only were they the class clowns, but they also aced tests in almost every subject I'd learned.

English was a new challenge, however. They came to the school with as much exposure to English as the other students in the class—little to nil. But, they took an immediate liking to me, and began from day one demonstrating an intense interest in learning about me and this language I spoke.

And, by intense, I mean they took the initiative like you wouldn't believe. They were classic examples of why I ceased assuming anything about what Japanese people know or don't know, or were capable of, especially students. They started by not watching, but studying English movies and TV shows, especially comedies and rather racy stuff, and stopping me in the hallways to explain to them the meaning of words or running the expressions they'd learned by me to see if they had gotten it right.

That first year, I remember Yuuji stopped me in the hallway one day and said, "Good Morning Loco-sensei! How are you?"

"I'm fine, thank you, and you?" I replied, like I did a thousand times a week to my kids.

"I'm fine, thank you."

It was just as I had taught him and his classmates a few weeks earlier, straight from the textbook. And I was about to praise him on his voice and diction when I noticed Kintarou coming our way. Yuuji was looking in my face, the perfect expression of a student awaiting a pat on the head, when he turned and saw Kintarou like he'd sensed his approach.

Suddenly, Yuuji burst out yelling, "You son of a bitch! I ought to kick your ass!"

Kintarou turned and hissed like a snake and assumed a battle-ready stance. "You just try it, you fat fuck. I'll wipe that stupid look off your face!"

I stood there with my mouth open in shock. I'd never seen such aggression from Japanese people except in movies or maybe a K-1 fight. Suddenly, they were grappling with one another, and Yuuji got Kintarou in a bear hug and was squeezing him, pumping him from the rear like a steroid-addled troglodyte, and yelling, "How do you like that? Huh? How do you like that?"

An audience of students started to draw near, but no one intervened. They just stared half-amused and half-shocked.

Kintarou's face had turned red and he looked as if at any moment he might pass out so I stepped over and told Yuuji to let him down.

In English.

That's when I realized that I'd understood perfectly everything they'd said because they too had been speaking English!

What the fuck!

Yuuji was watching my face and started laughing as he set Kintarou down. Kintarou still had the crimson hue of someone who had just got the life squeezed out of him, but he was laughing, too.

Two professionals.

I was speechless. They both nodded like they understood what I hadn't said, 'you guys are gifted!'

Kintarou and Yuuji kept this up for their entire first year of school. Their conversational English was still at a very basic level, but they were learning many natural English expressions on their own, and incorporating them into their everyday conversation. Each expression had been chosen for its shock value and they rarely failed. I'd ask them, as I ask all students every day, "How's the weather today?" Most students would say sunny, rainy, cold, or cloudy. Some students might remember to say "it's" before the weather condition. Most didn't, regardless of how many times I tried to re-wire their minds on the matter. Yuuji would make my day and say something like, "It's cold as fuck!" and Kintarou might say, "Who cares? We're inside!" With those two, you never knew what you were gonna get. Even when I'd expect the unexpected, they'd figure out a way to catch me off guard, or they'd do nothing and have me second guessing everything.

In their second year, they took to hanging out around the bathroom between classes with a mob of fans and friends. When I'd walk past, they'd grab me by the crotch and try to drag me into the bathroom. Like most Japanese kids, they had no qualms about playing grab-ass and possessed no homophobic hang-ups like we had back when I was a junior high school student. So, I was subjected to all kinds of sexual assaults when I walked by. One time, I let them drag me into the bathroom against my better judgment, just to see what they were up to in there. Four of them pulled me in where another ten or so were standing around like a scene from any American school movie ever made—only no one was smoking, drinking, writing graffiti on the wall, or anything like that. It was just a bunch of kids hanging out in the toilet.

One time I was flung into this mix and the students who were already in the bathroom froze guiltily or jumped about like I'd caught them doing something. From their reaction, I wouldn't have been surprised to find one of the female students on her knees in one of the stalls giving them each blow jobs in turn. I looked hard, but I couldn't see, hear, or smell anything amiss. So, I figured maybe it was some kind of group masturbation. If shoving their fingers up my ass (called "kancho") was OK, who knew what else went on with these kids when no adults were watching? I certainly didn't.

"Nani shiteiru (what are y'all doing)?"

"Nani mo nai yo (we ain't doing nothing)."

I knew the Japanese word for masturbation, so I said, "Yappari. Onani shiteiru deshou (probably whacking off in here)!"

"Chigau (hell no)!"

Since I'd gotten a rise out of them, I figured I must have struck close to home.

Of course, Yuuji thought this was the perfect time for some hijinks. He started pretending to give Kintarou a hand-job. And Kintarou looked perfectly like someone trying to pretend he wasn't receiving a hand-job while he was experiencing intense pleasure. I almost fell out laughing.

"The Onani Brothers!" I called them, and they loved it. The name stuck.

Now, in their third-year, their skits were much more sophisticated. And much dirtier.

★ ★ ★ ★ ★

The day's grammar point was, "I'm too (adjective to verb) or "I'm so (adjective) that I can't (verb)." My instructions to the class were to pair up and prepare a skit, but feel free to expand beyond the guidelines.

"Let your imaginations run wild!"

I had already taught them the grammar the previous week, so this was kind of a review and an opportunity to demonstrate what they'd learned. This was my English elective class, so the students were mostly the ones who loved English or were pretty good at it.

At first, I was going to have them perform their skits before the entire class, but I changed my mind. The potential embarrassment often restricted the weaker speakers or shyer students' imaginations, and they'd likely stick to the safe and simple instead of spreading their wings a little, which is what I liked to encourage them to do. So I told them that they need only perform it before me or the Japanese teacher. If they did, they'd get a stamp, and if they used some imagination, they'd receive two stamps. The kids loved stamps. I had a Snoopy stamp I used for the really good ones.

"Is that OK with everybody?"

There was no response which could either mean "yes" or "no", depending on the quality of the silence, which I still had trouble reading.

"OK, let's make pairs!" I said and held up two fingers. My kids know a lot of classroom instruction words like "make pairs", "make groups", "sit down", "stand up", "answer the question", "shut up", etc. But, they'd choose to disregard the meaning whenever it was convenient. Some girls liked to work in groups of threes or fours. Some guys liked to work in a mob. Pair work was just not "group" enough for some kids. So I had to walk around the classroom breaking trios, quartets, quintets, and mobs into duos for a few minutes.

Kintarou and Yuuji naturally paired off—no arm twisting necessary. They were "manzai", the Japanese word for a stand-up comedy team. And I could see in the purposeful expressions on their faces that they had big plans for my guidelines. I couldn't wait to see the result. To be honest, sometimes I designed lessons with those two in mind because they were always pure entertainment. Though not always fun for the whole family, they generally kept it PG-13. Whenever they'd upgrade to R-rated or even X-rated, even though I was the only one in the class that could understand them most of the time—Kawaguchi-sensei usually left the class to me—I'd cut them off mid-sentence or mid-word and say, "Okaayyyyy, thank you very much, Kintarou and Yuuji! Next!" if I could stop laughing long enough to do so.

After about 20 minutes or so, the higher level students started coming to where I was at the head of the class to perform the skit they'd written. Most were about shopping, purikura (photo sticker machines), baseball, or karaoke. One example of this is as follows:

"Hey Natsuko, let's go to purikura. *Sorry, but I'm too tired to go to purikura.* Hey, Let's go shopping. *I'm so sleepy that I can't go shopping.* OK, then." Some of them were pretty good, but most were safe and exactly what I had asked for minus the "let your imagination run wild" part.

This was leaps and bounds beyond the regular English classes, though. It would just be plain facetious if I gave that type of instruction to a regular class. Most kids, and adults, at least when it comes to doing so in English, have about as much imagination as a bowl of rice. I'd expect more than half of the class to make skits without changing a single word from the example I give. Another quarter of the class would change maybe a word or two if I incentivized it somehow. The others will sleep or sit there with blank, unreadable expressions, their imaginations unable to extend beyond the operation of their mouths and nostrils in tandem to breath instead of their mouths alone.

I gave out a lot of single stamps that day. Only a couple of students' work warranted double stamps.

It was one minute until the bell and Yuuji and Kintarou were still at it, rehearsing and re-writing. Watching them was like having a behind-the-scenes view of a brilliant comedy team like Richard Pryor and Gene Wilder, Lucille Ball and Vivian Vance, Jay and Silent Bob, or even Beavis and Butthead. I would have loved to watch them a bit longer, but the bell had begun to chime.

The students all returned to their seats and we closed the class as we always do, with a bow and a roar of "Arigatou gozaimashita (thank you very much)!" As I collected my materials to head for the teacher's office, a little disappointed that they hadn't finished in time, here came Yuuji and Kintarou.

"Loco sensei, can we do it now?" Kintarou asked.

"A little late, aren't you?"

"Onegai (*please*)," Yuuji plead.

"Ja, douzo (alright, go ahead)," I said, like I hadn't been eager to see it.

They faced each other, hands free, having committed the conversation to memory:

Yuuji:	Hey Keiko-chan, let's make love tonight.
Kintarou:	(in a high-pitched voice, pretending to be "Keiko") Sorry Yuuji-sama, but my pussy is too sore to make love tonight.
Yuuji:	Oh, I see. That's too bad.
Kintarou:	How about anal?
Yuuji:	That sounds like fun, but your anus is so tight that my big dick can't get in.
Kintarou:	That's true.
Yuuji:	How about a blowjob?
Kintarou:	Oh yes, that's a great idea!

Then, Kintarou looked longingly down at Yuuji's crotch and licked his lips. He was about to kneel when I grabbed his arm and said, "Just go get your books so I can stamp them!"

I gave them both double stamps, of course. I knew I probably shouldn't have been encouraging the dirty English, but I was just so damn proud of how they'd grasped the language. Besides, I would have hated to be party to anything that discouraged their pursuit of English fluency, or even their bawdy comedy, in any way.

12
Yes I Am
(Syouganai Junior High)

There were two haa-fu kids in one of the first-year classes I taught with Mrs. Betty. One was half-black. The other was half-white.

The half-black—to be precise, Nigerian—kid was born in, raised in, and has never stepped foot out of Japan. He didn't speak any language aside from Japanese and knew nothing, as far as I knew, but Japan. He was brown-skinned with mousy-features, a button nose, tiny, narrow eyes, thin lips, and topped off with a curly Afro on his head. His father had been deported to Nigeria, I'd heard, and his mother actually got married to a Japanese man who proceeded to adopt him.

I called him Webster.

He was *so* Japanese that he looked like a Japanese kid doing a daily one-boy minstrel show. I half-expected to see him on the street one day without the makeup on his face. When we first met, he looked at me the same way the other Japanese kids did—like I was the most amazing thing he'd ever seen and we had absolutely nothing in common. I'd experienced that reaction before, so I wasn't surprised. He was as Japanese as he'd ever be allowed to be.

The other haa-fu I called "Kevin" 'cause he reminded me of McCauley Culkin in *Home Alone*. He was tall, blond, blue-eyed, and there wasn't much about him that indicated he was half-*anything*. He looked like an exchange student from Norway. He didn't quite have those Japanese mannerisms down pat either, but somehow he fit in—maybe because, in addition to being fluent in Japanese, he avoided doing anything to stand out any more than he did effortlessly.

His father came up to the school one day to observe our class with a bunch of other parents, and after the class, as I exited the room, he pulled me aside.

"Mr Loco, I'm Mr. McCallister, Kevin's father."

"Nice to meet you."

We shook hands and he told me a little about himself. He was a contractor in Japan where he would remain indefinitely.

"My son, Kevin, as you know, is fluent in English."

"Uh, huh."

Actually, I hadn't known that.

I've had the opportunity to meet and teach a number of haa-fu students during my tenure here and, as I've mentioned, I learned to assume nothing about them. The only thing I'd place squarely on their list of commonalities was that I was their English teacher. Some spoke English. Some didn't. Some wanted to stand out and shine, others were very reserved. Others simply wanted to blend in and disappear among the masses.

I also endeavored to avoid placing a spotlight on haa-fus. I knew firsthand how challenging it was for visually identifiable minorities to make their way in Japanese society, and the last thing I wanted to do was complicate matters. So, I had never asked Kevin a thing and he'd never volunteered a thing.

The word around the Green Tea cooler in the teacher's office was that he was a haa-fu—even that had surprised me—and had lived *in the States* (ugh!) with his family for some time. How long was anyone's guess.

"Kevin says great things about you."

"Really?" I said with a little too much surprise.

"Well, yeah," he said, grinning oddly. "He says your classes are usually pretty fun and you don't half-ass the lesson. I could see that for myself just now. You're a good teacher! American, right?"

"Yeah," I said, a little uncomfortable with the praise. It felt like he was setting me up for something. My old New York survival instincts, rusted from disuse, picked up a weak signal.

"I thought so." He scratched his head, scanning the perimeter at the same time. "East coast, up north, I bet. New York?"

"Yeah, Brooklyn."

"I'm originally from Virginia, the DC area, but I've got family in Forest Hills."

"Ah!"

We both took a moment to acknowledge our commonalities, kind of nodding and smiling at one another. I still felt he was up to something, though.

"So, here's the thing, Mr. Loco—"

"Call me Loco," I said.

"Loco it is," he said and smiled like he'd won me over. That signal was getting stronger. "I'm Ron."

He reminded me of a seasoned blue-blooded Yankee recovering from a cocaine addiction—prone to fall off the wagon from time to time. Like he'd been the black sheep of a rich-as-sin family that made its fortune during pre-civil war producing tobacco by the ton—a family that tolerated his drug use but effectively disowned him when he took a Japanese bride. It was all in his vibe. He felt very familiar and likeable. I've always been fond of black sheep.

"So, Loco, I was wondering if you could do me a favor?" he began, leaning in. I almost leaned away. Yeah, he was definitely a grifter.

"What can I do for you?" I asked, keeping my cards close.

"Well, I'm very concerned about Kevin. He can speak Japanese fluently, as well. His mother made sure of that, so that's no problem," he said, suddenly sounding very nervous. He actually looked around, again, to see who was in earshot. "The problem is his English. I don't want him to lose it. I use English at home as often as I can, but I travel a lot on business and, well, all of his friends are Japanese. And all of his relatives—here in Japan, anyway—are Japanese, too. So I'm essentially the only connection he has to America, and to English."

"I see," I said, shaking my head, seeing where he was going now.

"Me and, of course, you!"

His eyes revealed a deep misgiving, almost panic.

I remember thinking that I'll probably find myself in a similar predicament someday. The longer I stay here, the harder it will be to go back to the US, and the more likely it is that I'll set up permanent shop in Yokohama. I'll probably take a bride and build a family and they'll be this language and cultural thing hanging over us. I had friends dealing with it and they all related similar tales of the challenges involved with raising children to be multicultural and bilingual in the midst of Japanese society as it currently stands.

Most succumbed to the overwhelming pressure and allowed the Japanese to dominate. Some found ways, through various means, to offset the damage.

Apparently, Mr. McCallister envisioned me as part of his means.

"What would you have me do?"

"Nothing, really," he said with a shrug. "Just talk to him. I mean, I know you have to keep a certain professional distance from the students. And, God knows I know they keep you busy, but if you have time, just talk to him—about anything, anything at all. He likes sports. He's on the basketball team here. Do you like basketball?"

Nice of him to ask.

"Yeah, I love it."

"Well, you can talk sports with him. Or anything, really."

I looked him in the eye. I could see thinly disguised anguish and it struck a sympathy chord.

Poor guy.

"You know what, Loco? Forget about it. I'm sorry I came to you like this. We don't even know each other."

Yeah, he was a hustler, but not an especially skilled one, unless he thought I was an idiot. But it had been so long since anyone had tried to hustle me that I felt almost nostalgic.

"I'll see what I can do, alright? I mean, I can't promise anything and I certainly won't push the issue, but if he's open to it, I don't see any problem with it."

"That's all I'm asking," he said with glee, and grabbed my hand and shook it. "I mean, you know how it is here. It's hard enough living and working and raising a family, but raising an English speaker? I'm lucky he still knows the alphabet."

I almost laughed. But he was so earnest.

"Thank you so much!"

"I'll do what I can," I said.

For the next few weeks, whenever I ran into Kevin, he'd be with anywhere from two to four Japanese friends, frolicking around. The first few times I'd greet them and try to give Kevin an eye—an eye he'd artfully dodge. There was no way to sneak in a question about the Cavalier's chances of getting to the NBA finals. He'd be gone before I could even form the question in my mind.

One day, I caught him alone in the hallway between classes.

"Hey Kevin, how's it going?"

"Eeeeto (hamana, hamana, hamana)!"

"Don't 'eeeeto' me! You speak English!" I snapped.

His eyes focused at my chiding, and he seemed to nervously lower his Japanese mask just a bit to reveal the American boy living abroad he'd hidden behind it. He checked to see if the coast was clear the same way his father had, then looked back at me.

"I'm fine."

"You've been following the playoffs?" I asked, trying to sound conversational. "Your father says you're into basketball."

"Yeah, I play for the team. I play power forward."

He didn't sound like he'd lost anything.

"Lebron James looks good," I said. "Maybe the Cavs will go all the way this year!"

"Nah," he replied, his hands in his pockets, still looking as nervous as a gazelle at a watering hole on an African savanna. "I'm going with Boston. Their defense is better and Rajan Rondo just keeps getting stronger. I think he's gonna be the best point guard in the eastern conference next—"

"Ke-bin, nani shiteiru (what are you doing)?" came the voice of one of his cronies from the staircase behind us.

"Nani mo nai (nada)," he said, donning his Japanese mask. He bowed appropriately and "Jya ne'd" me ("later").

That was our first and last conversation in the six months since we'd met. Every time we bumped heads after that, he was always in the company of his Japanese posse and would "eeeeto" me.

Then, today . . .

Before a lesson, I like to do a little warm up activity to get the kids thinking in English. Mrs. Betty, as had been her practice since she started substituting for Yamada-sensei, whenever we would team-teach, sat off to the side while I had the run of the class. Sometimes she'd even eerily doze off, looking like my grandmother who used to pass out on the couch watching TV—sometimes with lit cigarettes dangling between her fingers, an ash several inches long extending from its tip.

We played a game known as "criss-cross" in which I had all of the students stand and I'd ask them questions using grammar points we'd recently studied. If a student knows the answer, he should raise his hand. I call on the first one to do so. If they answer the question correctly using the grammar properly, they are then given the option of choosing left, right, front or back. Whichever direction they choose, the students seated in the row or column in that direction can join the student in being seated. The last student standing is the loser.

I usually start off with really easy questions to draw them in like, "what time is it?" or "what's today's date?" If those prove to be too hard, I might even ask "what's your name?"

For these games and just about every other activity, Kevin would usually opt out or find some way to make a dumb mistake that was beneath his English ability. I wouldn't give him any flack because, once

I knew he was fluent, I realized it was like asking a teenager to sing the Sesame Street song everyday.

But, to my surprise, Kevin was standing right along with all of his classmates today, and looking engaged at that! I figured maybe someone in my absence, perhaps even Mrs. Betty, had gotten at him about his lack of participation in games.

I went through a few questions and most of the class was seated. I was reviewing the verbs "to do", "to have", and "to be".

Kevin, however, was still standing.

I glanced over at Mrs. Betty, and her eyes, tiny through her thick lenses, looked like she was half-there and half-elsewhere, perhaps about to doze off. Lucky her.

Webster, who was off on the side near the back, was chatting freely with his full-blooded buddies and had his back to me. They had started getting a little loud and raunchy. With some of the unruly kids, I put them on the spot to shut them up, but, I'd never had occasion to single Webster out, and I hoped I never would.

"Webster-kun," I shouted, in Japanese, deciding "fuck it", because he was as Japanese as the rest of them, "Why don't you ask the questions?"

He was still talking and laughing—hopefully not ignoring me, but he probably was—so the other students had to get his attention for me and tell him what I'd said.

He spun around.

"Eeee! Me?" he hollered, jabbing his index finger at his nose.

"Yeah, you!"

The class laughed. He looked around, soaking up the jeers. Then, he threw back his shoulders and communicated something with his eyes to his cronies. They laughed. 'I'll show you' his body language hollered. 'You don't scare me!'

"Do you like ice cream?" he asked the room.

A girl's hand shot up first. I called on her.

"Yes, I am!" she shouted. Those who knew the correct answer laughed. Webster's boys fell on the floor howling. I smiled.

"Yes, I *am*?" I said, emphasizing the word that needed correcting.

"Ah sokka (ah, I got it)!" she exclaimed. "Yes, I *do*!"

"*Ex*cellent!" Webster shouted, just as my mouth was forming the same word, mimicking me perfectly. Everyone laughed. Even Mrs. Betty!

Webster, charged with confidence now, launched another.

"Are you Japanese?" he asked, using one of my go-to questions for testing the verb "to be". This time, however, exaggerating my intonation with his impersonation. It sounded like, 'Ahhh Yuuu JaPaNeeezzZZu?'

Everyone got a kick outta that, too. Even me. Then the laughter stopped just as suddenly as it had begun. I was looking at Webster, giving him a faux-scolding glare, but when the laughter had abruptly ceased I scanned the room to discover the reason.

It was Kevin, his hand held high!

He'd never raised his hand for criss-cross, and everyone recognized this.

He was looking at me intently, more intently than he ever had. I couldn't understand why. It was a weird moment.

I called on him, prepared to hear a "no" from this blond-haired, blue-eyed American. I mean, if I asked one of the Chinese students that same question, he'd shout, "*hell no*" like you'd asked him if he had three legs and walked in circles.

"Yes, I *am*!" he said, pumped with aplomb, a sly grin on his lips.

The class gasped. Apparently I wasn't alone in my presumption that he'd answer in the negative. I almost wasn't sure I'd even heard him right.

But, his eyes, challenging mine, seemed to assert, "Yeah, you heard me right, Mr. Loco. I might look different, and y'all might have other plans for me, you and dad. But, for better or for worse, these are my people. I've made up my mind! I'm Japanese!"

I smiled, and gave him a nod-bow. I was proud of him.

But, I knew Mr. McCallister wasn't gonna like it one bit. Poor guy.

Interlude

By the Time I Get to Yokohama

This morning I was on the train checking my email when we pulled into the station. It was packed to the gills and about to get more so judging from the queues on the platform before the door I was facing. I turned around and braced for the surge. And it came.

As usual, the surge swirled around me as much as it could, avoiding making contact with me—like I was an enormous boulder in the path of a stampede—but soon all of the available space outside of the bubble around me was filled by the surge. That is, those who hadn't decided to make their way to another equally crowded car began to brush against me. Eventually, one man turned completely around and, with his back and putting a little shoulder into it too, dislodged me from my position without apology or acknowledgement.

This was all par for the course. Sometimes, by the time I get to Yokohama, I've exercised patience that would make even Job think seriously about atheism.

A high school girl, caught up in this commuter pinball game, was shoved against me. She turned my way, clearly intending to apologize, saw it was a non-Japanese-style human, did a quasi-nod and curtsy combo, took a quick glance to her rear, and then turned back my way looking a little freaked out. She was dressed in the standard fare, a sailor-style uniform with the skirt hiked up pretty high on her thighs. She wore a surgical mask like many people do, probably to avoid spreading germs or catching the flu that was going around. Her eyes and body language were what made it clear that she was frazzled, though.

She was aggressively repositioning herself this way and that and it took a moment for me to realize it had nothing to do with me—not this time anyway. People often, upon realizing that they've been shoved into my vicinity, make strenuous efforts to remove themselves. I discerned that this girl's efforts were not to evade me, but rather to escape from someone else—the man behind her.

He was the runt of the litter, and not much taller than the schoolgirl. He was dressed in typical "salaryman" fashion with a briefcase in one hand and his cell phone in the other. His eyes were shifty, but his target was clear. There was no stealth to his game. He wanted her and was aggressively wading through the passengers in pursuit.

The girl slid in front of me and sort of peeked around me to see if he would follow, like I was a cornerstone of a building, or a bodyguard. She chose *me*, of all people. In a car full of her compatriots, she chose me. I wondered if any thought had gone into her decision. Had she had such an experience before, perhaps with this same guy, on this same train, and learned the hard way that Japanese men wouldn't lift a finger to protect her? If so, that was actually pretty clever of her, I thought. It would be like a woman being stalked yelling "fire" instead of "help me!" And if she had intended to use the Japanese-free bubble around me to dissuade her assailant, that would also indicate some unorthodox outside-the-box thinking on her part, bordering on genius.

I was intrigued as much as disgusted now. I turned just as the pint-sized perv realized what she'd done. His eyes scaled me slowly until he reached my eyes, and froze when his eyes made contact with mine—like a deer caught in my headlights. Maybe something in my eyes indicated to him that I was oblivious to what he was up to, or he was simply lust-driven and wouldn't be dissuaded, not even by the likes of me. Whatever went through his sick little mind, it told him to keep pushing forward and ignore me because he tried to slide in front of me and position himself between the girl and me.

I wasted no time closing the gap between her and I. If anyone were paying attention, it might have looked to them like *I* was the chikan.

Shorty didn't like that. Maybe he thought I was trying to move in on his action or something. So, he tried some old slick shit and used the continuing surge of boarding passengers and the sharp edge of his briefcase to wedge himself in front of me. This behavior, however, was very noticeable to everyone in the vicinity. However, instead of focusing on him and his oddly aggressive endeavors to get closer to a high school girl, our fellow commuters kept their indirect and suspicious, fish-eyed focus on me, the conspicuous threat.

Shit like this tempts me to say "fuck it" and let whatever will be just be. And, taking advantage of my moment of indecision, he wedged his arm between his prey and me.

As the train left the station, I could feel his arm between us adjusting with the movements of the train, only with determination. He was re-positioning it, and in doing so, was angling his briefcase into my groin to make space.

This motherfucker!

He was on my right side. I was holding a metal strap with my left hand. I switched to a strap on my right side and, as I did, I swung my right elbow low and caught him squarely in the forehead.

It didn't so much hurt him as it surprised him.

"Gomen nasai," I whispered and nod/bowed. He ignored my apology, probably sensing that my assault was done intentionally. A perceptive perv.

But his hand didn't budge.

My elbow was now above his head. My switching hands had actually made his access to the girl easier. I had anticipated he'd back off after I'd shown him my intention to intervene. He hadn't and, as a result, now had an almost unfettered and well-concealed entree to her.

The train swerved a bit and everyone was tossed to the left, myself included. He apparently had been anticipating the swerve and used it to slide closer to his potential victim. I realized he wasn't going to use his hands, though. He'd wanted to get directly behind her for some reason. And now he was, as I had been shoved further to her left by the swerve.

I couldn't see what was going on below, but I could tell by his face that something was up as he was trying much too hard to look nonchalant. The girl had ceased all struggling and jostling and had accepted her fate, whatever it was. She was looking at her cell phone, eyes locked on it. Some of the other passengers would occasionally glance over to check him out, but most kept re-confirming their proximity to me, feeding their curiosities, or relieving their suspicions as to what my motives might have been for being among them.

By the time we got to Yokohama station, I'd had just about as much as I could take of the misplaced suspicion around me. Will these people ever learn?

But, as the doors opened I saw a flash of movement and heard a ripping sound. It looked like the man suddenly snatched something from the girl. Her panties? I'd heard about pervs using scissors and box cutters to slash women's skirts open, and even of women's underwear being stolen off of clotheslines, but I'd never heard of pervs pilfering panties in person!

They tussled a bit to separate like their headphone wires had gotten tangled. Then, he tore away from her, making it appear like a classic NY-style purse snatching, but all the girl had was a school book bag and she was still holding that. He'd done something wrong, that was for sure!

As he tried to shove by me and make his exit, I stuck out my foot and tripped him. He lunged forward, but the crowded conditions kept him from falling. He did knock over several people in the process of making his escape, though. Several passengers spilled out of the car onto the crowded platform. He stepped on a couple of the fallen people and stepped over a couple of others, but once his feet were on solid ground, he was Usain.

I thought to pursue, but I wasn't about to climb over fallen people to do it. I watched as he shoved through the swarm of commuters for the escalator. But the girl, she was not as reticent as me. She apologized and pardoned her way through a few people, shoved her way through others, and took off after him. By the time I reached the escalator, the guy was nearly at his top running speed and the girl was hot on his heels. She must've run track.

By the time I reached the top of the escalator, I saw a few heads turned in the direction they had run, but the man and the girl were gone.

13
Hurricane Betty
(Mendokusai Junior High)

When I arrived at work today, Akiyama eyed me from the door all the way to my desk, which I'd learned meant she had something to tell me. It was something white hot, and probably something secret, her pursed lips informed me.

But, at 8:25 am in the teacher's office, it was neither the place nor the time.

So, I had to sit there through the 15-minute morning meeting, only half of which was comprehensible, trying to guess what today's drama was. Every few moments, between bites of her breakfast rice ball, Akiyama would look at me and shake her head regrettably. This was her way of letting me know I wasn't gonna like it, not one bit.

Mrs. Betty hadn't arrived yet. She usually dragged herself into the office around 8:45, after the meeting had finished. I wasn't exactly sure why she didn't have to be there for the morning meetings, but she never attended. Akiyama caught me eying her empty seat and her eyes widened a bit.

This meant the news was about Mrs. Betty.

Damn.

Even though I knew it couldn't be what I feared most—no way Akiyama could keep something like that in, and eat breakfast over it—I still felt a very unsettling feeling.

The VP was droning on and on about some weather-related issues. Apparently, the unusually hot conditions had caused problems in several schools in the area. There had been black outs, power outages and student illnesses. Watching them running around in this humidity for P.E. Class, I wasn't surprised.

Not to mention the typhoon that was headed our way . . .

After the meeting broke up and the homeroom teachers hustled off to their classes to take attendance and whatnot, the office had cleared out. Akiyama and I were practically alone.

"What?" I begged.

"Betty-sensei wa nee," she began. Akiyama would make a great storyteller, if she could find an audience with sufficient patience. "She's in trouble."

"What happened?"

"Yesterday wa nee," Akiyama had this habit of sticking English words in Japanese sentences, and sucking air when she had something to say.

Usually I really dug her style, found it kinda cute even, but at the moment I wasn't really feeling it—not where Mrs. Betty was concerned.

"Just tell me!" I snapped. I was really worried about Mrs. Betty. I'd grown quite fond of her. In fact, she had basically become my adopted grandmother.

"OK, OK," she sighed. "Yesterday, right? Yesterday the principal received a letter from a parent. Actually it was a fax from the mother of a student in one of Betty-sensei's English classes."

"Oh no!" I said, and didn't really need to hear the rest. I already knew exactly what had gone wrong.

Every time Mrs. Betty and I team-taught a class, there wasn't much teamwork involved at all. She'd arrive at the class, find a seat off to the side, plant herself in it making herself as comfortable as an elderly woman can in a wooden chair designed more for endurance than for comfort, and she'd stay awake, sometimes. Consciousness was about the extent of her contribution to our team effort.

Of course, I had absolutely no problem with this. As far as I was concerned, she was a retired teacher and just doing the school a favor by filling in for the wayward Yamada-sensei. But, go figure. Parents actually expected her to teach something, and for their precious brood to learn something.

What happened in her classes the two weeks I'd been at Mendokusai and absent from Syouganai—when she'd be alone with the students—was a mystery to me. I presumed she was doing what she'd been doing for damn near half a century, with some modifications for age and health.

"The student apparently told their parents that Mrs. Betty doesn't do anything in the class."

"I see."

"Yeah," she said, nodding, mock astonishment on her face. I could tell she wasn't surprised, either. Just going through the motions. "The parent said the student told them that she wasn't teaching the grammar points at all. Just playing games and having them read the textbook—that she hardly even stands up during the entire class."

I just shook my head.

"Did you see this fax?"

"No," she said.

"Did Mrs. Betty see it?"

"No."

"OK," I said, smelling a rat.

The office door opened and Mrs. Betty came hobbling in. My heart raced out to her, but my body remained seated. She didn't like to be fussed over.

"Does she know?" I whispered before she was within earshot.

"Yes, the VP spoke with her about it yesterday," Akiyama breathed. "She was very upset about it."

"Good morning, Betty-sensei," I said in English as she limped past me.

"What's so good about it?" she snapped, in Japanese. "Haven't you heard? A typhoon is gonna piss all over us today!"

I recoiled, but kept smiling. My grandmother would get like this sometimes, too. She could be as cantankerous as the Grinch. I always thought it was funny though and never knew if she was serious or not. There were a couple of other teachers in the office and their heads popped up at this old-school Japanese-style profanity.

Akiyama, a smile painted on her face as well, greeted her in Japanese with honorifics and all, much more in tune to Mrs. Betty than me, and Mrs. Betty replied in Betty-ese. Akiyama blanched.

Akiyama had explained to me one day why I had trouble with my adopted grandmother's Japanese. She'd told me that "Betty-ese" was actually chock-full of idioms, euphemisms, exaggerations, and embellishments. That made sense.

Mrs. Betty always wore a crooked smile or a poker face. But, today she openly bore the countenance of someone with a lot on their mind.

I decided to let her be, and started fooling around on my computer. Akiyama apparently had had the same idea. She pretended to prepare her lesson for first period, though we all knew she had probably had it prepared since last week. The woman lived to teach, an educator by design.

"Akiyama-san!" Mrs. Betty said sharply.

"Hai!" Akiyama replied, snapping to attention.

Mrs. Betty proceeded to release the dam and a flood of Japanese was let loose.

I watched Akiyama out of the side of my eye. She was nodding and "hai-ing" over and over, each "hai" an octave higher than the previous.

"Hai, wakarimashita (OK, understood)," she cried, finally, with a bow.

Then, Mrs. Betty rose gingerly, clutching at everything for balance. I hated to see her like this, angry and helpless-looking. I glanced over at the VP at the front desk. I was sure he'd done the honors. The principal would have farmed this responsibility out for sure. The VP was sitting there, shuffling papers and trying to pretend he hadn't heard all the language Mrs. Betty had just filled the empty office with.

And then Mrs. Betty was off, getting her head start to her first period class. Akiyama and I followed her with our eyes. As soon as the door slid closed behind her, I turned to Akiyama.

"What did she say?"

Akiyama looked at me, kind of misty-eyed. Then she glanced around at the VP. Seemingly on cue, the man rose and went into the principal's office, on official business no doubt. Then she turned back to me.

"Eeeto ne," she said.

"What?" I yelled. "Tell me!"

"I don't know how to say it in English!"

Great.

"Well, is she okay? She looked pretty upset."

"Oh, she's fine," she said, and then proceeded to tell me in easier Japanese what Mrs. Betty had said.

Her words made me proud to know her. I laughed, hard because I had actually been worried about Mrs. Betty, this force of nature.

Silly me.

I caught a flash of the VP peeking out from the principal's office. Our eyes met for a micro-second, and then his face disappeared back into the office.

What she'd said went a little something like this:

"I've been teaching for over 45 years, dear, and never, and I mean *never*, in that time had a parent ever complained about me. If they had, Lord knows, it never got back to me. You know why? Cuz Mrs. Betty knows how to teach! I am well-respected in the teaching community, by students, teachers and faculty. *Well* respected! I have students that are grown men and women now with grown children of their own coming to visit me and pay their respects. You-know-whut-um-sayin' dear?

So, if a parent ever even thought to contact a principal about me—out of respect—that principal would have handled that situation without dragging me into it. Out of respect, I tell you, they would've told that parent that if she or he had a problem with their child's education, don't be faxing it over! What kind of sugar-honey-ice-tea is that? He'd have told that parent that the best way to ensure your child is getting the education they're entitled to is to get off of their cowardly, fat, faxing asses and come see to it!

Lord knows, I miss the old days when teachers got respect not only from students, but from their parents. *And,* they got it from puffed-up bureaucrats, scared to death of a piece of paper what came through a damn machine!

I'll sho' be glad when that Yamada brings herself back. Bless her miserable soul!

Now, let me go see to the little darlings. Jesus, give me strength!"

★ ★ ★ ★ ★

The following day, Mrs. Betty informed Akiyama and me that she'd be spending most of the day at the doctor. She'd been having problems with her left knee. The trouble she had walking persisted and she'd been in pain most of the day. Beyond my concern for her well being, which was considerable, it also meant, I was informed, that I'd be teaching the five classes of first-year students that we would generally have taught together alone.

And one of these precious angels would be the the little pissant that told his parents Mrs. Betty wasn't making the grade!

This would be, actually, the first time in my tenure as an ALT that I was called upon to do such a thing. And, the more I thought about it—and considering the environment I worked in—the more I realized that it was a sign of trust as well as a leap of faith on the part of the principal and the English teachers. The decision was made as much out of necessity, as there really wasn't anyone else available to do it, as it was out of their belief that I could handle it.

Akiyama and Mrs. Betty had been behind this show of confidence, of course.

There had been a meeting held to discuss what to do in Mrs. Betty's absence. The faculty met about *everything*, at least once. And, after all, this wasn't just one period; this was an entire day of me, on my lonesome, with PTA-members marching hither and thither around the building at will.

★ ★ ★ ★ ★

Akiyama met me that night after this meeting. We'd taken to going to dinner and occasionally drinking after work at least once every two weeks. It was great having a friend who "got" me, particularly a Japanese one. Sometimes I'd get this feeling that, to Japanese, I was simply "un-gettable". But Akiyama did, and how, and to top it off she was actually fun to hang out with. Her tastes were a little pricey for me, though. I favored dining on the cheap at Japanese family restaurants, but she liked to go to ritzy joints with tablecloths and place settings.

That night we split the difference and went to a TGI Fridays near Yokohama station.

As she broke the meeting scenario down, I could see it playing out in my mind with the two of them, Mrs. Betty and Akiyama, tag-teaming those effete leaders of ours.

"I wonder if this is a good idea," the principal had said, to test the waters. "He's only an ALT, after all."

"Loco-sensei can handle it, sir," Akiyama said. "He's taught classes by himself before, and did very well."

"I don't know about this," he said. "I mean, what if the kids are unruly? Can he handle it?"

"Can *he* handle it?" Mrs. Betty jumped in and said. "Christ in Heaven! Can *you* handle it? *You* can't even handle a fax from a parent!"

"Now, Betty-sama, there's no need to get—"

"Don't 'sama' me! I ain't no VIP!" Betty hollered at the man. "I'm a teacher—a damn good one, too! And, it takes one to know one. And, Loco-sensei is a fine teacher—with a spine! More than I can say for half of these spine-less bureaucrats in this office, letting these kids run around all crazy! Have you looked around at your school recently, Mr. Man? In case you haven't noticed, the damn lunatics are running this asylum! And all you can do is question the classroom management skills of one of the few teachers around here who isn't afraid to step up at a time—"

"OK, OK, OK," the principal said. "You're right, of course."

Akiyama and I laughed and drank 'til the last train.

LOCO in YOKOHAMA

★ ★ ★ ★ ★

So, yeah, when I walked in that morning, I kinda felt like I had to represent.

I wasn't even sure if this kinda thing was in my contract, but I wasn't inclined to get *The Company* involved. The last thing I needed was the Silky One getting all hot and bothered about the situation and possibly complicating it with some legalese.

I *wanted* to do this!

I had arrived early that morning and prepared everything. I wasn't nervous, though. I just didn't want to let Mrs. Betty down.

In the first-year teacher's meeting, after the main morning meeting, Akiyama stood and reminded the other first-year teachers that I would be on my lonesome.

"If you find yourself with some free time, please look in on Loco-sensei and give him a little support if he needs it."

All eyes were on me.

I didn't know what to say. I mean, I didn't anticipate needing any support, but you never know, you know? So, I went with the default, "Yoroshiku onegai shimasu," (I'd be much obliged) and smiled. It's a phrase you can pretty much use in any situation where you want people to do something for you and want to express your gratitude for their doing so. The smile can do the rest.

Midway through the first period, Ozawa-sensei came by and stood outside the classroom in the hallway, visible through the open doors and windows. And watched us.

Watched us having a ball!

I hadn't noticed when Ozawa left. His halitosis hung around a lot longer than he had, so I actually thought he was still there.

The kids, especially the first-year students at Mendokusai, loved themselves some Loco-sensei, especially when there was no other teacher around. And, they had me for a full 50 minutes, a very rare treat indeed. I got to know the students better in that 50 minutes than I had in the four months since I'd met them. Even the ones I knew to be knuckleheads lightened up. Once I had established that while, yes, I was alone today but, no, this would not be "show your ass" time, and, yes, I too wanted to avoid tedium with extreme prejudice but, no, I would not forfeit the lesson to achieve that goal, all went very well.

The same held true for the second period class. However, during this class, the principal himself came up to watch unobtrusively. I spied his approach before he saw me, and proceeded to pretend I hadn't seen him at all. And he couldn't have come at a better time. We were engrossed in a game I used to teach English adjectives in which I stick the words and representative pictures on the blackboard and have the students stand and clap while I say the adjective and point to the picture. If I say the wrong adjective, they shouldn't clap; for example, I'll say "tall" and point to the picture for "short". If they clap, they must sit down. I can adjust the speed according to the skill of the students. The last one standing is the winner.

They were having so much fun that they didn't even notice the principal. A couple of minutes later, I forgot he was there, too, as I was so caught up in their enthusiasm. After a few minutes, I caught some motion out of the side of my eye. Apparently he'd been satisfied that all was well, and just as unobtrusively as he'd arrived, he departed.

During the third period, no teacher or administrator came by.

After three periods, it was lunch time. I ran into Akiyama in the office.

"How's it going?" she asked, beaming.

"So far so good," I said, modestly.

"Ne, ne, ne," she said, and leaned in. "The principal came by your class and watched you!"

"Yeah, I thought I saw him," I said.

"He called me in the office just now. He said you were doing a great job!"

"Really? That's nice."

She'd said it like there was job offer as a permanent teacher or some kind of bonus attached to his praise. As far as I was concerned, I was doing this to help her and Mrs. Betty out, not to impress any of the brass

"You are great!" She was so excited for me.

I didn't want to be a killjoy so I smiled and said, "The kids were pretty well-behaved today, lucky for me."

By the time 5th period came around, my medicine was starting to wear off.

I'd had a tooth extracted the previous Friday, and with the pain came a little irritation. This was exacerbated by what had to be the worst class of the six first-year classes. In this class, there were a couple of students reminiscent of Matsui-kun and company over at Syouganai. To them, me on my lonesome meant "party time!"

Every instruction I gave was met with "wak*kan*nai!" Said the way they said it, the best English equivalent would be, "you're not *really* expecting to be taken seriously, are you?"

My mouth was aching, and from the 90-minute wrestling match my dentist had with my impacted tooth—he won, by the way, with the aid of a tray full of tools that looked medieval or better suited to a mechanic than a dentist—my whole head was throbbing, and my patience with these two knuckleheads was rapidly waning. The wall clock told me I had 20 more minutes, but my patience clock contradicted it and said, "20 more seconds."

Mrs. Betty could not have chosen a better time to make a dramatic entrance. She hobbled into the classroom through the back door just as one student, the worst of the bunch, Taro, was sticking things in the lone oscillating fan just to hear them rattle around the blade's cage.

"Now, now, young man, I know you're not behaving badly after our last talk," she said calmly in Japanese, like everything was well under control. I had a strange feeling right about then that Taro-kun was the little ratfink that caused the hubbub the other day, and that Mrs. Betty had felt it, too.

Taro's head whipped around, as did every head in the class. He looked back at the rattling fan, then at everyone else in the classroom just as everyone looked at him, then back at Mrs. Betty, and down at her cane. I remembered at that moment that it was the one she had threatened to go upside his head with if he didn't join in the game on her first day teaching at the school. He looked the way kids look when they're bumfuzzled, racking their brains for an alibi, and coming up with nothing for the effort.

"I. . . I. . ."

"No need to explain. Just turn off the fan and take your seat like a good lad."

He did as he was instructed this time. Post haste.

"Mr. Loco," she said to me, as Taro took his seat for the first time in 40 minutes. "Would you mind very much if I took over from here? I need to return some quizzes and such."

"Of course not," I said. Watching her painful steps, I felt almost ashamed to think my tooth pain was significant. "Are you OK?"

"I'm fine, dear," she replied. "Just old, is all."

She slowly made her way to the front of the class, all eyes following her. She greeted the students and then turned to me.

"You don't have to stay," she said, smiling that beautiful crooked smile of hers. "Go on down to the office, and take it easy. I'll be down in a bit. English class is over for today."

"You sure?" I asked. "They're a little wild this afternoon."

"Who? These little angels?" She said, her voice high, and as icy as a typhoon cutting across Mt. Fuji in the dead of winter. I could feel the chill in the gaping hole in my mouth where my molar used to be. "Don't worry about me, Mr. Loco. They know better."

14
Long Live The King
(Syouganai Junior High)

LOCO in YOKOHAMA

I had just finished teaching a class and was sitting in the teacher's office when I received a text from a friend of mine informing me that Michael Jackson had died.

I immediately deleted the message. I don't know why. Maybe, stupidly, I thought that if I treated it like junk mail it might become as true as most spam. My mind sought supporting evidence that it was spam. I scanned the office, for surely if it were true, there would be something different. Screaming in the street, crying children, shattered windows, maybe a black hole would've appeared in the wall and commence to sucking all of the joy out of the world.

But nothing had changed.

My fellow teachers in the office were still in workaday mode, sitting at their desk or sipping green tea or chatting with one another. Some were even laughing. Nah. Michael must be alive and kicking, I thought. Otherwise, the world would have taken a moment of silence.

But, just to make sure, I checked the internet expecting to find that it was perhaps some kind of international hoax.

My heart was racing as MSNBC's homepage began slowly loading and a full-page photo of MJ slid into view from the top of the screen. The headline read: "Michael Jackson dies at age 50".

I didn't want to read anymore but felt strangely compelled to. Reading somehow soothed the ache in my chest, and it kept alive the hope that the media had jumped the gun, again, like when they'd called the 2000 election for Al Gore before the Florida count was in. Maybe Michael was on some operating table fighting for his life.

I bounced around to CNN and other news sites, all bearing similar headlines, almost all of them mentioning that he *was* "The King of Pop".

Was. The. King. Of. Pop . . .

I hated the idea of Michael being spoken of in the past tense almost as much as that bogus ass title. Though it was his request to be called that, I always felt *The King of Pop* had that cloying feeling of a contrived decision made by handlers or marketing mavens, or was made in a moment when MJ's faculties weren't operating on full-thrusters. It felt like self-sacrilege the first time I heard him use it, and like a slur every time the press did. Even these tales of his demise felt like the reporters were getting in their last licks, angry that their favorite slab of red meat—one that they relished gnawing on at every opportunity—left the paparazzi party prematurely.

All of the stories mentioned the scandals within the first paragraph or two, of course, each with a hint of, "that child molesting freak is among us no more!"

★ ★ ★ ★ ★

I turned away from the monitor to the teachers' office and I saw that the television was off. That was not the case when the swine flu had landed in nearby Kawasaki, or when Japan was playing the U.S.A. or Korea in the World Baseball Classic. I figured none of them knew yet.

And it made me feel very alone.

"*You are not alone,*" Michael sang in my head. I hummed it in my heart like a silent musical vigil as I made my way to the vice-principal's desk.

"Can I turn on the TV for a moment?" I asked the VP.

"Why? What happened?"

Another teacher chimed in, "Oh, Michael Jackson passed away."

I was shocked! Someone knew? In fact several teachers knew. They looked at me as if I might give them some hint as to how they should feel about this news. One of them turned on the TV and started flipping through channels. There was no breaking news or banners racing across the top or bottom of talk shows.

"I'm so sorry," Takahashi said walking over to me, like MJ was a friend of mine or a family member. Usually, this kind of thing would irk me, like the slew of congratulations I received when Obama was successful in his surprising ascension to power. But, somehow, I felt it was appropriate this time around because I truly was beginning to feel like I had personally suffered a terrible loss.

"Thanks," I said, tried to smile but couldn't.

Instead, I went and took the remote and flipped through the channels once again, yet saw no news. As soon as I sat down at my desk, the bell chimed for the next class. I had totally forgotten about it.

"Shit!" I grabbed my lesson materials and ran up the four flights of stairs to the classroom—arriving just a little late. I looked out over the faces of the children while I huffed and puffed from my exertions, and was reminded of what Michael must have encountered on his many visits to this country—a sea of adoring Asian faces, crying, screaming, and fainting.

My kids were anxious about the test they were about to take, though.

Takahashi, who seemed to have an inkling of how I must've been feeling—because my eyes unfortunately tell my whole story sometimes—looked at me anxiously.

But I threw on a brave face and plodded through the greetings.

Everything was so ordinary in the class that it felt unnatural. Takahashi had to repeatedly clear her throat to get my attention. All I could think was that something was wrong in the world. I just couldn't put my finger on what it was.

While the students were taking the test, I sat on the teacher's desk and watched them.

They would hardly know who MJ was, I thought. He would be just another strange American pop idol, if they even knew that much. And Takahashi, in her mid 20s, was just old enough to have heard stories about his plastic surgeries, those child molestation charges, and his eccentricities. No, she wouldn't understand, either. This exacerbated the loneliness I felt until it seemed to be collapsing around me like a wormhole.

I turned away from the class and faced the board, 'cause I couldn't hold back my tears. Takahashi was beside me and asked if I was OK. She touched my shoulder, even, and in her eyes was deep sympathy . . . *for me,* but nothing for Michael. He'd touched so many people, but none of them were in this room.

I didn't want to cry there, not amid those who didn't get it.

"I'm fine," I told her, and wiped my face with my sleeve. "Just tired."

I turned back to the class. They hadn't noticed a thing.

Towards the end of the period, once they were done testing, we began an exercise, but I still couldn't focus. I kept contemplating a world with no MJ. His words kept bouncing around inside my head until one of his songs got trapped in my mouth.

It was *Beat It.*

I started singing it under my breath right there in the class, but I was loud enough that the kids in the front few rows could hear me. They looked up from their note-taking and listened.

"Whose song is that?" one girl, Harumi, asked, bobbing her head, clearly enjoying it.

"Michael Jackson's," I said. "You don't know *Beat It?*"

She shook her head and shrugged her shoulders. The song is older than her by more than a decade so I shouldn't have been surprised. But I was. It's so incredible to talk to people who don't know his work. We use English songs in class quite often, so the kids are used to singing in English. But usually the Japanese teachers choose the songs and they invariably use songs that the kids are familiar with already, either from their use in famous commercials or popular TV shows.

But they don't know *Beat It*.

Just singing it made me feel better. And the students somehow sensing and acknowledging Michael's magic made it feel even better, suggesting to me that even if he had been born in this time, he would have still been the greatest ever.

I started doing some of the more basic dance moves from the *Beat It* video.

When Takahashi noticed me dancing, she looked relieved, and the kids loved it. Some of the wilder students got up and tried to do Michael's moves, too. Some knew them better than me. They didn't know MJ, but knew his moves? Maybe they'd filtered down to some J-pop group or maybe they knew Usher, or something, I figured. They didn't know MJ was dead, either. To them, he was alive. They could see the MJ in me.

★ ★ ★ ★ ★

By the time I returned to the teacher's office, the TV stations had finally gotten around to reporting his passing. MJ's name was on everyone's lips. Most of the teachers grew silent and looked to me with half-condoling, half- "it's nice to have something to talk about besides the rainy season" expressions on their faces, confirming that—at least in that office—MJ was my loss and mine alone.

"*How does it feel, when you're alone and you're cold inside? Like a stranger in Moscow,*" I sang, softly, as I sat at my desk feeling a growing solitude.

"Must have been suicide," I heard one teacher say, with a tone in his voice like over-medicating was the American version of popular Japanese *splattercide,* in which one decides that now is as good a time as any and hops in front of a racing commuter train during rush hour.

"He was using drugs," another said, with haughty contempt laced with pity, like it was something so shameful that neither he nor anyone he'd ever met, nor any Japanese in their right mind, would ever do for certainly they would share Michael's fate if they did.

I pretended not to understand, to not even hear them. Several people asked me, sincerely, if I were OK.

"I'll be alright, thanks."

"Did you like him?"

"Like" ("suki" in Japanese) has a different meaning. It's actually substituted for "love" quite often. Aiko used to say, "Suki yo!" to express her feelings for me, and I knew she would have done anything for me. I used to sing MJ's songs for her. She loved it when I'd serenade her with his words—"*the way you make me feel, you really turn me on, you knock me off of my feet, my lonely days are gone. . .*"

"Yes, I liked him very much," I replied.

"He was the King of Pop," Takahashi whispered to me, while her hand gentled my back—as if acknowledging him as royalty would mollify my grief somehow. I looked over my shoulder at her. She must have seen something in my eyes 'cause her hand stopped stroking and retracted.

The King of Pop?

The Godfather of Soul! Now that's a fucking title! That's a throne to plant your ass on forever and sit contentedly. When James Brown passed, I didn't grieve. Hell, I wanted to party! I had ants in my pants and I needed to dance! He'd done some questionable shit, too, but James spent his whole career bringing the noise and bringing the funk and I'd be damned if I was going to desecrate his legacy with sobbing. He died as he lived, saying it loud, 'I'm black and I'm proud!'

There was nothing sad about James.

But, Michael, seemed to shun his own skin. Maybe when he looked at the man in the mirror he couldn't see how beautiful he was. When I reflect of MJ, I think of a story I heard in a film called "Basquiat" where a little prince with a magic crown gets locked in a tower by a warlock who took away his voice. There was a window made of bars and the prince would smash his head against the bars hoping that someone would hear the sound and find him. However the crown made a sound so beautiful that people wanted to grab the air. He never escaped from that room, but the sound he made brought joy to the world.

That's what Michael did for me. He filled everything up with magic and beauty. My sadness comes from his never being able to escape—but man did he try, and the harder he tried the thicker the bars got. And that evil warlock that had MJ locked in a cell? I believe *he* was "The King of Pop".

★ ★ ★ ★ ★

The students generally have lunch in their respective homerooms seated at their desks. While they dine and chat, they listen to J-pop pouring down from the loud speakers. The music can be heard everywhere in the school except on the first floor where there are no classrooms, only offices. The songs are selected by student DJs. Occasionally, I join the students in their homerooms for lunch. I enjoy this time because it's a great chance to get to know the student's better.

But, I had MJ on my mind and didn't feel like being around the kids, so I decided to eat lunch in the teacher's office and surf the net. I was trying to find some stories or testimonials that didn't read like his death was a tragic end to a failed comeback attempt or the hardly gratifying, not-even-in the-same-vicinity-of-being-just-desserts of a *publicly* convicted child molester who'd escaped justice, a la O.J.

I found a number of stories from people who felt as I do and that lifted my spirits a bit. While the mass media seemed to be mourning the loss of one of their favorite targets, the public at-large, at least from what I'd scanned, seemed to be truly shocked and grief-stricken, liked they'd been hoping and praying, as I had, that he would have lived long enough to be publicly vindicated of this stigmata.

A couple of links led me to Youtube and I wanted so badly to hear his voice, but that might have caused a disturbance. So I settled for soundlessly watching him teach Michael Jordan how to do his dance moves in the "*Jam*" video. Man, what a moment! I felt myself welling up again. Watching him, so alive, so joyful, was a little more than I could deal with at the moment, so I left the office and decided to roam the hallways alone. Lunch is only 20 minutes so I only had few minutes remaining.

As I approached the stairwell, I thought I heard Tina Turner's voice which, it goes without saying, has no place in a Japanese junior high school. She was singing, ". . .*we are all a part of God's great big family. . .*" and I knew suddenly what it was I was hearing and what would come next for I had heard that line of hers about 10,000 times over the past

20-some odd years. Then it came, Billy Joel singing, ". . .*and the truth, you know, love is all we need. . .*"

By this time, I was taking the steps three at a time because I knew what was next! I could even see him, with his Jheri Curl and his gold-braided military-style jacket, high-water slacks, loafers and that damn glove of his!

I could see him!

"*We are the world, we are the children,*" came MJ's exquisite voice. But, he was not alone. I could hear his words spilling out of the third-year students' homerooms, from the mouths of the students!.

They knew the words!

Of course they knew the words, I realized, my heart racing.

I'd taught it to them!

We had sung the song at the beginning of every lesson for over a month, two years earlier, when they were first-year students.

I'd never heard an English-language song played during lunch in my three years of working at the school so I wondered, for a second, if it were a fluke or if the kids had learned of MJ's passing and decided on their own to play the song.

I would later learn it was Takahashi who had been the DJ that day, and that she'd dedicated the song to Michael Jackson.

I stood there in the hallway, grateful, and as enchanted as I'd been the first time I heard MJ's beautifully simple message to the world, I listened to it sung the way he had intended it to be sung, by the most profound beings on earth, the children of the world. And though he had feeding the children of Africa in mind when he wrote it, his inspired heartfelt message expanded and extended itself so that it could feed not only the famine-ravaged regions of Africa, but a world starving for inspiration and goodwill.

This world has been fortified and nourished by Michael's heart. And, even though he has passed on, his music and energy will live on, forever. Long Live King Michael!

Interlude

You're Too Kind

LOCO in YOKOHAMA

One summer day at about 12:00 pm, Mrs. Betty picked Akiyama and me up at Yokohama station. Then, 20 minutes later, we rounded up her daughter-in-law and grandson of 15, who were waiting at Mrs. Betty's modest two-family home. Betty lived on the ground floor and her son's family occupied the upstairs. He, however, was away on business and wouldn't be joining us. After a moment to make sure all was in order, her daughter-in-law took the wheel and—as she'd promised back in the spring—off we went. The five of us set out on a two and a half-hour drive to the Izu peninsula.

After we got through all the introductions and awkwardness, which didn't take long, the ride was wonderful. I could tell that Mrs. Betty had undoubtedly spoken about me quite a bit, but nonetheless, both mother and son said things like, "Oh, you're American?" and "You're from New York City? Wow!" and pretended they hadn't already interrogated their aged mother and grandmother about this foreign stranger who she had invited to come and sleep overnight with them.

Though both Akiyama and Mrs. Betty could speak English well, the conversation was exclusively in Japanese. I could catch about 70% of it, which was pretty high for me.

It turned out that Betty wasn't the only one in the family with the travel bug. Her grandson, Shintarou, had run off a list of countries he'd gone to—with and without Mrs. Betty—including France, Belgium, Spain, Italy, and England.

"I liked Spain the best!"

"Really? Why?" I asked.

"I loved the Covadonga. It was dokusouteki."

"Dokusouteki? What's that?" I asked Akiyama.

"Nan darou, like, I don't know. Look it up!"

I pulled out my cell phone and checked the meaning in the dictionary. It said "original, creative, ingenious," Three words with different meanings to my understanding.

"Original, creative, *and* ingenious? At the same time? Like, can I say 'Michael Jackson was dokusouteki'?"

"Exactly!" Shintarou snapped. "That's exactly right! You're great."

"Nah, just lucky," I said.

Yeah, he and I hit it off immediately.

257

I got to know the daughter pretty well, too, during the drive, and they me, so everyone was relaxed by the time we arrived in Izu.

From the outside, it looked like your typical Japanese-style upscale "mansion". I had envisioned a home, but it was actually a 3-bedroom condominium with a lobby from which you could probably skip stones on the sea.

After we unpacked the car of about 50 bags of God-knows-what, Shintarou gave me a quick tour. He was a great kid and had a way about him that let you know that he had no idea how well-off he was. He was not spoiled, nor bombastic, not even shy, but just matter-of-fact, with a warm and curious smile. He spoke no English but didn't behave as if that was a handicap like many people here do.

"Here's the pool," he said. "There's no lifeguard though, so we have to be careful."

"Uh, huh."

"And there's the beach over there. It's about a 10-minute walk. I don't like beaches, though."

"Me neither, too many, er, creatures."

We had an easy laugh, like we'd known each other for years.

Hovering over the beach and over Hatsushima Island in the distance, was a yellow-orange harvest moon that had just risen. I was mesmerized at its majesty.

Shintarou had already moved on.

"The hot springs is this way," he called from down the hall a ways.

"Yeah, OK, right. I'm coming."

"Everyone in the building can use the hot springs, but," He peeked over the railing at the parking lot below. I followed his glance. The only car there was a green BMW, the car we'd arrived in. ". . .looks like we're the only ones here. Guess cuz it's a weekday."

"That makes sense."

"You want to get in the hot springs now?" he asked, probably sensing my excitement at the news that I wouldn't be a spectacle for other bathers.

"Sounds like a plan."

"Cool!"

We sat in the hot springs for half an hour or so chatting in the glow of the moon outside the window, and to the sound of the surf smashing against the rocks at the shore. While the steamy bubbling of the hot spring water filled the huge tub, we learned we had a number of things in common. He wanted to be a writer. He loved manga, especially "Shonen Jump" and "One Piece", and wanted to write his own stories. I was impressed, as was he when I told him about the book I was in the process of writing, and how my love of writing was first ignited by comics as well, namely "Spider Man" and "X-Men".

By the time we got back upstairs, Akiyama and Betty's daughter had prepared vegetables and assorted meats on a barbecue on the terrace while Betty sat in a chair and basked in the cool breeze circulating the room.

"How was the hot springs?" she asked.

"Heavenly, Mrs. Betty," I said. "Simply perfect."

"Oh, you do an old woman's heart good, dear boy!"

With a little—actually, a lot—of help from her daughter, she got to her feet, went out on the terrace, and started helping with the barbecuing.

We all ate heartily. After dinner, Akiyama and Betty's daughter went on a hot springs run while Shintarou, Mrs. Betty, and I played Scrabble—in English! I was thinking they were gonna whip out a Japanese version when they'd suggested it for some reason—maybe because Shintarou couldn't speak English a lick.

It was a competitive game. They played often as a family, so it was a treat and a first to have a native speaker join in. I won, but they didn't treat my victory as a foregone conclusion, and the score was tight! I'd made the word "fruit" at one point and Shintarou, shocking the shit out of me, had extended it to "fruition."

After the game, Shintarou and I braved the dark country roads of Atami and walked to the nearest convenience store. We wound up buying ice cream for everyone. Actually, I'd just wanted to get away for a smoke, but once we'd seen the ice cream, Shintarou thought it would be perfect, and I agreed. Haagen Daz for everyone.

After another dip in the hot springs, I was beat and crashed in a room with Shintarou to the sound of waves breaking against the shore. "Nothing like this," I thought, laying there trying to think of the last time I'd felt this at peace with the world.

The next morning I woke up late. Having slept like a baby, I'd overslept and missed the sunrise I'd wanted to catch. The women were at it again. They'd prepared a smorgasbord of bread, meat, salad, and fruit for breakfast. Shintarou was still out like a light.

I excused myself and went down to the hot springs again alone, where I bathed, showered, groomed, got dressed. Then I bought a can of coffee from the vending machine, sat in the picturesque lobby and had my morning smoke. By the time I got back, breakfast was all laid out.

We discussed plans for the day over the meal.

Shintarou's mom decided that the excursion would be incomplete without a stop at the beach. I wasn't about to protest.

"Sounds good to me."

Mrs. Betty was seated in a chair and looked very frail. The harsh and humid summer had not been kind to her. Her movements seemed much more strained and painful. I couldn't imagine she'd be able to return to school in the fall, but she certainly intended to. I was half-relieved when she told us she would not be making the trip to the beach. She didn't need to be out in the heat.

"I'll just be a burden. You young folks go ahead. I'll be fine right here."

Her daughter and grandson protested, to no avail.

"No, that's final, now," she almost shouted. "I'll be fine, y'all go ahead, go on, now. Get!"

Her daughter explained to her how to use Shintarou's cell phone to call if she needed anything and, after breakfast—and after she and Akiyama cleaned everything up, as my offers to help were flat-out rejected—we headed out.

★ ★ ★ ★ ★

The beach was not so crowded, and very hot. We laid out our blanket and hoisted an umbrella. I kept looking at the sea. It looked pretty good to me, despite my abhorrence of often furtive living things like seaweed, crabs, jellyfish, and gawking Japanese. I couldn't resist. I took a peep at Shintarou. He looked like the same thoughts, minus the gawking Japanese, were going through his head. We got up together and walked towards the shore. I stuck my feet in the water.

"It's warm!" Shintarou said, voicing my thoughts.

"Sho'nuff!" I said.

LOCO in YOKOHAMA

I turned and headed back to the blanket and grabbed my trunks out of my bag as I'd brought them "just in case". I slipped them on over my boxers and sprinted back to the shore and dived in headfirst. Shintarou was right behind me.

We swam around for a good 45 minutes, doing handstands, and diving off a floating pier some ways out.

The seaweed was long, clingy, and wrapped around your legs and feet like tentacles. But there were, thankfully, no crabs or jellyfish. There were plenty of gawkers though, but fuck 'em. I was in heaven! I'd forgotten how much I loved the beach. It had been about 3 years since I'd gone swimming at one.

We came back to the condo to find Mrs. Betty still seated in her chair, watching TV.

"How was the beach?" she asked.

"It was heaven, Mrs. Betty!" I said. "Just perfect!"

"You look so radiant, Mr. Loco! Doesn't he, Akiyama-san?"

"He is glowing, isn't he?"

"Y'all two need to stop!" I said, smiling, mildly surprised that my joy was so easily discerned.

"Let's hit the pool!" Shintarou said. Another great idea. He'd gotten about two shades darker, and looked like one of those hostess playboys you see in Tokyo red-light districts.

"OK, let's go!"

We hung out in the pool for about half an hour, racing and fooling around. We had the whole thing to ourselves. Once we were done, we showered up. While showering, I noticed that there was a strange-looking fountain in front of the shower area.

"What's this for?" I asked him. It didn't look like it was for drinking or washing.

"It's for washing your eyes out," he said.

"Get the fuck outta here," I'd said in English.

"Eeee?"

"Really?" I said. "I've never seen one of these before."

He demonstrated its use.

"Wow, how cool is this," I said. "I've always just walked around with red burning eyes for half the day, unless I had some Visine or something."

He laughed.

We returned to find the ladies had prepared yakisoba (Japanese fried noodles) in our absence. "I could get used to this," I remember thinking.

"How was the pool?" Mrs. Betty asked, still lounging in her chair, remote control in hand.

"It was—" and I looked at her. "You know how it was."

She laughed. I loved the way she laughed. Her whole body rocked. Then a dark thought came over me, and I couldn't push it away. My God, she's gonna die! Not today, not tomorrow, but one day . . . I almost started crying right there. She noticed, and stopped laughing.

"What?" she gasped, with such concern in her voice that she made everyone look at me.

I looked around at these people, half of whom I had only known for less than 24 hours and the other half for a sum total of not much more than that. And, they had shown me nothing, and I mean *nothing*, but kindness and generosity of the likes that's rare even here in Japan. I looked down at this wise, old, rickety woman, Mrs. Betty, and I thought, "Wow, I love her!" I didn't know when it happened, or how, but some time between the day she hobbled into my life and that moment, we'd made a connection, much the way Shintarou and I had made a connection. I looked down at the yakisoba on the table, little cobs of corn piled on another plate, and leftover bread from the spread I'd been served for breakfast. Then, I looked at Akiyama, her smile informing me that she knew what I was thinking right then.

I was having a moment.

It was a moment of reflection, and of pure appreciation and gratitude for all the wonderful energy around me. It would have been overwhelming if it weren't for Mrs. Betty rising from her seat for the first time since the start of that morning.

I rushed to assist her.

"What is it? What do you need? I'll get it for you," I cried.

As I helped her to take her seat again, she was grasping my shoulder, and I could feel her power. All those years of globetrotting, and all the amazing things she'd seen and people she'd met.

She looked up at me and said, "You know you can come here any time, right? I don't use the place much. You should bring your girlfriend."

And, she smiled, that crooked stroke patient smile of hers.

I kissed her on the cheek.

"Thank you, Mrs. Betty," I said, my heart swollen and eyes welling. "You're too kind!"

15
Forever Cute
(Syouganai Junior High)

I was about to crash for the night when I heard the tone on my phone indicating that I'd just received a text message. It was from Akiyama and it read, "Betty-sensei is leaving and that useless bitch is coming back tomorrow!"

At first, I sat there re-reading the message, saddened by the news. Mrs. Betty was a temp, after all, so I knew her days at Syouganai were numbered, but I'd avoided thinking about it. I guess I was secretly hoping that Yamada would have to extend her leave or would jump in front of a train or something. But, there was no way around it—Yamada-sensei was returning to Syouganai.

It had been about five or six months since our minor altercation in which I'd asked her, as politely as possible, to stop telling the students to call me "Loco" thereby denying me the respect that every other teacher in the school received without having to ask.

I had no way of knowing if my confronting her had anything to do with her sporadic and sometimes prolonged absences.

That is, until the following Friday.

She'd returned on Monday, looking literally "in the pink." Though she was looking a great deal slimmer than I recalled—like a doctor could examine her internal organs without the use of an x-ray—her eyes were clear and her smile was bright. She'd brought some sweets for everyone—a tradition in Japan. I guess it was to thank us for picking up the slack while she was out. Everyone had welcomed her back warmly, even Akiyama and Mrs. Betty.

Monday through Thursday, my schedule had been booked up with classes with the other English teachers at Syouganai. Despite the 3-day upcoming weekend—Monday would be a national holiday—I was not looking forward to Friday.

It came anyway, though.

On Friday morning, before Yamada arrived, Akiyama and I were chatting.

"So, you'll be teaching all day with Yamada today," she reminded me with a sympathetic smile.

"Looks like it."

I must have been frowning 'cause she added, "ganbatte (hang in there)!"

"Thanks," I said. Then, something occurred to me. "Do you think what I said to her back in April had anything to do with her absences?"

"I don't think so, but you never know," she almost laughed. She hated Yamada and didn't conceal it well. "Why?"

"Do you think I should be extra careful how I speak to her?" I asked. "I mean, do you think she's extra fragile? She doesn't seem so, but you'd know better than me."

She laughed.

"I'm more worried about how the students will affect her than how you will," she replied. "Most of them have practically forgotten who she is. And, they've gotten used to Betty-sensei's style. With her not in the room, who knows how they'll act up."

She had a point.

★ ★ ★ ★ ★

At the start of the class, as the bell chimed, Yamada and I stood before the uproarious students. After the final note of the tune, she started counting backwards from 10 in a stern voice.

"10, 9, 8, 7, 6, 5, 4, 3, 2, 1!" As she was counting, students settled down and took their seats. There were still several seats sans their occupants by the time she reached "one" and these students came racing into the room from wherever. She gave them disapproving looks. They apologized—at least, some did. The others returned her look with blank stares as if to say, "Who the hell do you think you are? Betty-sensei? Not even close, sister!"

"OK, let's begin English class!" she said with mock gravity, as if this was some time-honored traditional phrasing. Is she delusional, I wondered. Some of the students routinely ignore English and kept that tradition alive. The others just ignored her. Most looked to me as if I would give them a hint about how to deal with this "returnee" whose authority they hardly recognized.

I was about to speak when Yamada cut me off and said, purposefully, "OK, class, today," and she gestured and turned to me, "we have a *very* special guest!"

"Mata fucking ka yo (Oh, Fuck, here we go again)!" I actually murmured under my breath.

Most of the students were dumbfounded. They knew the words "special" and "guest", but they saw no one in the room that fit that description. Some of the brighter ones even looked around, thinking this "very special guest" might be in the back of the room or waiting in the hallway to make an entrance.

"Loco-*sensei* is here!"

She'd put so much English on the word "sensei" that it was hardly recognizable as Japanese. It sounded the way Americans in a judo class in Brooklyn might say it. She turned to me, smiling. Our eyes met, and in that moment, I had the distinct impression that she was trying to telepathically convey the message, "See! I remember what you told me."

I returned the smile, and it hurt to do so.

"Say good morning to Loco-sensei, please."

This had a crippling effect on the students' communication ability, as it had been our custom for me to say good morning and for them to reply, "Good morning, Mister Loco," as Mrs. Betty had them well-trained to say. Only a couple of students followed Yamada's instructions.

She looked at me following this development, worry in her eyes, like this had been her concern all along—like even way back at the beginning of the school year, she'd known that Japanese children would never take to calling a foreigner "sensei." Or, this was a sign of a deep discipline issue she wasn't looking forward to, but had anticipated facing, and not just a matter of her arriving at a party six months late.

She turned back to the class.

"Repeat after me, "Good Morning, Loco-sensei," and raised her hand like an orchestra conductor might.

"Good Morning, Loco-*senseiii*," the class repeated, exaggerating the way she'd unnaturally stressed it.

I bit my lip to keep from laughing. I think I drew blood. The students kept no such decorum.

She would do this exactly the same way for the remaining four classes that we taught together. I didn't pull her coat on the "very special guest" business this time. But, I was thinking that maybe I should get in her face again, 'cause maybe then she'd get sick again, you know? And Mrs. Betty would stick around longer.

But, that would be a fucked up thing to do.

Wouldn't it?

★ ★ ★ ★ ★

A couple of weeks later, Yamada-sensei, her mother in tow, entered the principal's office and didn't emerge again for two hours. Actually, it was longer than that, but I'd gone home after two hours of waiting for the explanation of this latest drama. It wasn't until two weeks later, upon my return to Syouganai, that I learned the result of that meeting. Yamada had officially taken yet another leave of absence. This time, it would be until the end of February.

"What about her mother?" I asked. "Why was she here?"

"Beats me," Akiyama said seated at her desk beside mine. "I guess it was for moral support, but it's all so strange. Did you say anything to her?"

"What? It wasn't me, I swear!"

After a long-ass second of holding a seriously concerned face, Akiyama burst into laughter.

She was yanking my chain.

"That's not funny," I said. "The last thing I need on my conscience is the mortality of some feeble-minded woman."

"Well, her students don't have your conscience, apparently. They chased her butt outta here!"

"That's fucked up!" I said. "So what's going to happen—"

At that moment, a woman I had never seen before came through the office's sliding door, damn near dancing on air, and sang, "ohayou gozaimasu" to everyone watching or listening while doing a little curtsy before the principal and VP. "Ohayou gozaimasu," she sang again at them, probably because they hadn't responded the first time.

The VP replied, "Ohayou," and the principal grunted, "Uisssu (mornin')."

As she continued towards Akiyama and I, I could see the pair of bosses following her with their eyes.

Their smiles said, 'what an interesting woman.'

Their eyes said, 'the BOE needs to start drug testing *all* teachers, not just the gaijin!'

Akiyama nudged me, and grinned sheepishly. "Oh yeah, I forgot to tell you . . ."

"Are you serious!"

"What?" she said, as this vision in pink walked ungracefully down the center aisle of the office towards us. Facially, she wasn't hard to look at, not at all—very attractive with a smile that revealed nice white teeth with a cute little snaggletooth poking out of the side. She filled up her sweater, which is neither here nor there in Japan where padded bras are standard issue, but it looked good. However, as I worked my eyes downward, I noticed that she was pigeon toe'd and knock-knee'd, so she kinda inched forward with the gait of an invalid, or a half-wit who'd been told by her parents that her greatest value to a future husband is her virtue, and that walking this way would enable her to keep her hymen intact.

"She's the substitute teacher?" I asked through my teeth because she was almost upon us.

"Ohayooooo gozaimasuuuuuu!"

She tossed a big smile at me followed by a faux high-pitched grating singsong voice, like a soused Minnie Mouse guest-starring on The Muppet Show.

I couldn't even fake a return smile. I didn't know what to make of this. Was she for real, or were there hidden cameras in the office recording this for one of those wacky Japanese comedy shows? Or were my co-workers pulling a wicked prank on me? That was a possibility, 'cause at a glance I could see most of them—knowing this was to be our first meeting—were either openly or secretly looking my way, clearly eager to see my reaction.

My reaction to what?

Well, my reaction to the pink sweater with hearts on the pockets, and sleeves. The pink blouse beneath it with the heart-shaped buttons, pinker than the shirt. The heart-shaped purse, which was black with little pink hearts, and a cell phone protruding from the top of it, also pink, of course, with little pink doodads on it and lipstick a little pinker than a professional anything—aside from a model, actress or a hooker—should wear, and topped off with a pink heart-shaped necklace around her neck.

I felt my stomach twitch.

She really wasn't all that shocking, at least not for Japan.

She was actually a "type." I call them the kawaii-sugiru gyaru ("too cute" girls), and if she were a good 15 to 20 years younger, I wouldn't have even given her a second look. But, she was jukujo—women of a certain age, late 30s to mid-40s, and usually fairly attractive. And if jukujo had kids, some men in the US might refer to them as MILFs or

"Mothers I'd Like to Fondle or Fuck". Among Japanese men, though, it was synonymous with "wayyyy past her prime" and, if unmarried, a spinster.

That makes Japan pretty much a MILF Paradise!

But this pink business. . .

She must have caught my stupefaction and figured it meant I hadn't understood her greeting, so she switched to English. Kinda.

"Good morning. You are Loco-sensei, I know. You are a big man—dekai (big)—and such handsome." She smiled, confident in the success of the first impression she was making. She peeked over at Akiyama, who was sitting beside me nodding her agreement while gagging on the laughter she'd swallowed. It swelled her eyes like she'd come down with a case of Graves' disease.

Then, the MILF in pink stuck out her hand for a shake.

"I am Nakano. Na-ka-no!" She said very carefully, leaning in closer.

"Nagano?" I replied, fucking with her. "Like the city?"

Akiyama guffawed, but disguised it as a cough.

Nakano shook her head slowly.

"No, not Na *ga* no. Na *ka* no! Nakano desu!" and she bowed like that was the end of the story and she'd made her point sufficiently.

"Ha-ji-me-ma-shi-te-you-ro-shi-ku-o-ne-ga-i-shi-ma-suuuuu (it is my great pleasure to make your acquaintance)!"

Nakano-sensei's pinkness was hard to look at with a straight face. So, with some relief, I stood up and bowed to hide my face and echoed her words of introduction like someone who'd been introducing himself in Japanese for several years.

She looked genuinely shocked!

"You are great Japanese speaker, I know!" she said.

I had a feeling that she was going to keep saying 'I know.' In fact, I knew it. I mean, we all have our thing when we use a second language. Some of us have more than one thing. Mine are 'deshou?' and 'sou desu ka' ("right?" and "I see"). These are my go-to words when I want to sound natural. I stick 'deshou' on the end of sentences sometimes just for the hell of it. Can't follow a speaker well, but don't want to make them repeat what they've said and fuck up the rhythm of the conversation? Stick a 'sou desu ka' in there. It works very often—in the same way that 'right' works in English.

But I had no idea where she got the notion that 'I know' was a phrase that could be thrown into virtually any sentence.

★ ★ ★ ★ ★

Once Nakano-sensei had headed to her homeroom to take attendance, and as the office door slid closed behind her, I wheeled on Akiyama.

"What?" she gasped again, high-pitched and guiltily, like I'd accused her of something.

"Where's Betty-sensei?" I asked. "She's not coming back?"

"Betty-sensei wa ne," Akiyama began, crest-fallen suddenly in that dramatic way of hers, scaring the holy shit out of me. "She's decided to retire for good."

I exhaled. I hadn't realized I'd been holding my breath. I missed Mrs. Betty more than ever now that I'd met her replacement.

We both sat there in silence for a moment, shuffling papers and acting like everything was normal.

Akiyama broke the silence first, saying, "She's not so bad."

"Who?" I said. "The jukujo in pink?"

"That's not nice," Akiyama said after a discreet bout of the giggles. "She was married, you know, and has two daughters."

"I see," I said. "And do her daughters know that she raids their wardrobe?"

"Actually, it's a popular trend among Japanese women *her* age," she added a little somberly.

I'd heard the stress on "her" and realized the cover-less manhole I was about to step in, and froze in place.

Akiyama, though she had yet to reveal her exact age to me, was most certainly in or desperately close to that "women of a certain age" bracket, as well—way beyond youth, but not out of the game yet. Only, she had no husband or kids, or any real prospects, either. She'd hinted at the resulting bouts of loneliness and dating frustrations she had experienced a number of times over the course of the past year during which we'd worked side by side. She wasn't unattractive, and knowing her as I did— her intelligence and charming personality, her wit and sass, her worldliness and common sense—I'd always respond to these hints with optimistic sentiments like, "You spent too much time abroad, and now you're just too damn international for these locals here. You probably intimidate the hell out of them." She'd just nod and smile warmly, like she appreciated the support, but I just didn't get it.

But, I did get it. Japanese men—hell, most men around the world—are fixated on youth, and women of a certain age are always going to have to step it up a bit, if not to maintain their self-esteem, to attract and hold on to men.

"Bimajyo," she said.

"Be your *what*?"

"No, bi-ma-jyo," she repeated. "That's what the trend is called. There are whole magazines dedicated to it. It's the beauty trend for jukujo, but don't say jukujo. That's not a good word."

"My bad," I said, repentantly. "Bimajyo, huh? So, these women dress in pink like teens on acid because Japanese men are fixated on little girls?"

Though I'd said it in English, my voice had risen a bit, vexed as I was that my friend couldn't find a man and may spend the rest of her days alone due to this mentality.

Akiyama scanned the room quickly, as did I. A couple of heads turned and I made a mental note of whose for that meant that they might know a little more English than they let on. I'd been there before.

Akiyama pressed a finger to her lips.

"Not only pink. Not only fashion. It's a lifestyle! Sexy, glamorous, sophisticated, youthful—"

"And the cartoon voice? And the curtsying? And, my god, that walk? And those accessories? That's all part of this lifestyle!"

"Not all of it, but some of it, yeah," she said, grinning again, only ironically this time. "We call it issyou kawaiiko."

"Cute girl for life?"

"Yes, that's right!" she said, beaming at my translation. "Forever cute!"

For the next three days, Nakano-sensei, true to her trend, came to work "forever cute" to the nines. She didn't wear all pink everyday, but she always had a little something that drew attention to her efforts to be "cute" forever—some kind of accessory that screamed, "look at me!"—a flaming pink leather belt, a pink cashmere scarf, socks, or pink blush on her cheeks.

If there was an award for issyou kawaiiko of the year, I was sure she was gunning for it!

It wasn't 'til Friday that we taught our first class together.

I arrived at the classroom just as the chime was coming to a close, trying to avoid this moment for as long as possible. As I walked in, to my surprise, all the students were already seated, whispering among themselves and staring at Nakano-sensei. I was accustomed to my entrance sucking all of the attention. A gasp en masse of "Loco-sensei!" was my general welcome, and I must admit, though I used to process this as something students did that made me feel like a special guest as opposed to just another member of the staff, I began to look forward to it because I'd come to interpret it as an indication of the joy they felt at having my class.

But, it wasn't to be.

It turned out this was this class's first time having Nakano as a teacher and I figured they were still experiencing the same shock waves that the teachers and staff in the office were. The girls seemed to approve of her style, though. I could hear whispers of "kawaii (cute)" emanating from them. The guys, however, were either gawking, mouth-breathing and slack-jawed, or were laughing at the ones who were.

One of the boys, Taro-kun, who had been neutered by Mrs. Betty into puppy-like gentleness, arrived a few seconds after me—clearly having returned to form in her absence. He ran to his seat, sat, faced forward, took a look at Nakano-sensei—all cutie-pie'd up for TGIF, planning to go boozing with Team Bimajyo after work, no doubt—bulged his eyes, leaned forward and yelled, "Donbiki (this chick gives me the fucking creeps)!"

I knew exactly how he felt.

16
Apeshit
(Mendokusai Junior High)

I was trying to imagine what the people on the street thought when the trash can landed at their feet. Or what was going on in the minds of the housewives thwacking their futons on the verandas of the apartment complexes nearby, or the elderly people in the park across the street playing ground golf with Senior PGA Tour intensity. What did they think when the garbage pail came sailing off of the school's fourth floor terrace, accompanied by a teen's primal war cry of defiance?

Probably, "Kids these days," or "son of a bitch ruined my putt!" or something like that.

They probably would have liked to know why, I bet.

Wouldn't they have been surprised to learn that the trigger of the tantrum that resulted in the launch was something as simple as Matsui-kun having not received a print-out that the rest of the class had?

I was in the teacher's office relaxing along with five other teachers when it happened. I heard a loud noise outside the window and was startled right along with everyone else. The five of them rushed out of the office to investigate. I kept my seat.

Why?

Well, at the very same moment, a visiting supervisor from the Board of Education—but not the BOE lady—and his underling were in the principal's office. They'd been there since first thing in the morning. I'd noticed the hushed tones everyone spoke in when I'd arrived and I knew something was up. I just didn't know what.

At the start of the morning meeting, the principal had emerged from his office, looking antsy, followed by two men. Everyone had stiffened a little. The principal of Mendokusai, normally a rather confident man, looked like he'd been detained and tortured in Guantanamo Bay over the course of several months—ready to cough up all kinds of government secrets and terrorist plots.

After he'd greeted everyone, he turned the floor over to our special guest, the Board of Education guy, who looked all swollen with self-important humility. After introducing his underling the BOE guy began explaining the purpose of his visit, of which I could only grasp enough morsels to piece together a partial understanding. But his body language answered many of my questions. The way he'd come strutting out of the office, with his assistant humbly aping him, I just knew he was someone important. At least, he thought so, which is often enough to be treated as such.

I had been warned by The Silky One himself that this might happen. Usually it was the BOE Lady who would make these visits, but he'd informed all the teachers that that would no longer be the case. Someone from the main office, meaning someone Japanese, would be visiting unannounced someday, and they tended to be a great deal less lenient than *The Company*.

And there I was in all my laid back glory, looking like I'd just emerged from a mirror-less cave with a bushy mustache and an unshaven beard, wearing black Levi's, and a pullover polo shirt—totally under-groomed and under-dressed for the occasion.

Great.

But this had become my norm ever since I'd started seriously getting back into writing. I spent so much time practicing and refining my craft, I'd come to think of my teaching gig as almost a distraction from my dream.

I slid down in my chair to reduce my visibility and tried to look natural and as inconspicuous as that raisin garnish in your banana pudding. And I had remained low-key all morning, just waiting for the Board of Education personified to take his awfully fussy-looking self about other business.

After taking a tour of the facilities, he, his assistant, the principal, and his vice returned to the principal's office, shut the door, and pow-wowed. Every 15 or 20 minutes, the VP would emerge from the office looking haggard and stressed and make eye contact with the teachers sitting around trying to look busy, sending a coded message even I could discern, which was, "things are not going well in there." Then he'd grab some paperwork and duck back into the office.

Around the time of his fifth trip out to fetch paperwork was when the trash can came crashing down on all his dreams of an incident-free visit.

Ten minutes after the crashing noise, I heard screaming in the hallway—screaming from an unmistakable source, Matsui-kun. He was being led into the conference room across from the teacher's office. It was the equivalent of the Dean's office in a public school in the U.S., only there was no Dean, and the school counselor only came to the school once a week—not that it would have made a difference if she'd been there. It wasn't like she'd been trained to handle these kinds of situations, nor did she have a reputation for kicking ass and taking names—unlike my junior high school Dean, a former cop as legend has it, had. I really don't know what she was expected to do aside from assess the situation and report it to some supervisor somewhere, if anything.

My curiosity got the better of me, so I risked exposure and rushed to the door to witness the scene. It took three teachers to restrain him. He was kicking, swinging tiny little haymakers, and sometimes connecting! He kicked one teacher, Mrs. Tanaka, squarely in the abdomen. I felt it from a few yards away. She didn't take kindly to the assault, not one bit. She grabbed his little ass by the scruff and pinned him against the wall with unexpected power, speed, and ferocity for a frail-looking jukujo, er, I mean, bimajyo. It even shocked Matsui out of his tantrum. He chilled out from then on.

After they got him into the room, it was Tanaka-san who did the honors and called Matsui's mother.

I could only hear one side of the conversation, of course, but it wasn't difficult to imagine the rest:

"Good Morning, this is Tanaka Yuuko from Mendokusai. How are you doing?"

"Yes, the weather is quite warm today."

"Yes, it certainly does look like rain, doesn't it?"

"Oh, my health is as good as can be expected, thank goodness. And, yourself?"

"Oh, how wonderful! I'm so happy to hear that."

While she was talking, she was rubbing the area where Matsui had kicked her while still managing to bow and smile like Matsui's mom was there in the room. All the teachers in the office were not staring at her with their eyes, but their ears were peeled. After a solid two minutes of small talk, she finally began to approach the runway of the reason for the call.

"I'm awfully sorry to trouble you . . ."

"Oh no, all is well, thanks for asking."

"It's only your son . . ."

"Oh no, he is well . . ."

"He's doing his best in his classes. I'm told by his teachers."

"Oh no, he is an extremely bright and energetic student . . ."

Due to the congestion on the landing strip, she flew in a holding pattern for another five minutes.

"The PTA? Well, yes, we'd welcome you!"

"Oh no, everyone's input is most welcome! Most welcome, indeed . . ."

"Oh, you don't have to be concerned about that. I'm sure you have wonderful ideas."

"And, how is your husband? Is he well?"

"A promotion? Well, that's great news!"

"Is that so?"

About then I got bored, and went outside for a smoke.

★ ★ ★ ★ ★

The next morning, my back just went out. I wasn't doing anything strenuous or ball-breaking. It just went, like maybe the breath I took before it went was the last straw. It happened occasionally.

The Japanese call it "gikkuri goshi".

My mother used to tell me it was caused by stress.

So, since I couldn't walk, I called in sick using one of my vacation days to rest my back and pump myself full of that good ole reliable American drug, Advil—the wonder drug of wonder drugs. Japanese over-the-counter pain relievers are a joke, but Advil might make you forget you've been shot.

The following day, I returned to the office, still Advil'd to the gills, but able to walk. Everyone showed a great deal of concern. It was unexpected and quite moving, actually. I realized while I was sitting at my desk and receiving a procession of teachers coming over to me wearing expressions of concern more suitable to one returning from their first session of chemotherapy or the funeral of a beloved child than a backache, that, in fact, in three years at Mendokusai, I had not called in sick—not once. No wonder everyone looked freaked out. It was indeed an unusual occurrence.

I had never held a job in my entire life—including my previous job in Japan at NEON—when I was not prone to taking a three-day weekend every so often. But, for some reason, since I'd been working in the Japanese public school system, I hadn't. You might think that my working in an environment where the work ethos could be worded as, "look as if you work hard every day all day, drink copious amounts of alcohol 'til last train, then repeat" had rubbed off on me a little. And you'd be right, except for only appearing to work hard and the copious drinking part. When I'd decline their invitations to go tie one on after work because either I had to teach one of damn near a dozen private students that evening, or was working on a blog post for one of the two blogs I maintained, or needed to be clear-headed to do some editing on the book I was writing, they'd be shocked. Sometimes they'd even say, "Nihonjin ni nari tsu tsu aru ne (I was becoming Japanese),*" as if hard work and sacrifice to achieve goals were strictly Japanese traits.

I'd just smile and pretend that I took it as the compliment they'd obliviously intended it to be.

Anyway, during the morning meeting, I learned that it was official; Mendokusai junior high was now in crisis mode.

The principal explained to us, in no uncertain terms, that we should not put our hands on the children for any reason. The hitting of children would not be tolerated by the school nor by the authorities. I figured this had something to with Tanaka-sensei's violent response to Matsui striking her. I sat there thinking that someone, perhaps the principal himself, ought to tell the students that the reverse was in effect as well.

Tanaka's call to Matsui's mother apparently had fallen on deaf ears for it seemed that day Matsui was hell-bent on testing how far he could push things.

After greeting the students, Takahashi announced to them that Loco-sensei was suffering from back spasms, and all the students shot me looks of sympathy. Even Matsui, who had, along with Satou, taken to routinely ambushing me and assaulting my nuts, had called a cessation of hostilities—seeing as I was in no shape to fight him off.

Magnanimous of him, was it not?

As Takahashi returned some test papers, she told me I could take a seat if I liked. She was really worried about me. I took her up on her offer, but the furniture in the school just wasn't suitable for a man of my height and build. So, I told her I'd be in the hallway where there were benches against the walls and windows and I could rest my back against the bench.

When I slid the classroom's door open, two of the second-year teachers appeared out of nowhere to block my exit!

They had been expecting a student to emerge. When they realized it was me, they smiled and turned beet-red in embarrassment—like I'd seen them picking their noses and examining the goods, or pulling their bunched panties out of their asses—you know, like I had seen something I wasn't supposed to see. They'd get like that sometimes, the teachers at my schools. Sometimes I was a well-established, trusted, and respected member of the staff. But, sometimes I was a visitor from another planet being given a guided and narrated tour of earth, starting with a Japanese junior high school. At other times, I was a spy from another country involved in educational espionage. What I was to them depended on the situation.

They allowed me to pass and I took a seat on the bench. These two sentinels watched me wondering why I had come out there and assumed, safely so, that it had something to do with Matsui.

"My back!" I said, and winced.

"Ah, sokka (oh, I see)!" they replied, their concerns alleviated. My back pain was something they were not expected to do something about.

There were always at least four or five teachers in the office during every class because they had no class to teach during that period. Usually, this time was spent doing important stuff like preparing for classes later in the day or for the following day. But, it had become routine for these teachers—at least one, but sometimes two—with free periods to stand outside the doors of the classrooms where Mika or Matsui were being taught—posted like guards at the Tower of London—or to sit in the back of the classroom in anticipation of trouble. The other teachers would remain in the office, but poised to rush to the scene when needed, like Minutemen during the American Revolution taking up arms when a horse-mounted crier came tearing through town—"The British are coming! The British are coming!" Only in this case, there'd be some hapless, teary-eyed teacher crying the alarm.

A few uneventful minutes passed and I guess the two sentinels figured all was well, so they returned to the office. I sat there alone sweating in the muggy hallway, listening to the soothing sounds of education in Mendokusai. Students studying, teachers teaching and, geezus, Matsui screeching.

LOCO in YOKOHAMA

Suddenly, the classroom door was thrown open and Takahashi bolted out, Matsui hot on her heels with an umbrella held over his head. She stopped abruptly and wheeled around on him right in front of me. It seemed like she believed that, while he would certainly strike her in front of the other students, rabble-rouser that he was, he wouldn't do so in my presence.

Wrong.

What the fuck was she thinking?

He feinted like he was going to strike her ankle, but when she reached down for the umbrella, he cracked her over the head with it—not at full strength, but with enough mustard on it that I would be unemployed and possibly behind bars in some Yokohama city jail now, and Matsui in some Yokohama city hospital or morgue, if I had been dealt it. I sat there and watched this, having a sort of out of body experience.

There were many circumstances in Japan in which I believed it was in my emotional best interest to detach from my feelings, and I did so every once in a while. I found it alleviated stress. And I was of the mind that my mother had been right, and stress was partially at fault when it came to my back. Mothers know best sometimes. So I sat there, as objective as a human can be, and watched this scene play out.

She spat a few invectives at him. He spat some back, laughed viciously, ran back into the classroom, and locked the door. Takahashi stupidly tried to slide it open. She glanced at the classroom's rear door and thought to head for it, but apparently came to her senses and realized that Satou would have surely locked that one by then. The keys were kept in the teacher's office.

The screech of the teacher's desk being dragged could clearly be heard, as Matsui presumably barricaded the door from the inside. The windows of the door were frosted so we could only see a couple of determined shadowy silhouettes passing back and forth by the door's window and hear the sounds of other stuff being dragged and slid in front of it.

Takahashi glanced over at me, a queer look on her face. Somewhere between "resigned to accept this torment", "at her wit's end", and "happy to be away from that room out in the hall with a friendly face".

She came over and sat on the bench beside me.

"So, how's your back?" She said, like the calamitous violation of everything I'd just witnessed and she'd just endured had not occurred at all.

Because my feelings remained detached, I was able to bring myself to say, "It's been better."

★ ★ ★ ★ ★

And, it just kept getting better. The goddamn school was falling apart around us. Or, rather, students were tearing it apart.

On a daily basis, I'd be jarred from my lesson preparation by the thrown open door of the office and a frantic and distressed teacher screaming almost incomprehensibly . . . not that I needed to comprehend every word. I knew she was having a problem that she couldn't handle alone, and thus she'd left her class alone to enlist her co-workers' assistance.

And, in most cases, I knew this meant Matsui or Mika, the usual suspects.

The two of them had gone completely apeshit and had amped their acting up to a point way beyond disruptive and had become downright dangerous—that is, by Japanese standards.

I had to constantly remind myself to keep all of this in perspective.

The next day, my back was finally on the mend, thank God. I was having a snack when Okawara-sensei burst into the office nearly in tears, with the residue of fire extinguisher agent on her clothes, and perhaps in her eyes.

All hell was breaking loose!

And it couldn't have happened at a better time.

The Board of Education just happened to be scheduled to pay Mendokusai yet another visit that afternoon, only this time to specifically see what all the clamor was about. And, much to my chagrin, they would be accompanied by a representative from *The Company*.

Yep, Silky in the flesh!

Why were they coming again? Well, the principal had pleaded with them for help. Of course I wasn't privy to this conversation, but judging from the look on his face whenever there was an incident—and I got to see this look on a regular basis, a look of utter helplessness hidden behind an expression of terse restraint—and the stolid countenance on the faces of the BOE people as they'd toured the school a few days ago, I'd wager the convo went a little something like this:

"*Heeeeeeeeeelllllppppp!*" the principal cried.

"What seems to be the problem?" the BOE guys inquired obtusely.

"These two students are out of control and I'm powerless to stop them!"

"Oh, we see."

"One of the boys kicked one of my teachers in the groin last week!"

"That must have been painful."

"Are you going to help us?"

"Help you how? Send your problem to another school? He's entitled to an education, as you well know."

"But—"

"And, no one has been seriously injured. Boys will be boys, ne."

"But—"

"Listen, let's give it a little more time and see if this problem doesn't resolve itself, *ne*? I have confidence that these problems will go away if we just have a little patience, *ne*?"

"OK. Of course, you're right, as always, *ne*?"

So, here we were again, and the "little problems" had not miraculously vanished at the behest of a magician by the name of "Patience". They had instead escalated to a point Mendokusai was wholly unprepared to handle.

The fire extinguisher incident happened first thing in the morning. Apparently, Mika was not a morning person. It took several teachers to wrestle the fire extinguisher from Mika; she was a big girl. I didn't see how it started. I just heard the all too common commotion in the hall which was Mika screaming obscenities and swinging wildly at whosoever dared to come within her reach. Okawara's alarm had mobilized the remaining teachers/militia in the office/barracks to assist.

This was the kinetic energy the BOE guys, and Silky Tony, would walk through upon their arrival after lunch.

Takahashi-sensei, who sat in at the meeting held upon their arrival, would tell me later that the meeting went a little something like this:

"*Heeeeeeeeeelllllppppp!*" the principal cried.

"What seems to be the problem?" the BOE guys inquired obtusely.

"I'm at my wits end! These two students are out of control and I'm powerless to stop them!"

"Oh, we see."

"Mika-chan hosed down one of my teachers with a fire extinguisher just this morning!"

"That must have been awkward."

"Are you going to help us?"

"Help you how? Send your problem to another school? She's entitled to an education, as you well know."

"But—"

"And, no one has been seriously injured. Teens will be teens, am I right?"

"But—"

"Listen, let's give it a little more time and see if this problem doesn't resolve itself, ne? I have confidence that these problems will go away if we just have a little patience, ne?"

"OK. Of course, you're right, as always, ne?"

"We'd like to observe one of these classes, if you don't mind."

"No, of course not. By all means!"

After lunch the BOE guys, the principal, and Silky Tony came to observe my class. I was to teach Matsui and company.

I'd like to say my kids were intimidated by so many adult visitors—one of which was a strange foreigner wearing a shiny gabardine suit and slicked back hair—being in their midst, and thus were on their best behavior.

But, I'd be lying.

★ ★ ★ ★ ★

When Silky Tony arrived at Mendokusai, he had no idea what he was walking into. *The Company* didn't know my school was in crisis mode. And, to be honest, from the horror stories I had heard from some of my fellow *Company* employees, my school was the Garden of Eden by comparison. So, I was sure a veteran at this game like Silky wouldn't have been impressed or deterred even if he had been forewarned. He hadn't always a member of the brass. He used to be cannon fodder, just like me.

However, this observation being somewhat impromptu meant instead of having months to prepare for it, I had an hour. And Silky, accustomed to observing classes that had been cherry-picked for observation, was now subject to the raw! And that's exactly what he, the principal, and the two guys from the BOE got.

The rawness!

On short notice, I had put together a simple little game to illustrate the meaning and usage of the English prepositions: in, on, under, next to, and between. My materials included a couple of baskets and a few handballs— not Spauldings, like the ones I played handball with in the playgrounds back in Brooklyn, but those big yellow ones used in Olympic-style handball.

I'd been observed many times—by mobs of circumspect parents on open-school days, prowling PTA members, curious principals, and of course, annually by reps from *The Company*. So, I was kinda a veteran at these things, and knew just what was expected of me and how to please my varying audiences. But, I'd always had significant preparation time. Without it, and with not one, not two, but four pairs of agenda-bearing eyes dissecting my every move, I found I was just a little uncomfortable. That, plus, Takahashi's nervousness was palpable, and with good reason. The BOE and the principal were there to watch her more than they were there to watch me.

Poor thing. She was a wreck! And this was even before the bell had rung.

It was about to get much worse.

They gave the visitors standing in the rear of the classroom a once-over, and the majority of the kids got appropriately nervous and self-conscious. But, a handful, Matsui among them, looked eager to take center stage. I could see their energy. They could hardly sit still. They were just waiting for an opening, like predators.

But, so far, their mumbling was muted and they were well-behaved— for them.

I demonstrated the various prepositions by placing the ball in the appropriate place in relation to the basket, and stating its position. Once I was sure the majority of the students had gotten it, I began the game by telling them to clear the floor by sliding their desk to either side of the room, and making two lines. One line was "Team A" and the other was

"Team B". In the front of the room, directly ahead of the two lines, I set up a basket, a chair, and a ball. I had Takahashi pretend to be a student.

"The ball is in the basket under the chair. Ready? Go!"

Takahashi rushed forward, grabbed the ball, placed it in the basket and slid the basket under the chair. Then she grabbed one of the two fans off the desk and held it up.

"Where's the ball?" I asked her.

"The ball is in the basket under the chair."

"Ping-pong," I said, imitating the Japanese onomatopoeia for correct answer. Then, to the class, I said. "OK?"

Again, most of them got it, and they explained it to the head-scratching, mouth-breathers in Japanese.

Matsui and another student volunteered to go first.

Here we go.

"The ball is under the basket, on the chair. Ready? Go!"

Matsui raced forward faster than the other and accomplished the task so quickly you'd think I'd said it in Japanese.

"Where is the ball?" I asked him.

He stood there in front of the class with the fan held high in his hand and said, "It's under Taka-babaa-hashi's shirt!"

Takahashi's breasts are inordinately large. In Japan, she stands out about as much as I do.

The class roared, and I had to keep a grin off of my face, because I could feel that at any moment we were gonna lose control of the class. All it took was one successful outburst these days and that was it; the rest of the class would be spent trying to resume some semblance of order. I didn't look at Silky nor the other observers—and I noticed Takahashi trying not to, as well—as I tried to think of a way to regain control of my game and keep it going.

Matsui was having none of that, though, nor were several others. Takahashi's breasts were a running gag and a popular one at that. He grabbed the other ball from the student he'd just beaten and tried to get them both under his T-shirt—they were still in their PE uniforms. Only one would fit. One of Matsui's other partners in crime, Mitsuhiro, grabbed the other ball and slid it up under his shirt and pulled himself beside Matsui so that it looked like they had two heads, one torso, and the two balls were Takahashi's tits.

Matsui then started singing, in Japanese, in that annoying AKB47 J-pop voice, "It's so difficult to find a G-cup!" Either boy had a hand cupping his "breast". I peeked in the back for reactions. Silky had hid his face behind his clipboard and even the BOE guys had smirked.

"I think we need an H-cup," the other boy said. Pandemonium broke out. "H" means "sex" in Japanese for some reason. I'd heard several explanations. Some say it's short for "home run," and others say that it's short for "hentai." I always think "horny" when I personally use it.

Takahashi was plum red and almost in tears with embarrassment, as usual.

I grabbed the balls from the boys and told them to go get in the back of the line, but it was too late. Most of the boys were discussing cup sizes and the girls, most of whom were still in training bras, had joined in on the fun though and were trying not to laugh.

Around that time, the principal and BOE guys had seen enough and walked out. Silky and I made eye contact, and though his face was somber, I could see the laughter in his eyes.

I don't know how I squeezed a decent performance review out of that, but somehow I did. Maybe because the kids did, after all, learn the prepositions I set out to teach, and how to use them properly.

17

So, This Is Christmas . . . In Yokohama
(Mendokusai Junior High)

LOCO in YOKOHAMA

The English songs teachers play at the beginning of each class are played on a boom box, and each student is presented with the song's lyrics in English and Japanese for they are expected to sing them, or at least attempt to. These songs are, without fail, songs they are already familiar with either through their use in popular Japanese films, TV shows, and commercials, or because the singer has garnered international appeal that has somehow managed to reach the relatively tiny demographic of early teens living in Yokohama, Japan. This song selection changes once a month, and by the month's end, the students either know it or they'll never know it.

Come Christmas time, however, I annually find myself imploring almost every Japanese teacher I work with to please, please, *please* diversify the Christmas song selection. The staples and standards in the schools, and indeed anywhere you go in Yokohama, are as follows: Wham's *Last Christmas,* Mariah Carey's *All I Want for Christmas Is You*, Tatsuro Yamashita's *Christmas Eve* and John Lennon's *So This Is Christmas (War Is Over)*.

Even when you're out and about, anywhere you might find yourself—be it to a department store, an office building, a ride in an elevator, in some train stations, a stop for a bite to eat at a fast or slow food restaurant, even walking down the street sometimes, you name it—instrumental and Muzak versions, covers or the originals of one of these four tunes, are piped into your mental inner sanctum like some kind of musical Big Brother.

Throughout the year, I wage vigorous campaigns to alter the other staples—a seemingly random selection of songs, some Beatles songs, an Aerosmith song here, a Queen song there, and throw in *We Are the World* and a few others. However, I noticed during my second year that these same songs were being used again and again. They were not random at all.

I also noticed that there was resistance to my suggestions of alternatives so, pretty soon, I gave up. Resistance was indeed futile.

But, come Christmas, I amp it up a bit because, while the annual selection of staples is broad—by comparison—in the schools in which I've worked, the Christmas selection has been relegated to the above four tunes.

This year, I decided it was do-or-die. I was going to get them to switch or die trying—figuratively speaking, of course. I started planning my incursion just before Halloween. I sat down and looked over the two previous year's failed attempts determined not to make the same mistakes.

★ ★ ★ ★ ★

I hadn't noticed the redundancy until my second Christmas working at Mendokusai. Standing before a class, trying to fend off that throbbing urge to sob that I feel every time I hear that chorus of kids singing *War Is Over* again and again while John Lennon's anti-war Christmas sermon gets translated in my brain as: "while you celebrate the holidays with your loved ones, your turkeys and presents, please remember the world is a fucked-up place where innocent babies are being napalm'd . . . by YOUR government, with YOUR tacit complicity!" I finally decided enough was enough. Lennon gets me every time. Sometimes I even tear up and I'm sure the kids have wondered more than once what was up with Loco-sensei. If you listen to that song the way Lennon intended it to be listened to, it'll make you wanna take a stand for all the children of the world living in war zones, catch the next thing smoking to Afghanistan and sling bricks at UAV drones.

Looking out at my students I could tell that they were not experiencing anything vaguely similar. In "peacenik" Japan, Lennon's message of peace on earth is essentially preaching to the choir in a language the choir can't comprehend. Once translated, it transforms into an overstatement of the obvious clearly aimed at thick-headed warmongering Americans, Chinese, and North Koreans. So, here in Japan, though adored, this soul-wracking song has all the emotional impact of a jingle about flossing daily or washing your hands after using the bathroom.

At that time, I had no idea how fixed the teachers were on these selections. I mean, sometimes they'd even come to me for recommendations, so why wouldn't I think change was possible?

One time, Kawaguchi-sensei specifically got at me because she too had felt that here was a great opportunity to introduce the kids to songs popular with kids in Loco-sensei's sector of the globe.

But, me being me, I wound up outsmarting myself and fucked it up.

I mean, I'm no advocate of Christmas, anyway. I haven't celebrated it in any traditional sense since I was about seven years old. That would be the year my mother, in her infinite wisdom, introduced Kwanzaa to our family. We never looked back. Well, that's not completely true. We looked back, that is my siblings and I, but my family as a unit, never went back. We'd miss the toys and trees and lights and anticipation of Christmas morning, because instead of weaning us off of the yuletide crack pipe, my mother ended the tradition cold turkey, dragging us away kicking and screaming. One year, there was a Christmas tree, with lights, a star atop it and presents stacked beneath it, and the following year, there were seven candles—each representing some principle in an African language—a basket of fruit, and a bunch of crazy ass African songs sung by a group of miserable kids who longed for Kris Kringle and the joy the day would bring. The reflection in the mirror revealed that these miserable kids were me and my siblings.

"Loco-sensei, can you recommend a Christmas song that we can use for the class?" Kawaguchi-sensei had asked me that day.

I racked my brain for 30 seconds or so, thinking of a simple song the kids might get into. "How about *The Little Drummer Boy*? Do you know that one?"

"I think so. What's it about again?"

"It's about, er, it's about a, well, a little boy who plays a drum, er, for Jesus. Yeah, on the day Jesus is born, he plays the drum."

"*Jesus?*"

"Jesus Christ. You know, the reason for the season." I'd remembered that line from some gospel song or other.

"Eeeee?"

"Well, there are two Christmases you know. There's the Santa Claus Christmas and the Jesus Christ Christmas, and they both have their own songs."

I swore at the time that I was teaching her something, but actually, all I was doing was convincing her that it was simpler just to go with the safe staples like George Michael, John Lennon, and company, and avoid all this Western religious foolishness.

"Like for instance, you know *Silent Night* right?"

"Yeah."

"That's another song about Jesus," I said. I was starting to feel a little uncomfortable with all this religious talk. I usually avoid it, but for some reason, I felt it was important to point out the significance of the music to Kawaguchi-sensei.

"Now, songs like *Jingle Bells, Rudolph The Red-Nosed Reindeer,* and *Frosty The Snowman*—these would be songs just about Santa Claus and enjoying the Christmas season, nothing about Jesus."

"Uh huh."

"So, do you prefer secular, er, *un*-Christian songs or Christian songs?" I asked. "I like both kinds, personally, but I recommend the secular ones for the students."

"Really? Why?"

"Well, because they probably aren't going to understand the Christian ones very well unless they understand Christianity, and I'd wager most of them aren't Christians, right?"

"No, they aren't."

If regret could be personified, it would look like her at that moment.

"And I wouldn't want to be mistaken for a missionary."

"A *what*? Listen, Loco-sensei, I think we're going to just stick with something familiar."

Yes, my attempts to change the music selection that year were an utter FAIL.

★ ★ ★ ★ ★

The year after that fiasco, I tried another strategy. If I couldn't get them to change the play list on the strength of the songs I was suggesting, I thought maybe if I could somehow defame the staples or the artists that sang them, then maybe they'd be a little more open to my recommendations.

I hatched a scheme.

A brilliant one, I thought.

Since there's no Thanksgiving here, after Halloween is about the time Yokohama starts getting into the Christmas frame of mind. Christmas commercial campaigns get going and decorations get unpacked and hung. So it was about that time that I began the practice of walking around the school whistling or singing Christmas tunes like The Pogues' *Fairytale Of New York* and Prince's *Another Lonely Christmas.* Those were a couple of my favorites. Of course, I knew neither of these songs was appropriate for the kids, but nevertheless, I threw on my best mask of cheer and goodwill toward mankind, and waited for one of the English teachers to take the bait.

"What's that you're whistling?" Takahashi-sensei asked while we were discussing the December lesson plans.

"Oh, nothing. Only one of the greatest Christmas songs ever made, that's all."

"Really? I don't know it. Who sang it?"

"Prince and the Revolution."

"Oh, I know *Purple Rain*. He's great!"

I'm a die-hard "sleep in the rain outside Madison Square Garden for concert tickets" Prince fan so when I encounter these "he hasn't really done much since Purple Rain" people, my first instinct is to shove my iPod headphones into their ear drums and blast them with some *Sign of the Times, Emancipation,* or any of a number of other effin' brilliant albums he's done since then that these *Purple Rain* fans missed. It seldom works, though. They're a hard-hearted lot usually.

But, I maintained a smile and said, "It was a B-side of a *Purple Rain* single."

"A *B-side*?"

Takahashi-sensei was all of 24. She wouldn't know nothing about B-sides or cassette tapes. Hell, she might not have even known what a Walkman was if she weren't Japanese.

"Long story . . . anyway, it's great!"

"What's it about?" she asked enthusiastically. "Maybe we can use it in class this Christmas."

"Well," and this is where I started my maneuvering. "Ummm, well, it's about a guy who misses his girlfriend who died on Christmas day."

"Oh, that's so sad."

"It is, isn't it?" I said, shaking my head with mock grief. "Every Christmas, he drinks their favorite drink, banana daiquiris, and cries and wishes she were, um, next to him intimately and—"

"Eeeee, is it, er, is it *sexual*?"

"Well, not really, I mean, not explicitly. But, a little. I mean, it's Prince. You're a *Purple Rain* fan. You know how he is. What do you expect?"

"Hmmm. Well, I don't think a sexual song is appropriate. I mean, for the students—"

"Well, what do you think *Last Christmas* is about?"

"Eeeee? It's about Christmas, deshou?"

"Yeah, kinda. I mean, it's about a guy who had a Christmas one-night stand with his gay lover who doesn't even remember him a year later. I mean, if that's appropriate, I don't see why—"

"Are you sure?"

"Well, George Michael *is* gay so he isn't singing about a one-night stand with a woman, that's for sure."

"But—"

"I understand, though. I mean, he is an artist—a great one, at that—and a poet, to be sure. And I have nothing against gay men, but c'mon," I said. And then sang: *"A man undercover but you tore me apart."*

She looked at me like I'd just shown her photos of the principal and the VP in the sixty-nine position in the principal's office.

"Not very subtle, is he?"

Apparently I'd stumped her. But, come December, she pretended our conversation had never happened and continued to play the song and had the kids sing the lyrics. However, whenever the song reached the part when George Michael sang about being undercover and being torn apart, she'd glance at me and puff her cheeks.

★ ★ ★ ★ ★

I tried the same thing with Kawaguchi-sensei, who favored Mariah Carey's *All I Want For Christmas Is You*. We sat down to the formality of discussing what song we should use, though we both knew she had already made up her mind 80%.

"How about Nat King Cole's *The Christmas Song*," I suggested, going through the motions.

She screwed up her face into a mask of confusion.

"Nat-to Kin-gu Co-ru? Shirimasen (I don't know him)."

"He's very famous, and it's a very famous song. One of my favorites."

"Uh-huh. Is it about, um, Cristo?"

"Who? Jesus? No! It's about, well, it's not about anything really. It's just a Christmas song about, you know, Christmasy things—chestnuts roasting on open fires and such."

"Uh-huh."

I whipped out my iPod.

"Here, take a listen," I said handing her the headphones.

"Ah sooo! Shitteru (I know it)!"

"It's *very* famous," I reiterated, and braced myself. I knew the routine.

"But the students don't know it, I bet."

"Well, then, let's teach them something new," I said, grinning. "They might get a kick out of it."

"Sou da ne, demo saaaa . . . (that's true, but . . .)," and she made a face of helplessness that pretty much sighed "it's in Buddha's hands" which signaled the end of the meeting, at least for me it did.

I had planned to get into Mariah's mental meltdown and purported drug use at the time, but I'd felt pretty petty suddenly. So I let it go and prepared myself for another season of Mariah's high frequency ululations that only dogs or pre-teen girls should be capable of accomplishing.

My scheme had failed.

The following year, however, I came up with another master plan! And I wouldn't have to talk about John Lennon's tripping the light fantastic on acid or anything like that. The answer was simplicity itself and, like most of the answers to life's most puzzling questions, it was right in front of my face the whole time.

★ ★ ★ ★ ★

That following April would mark the first graduation where I'd known the students from the time they nervously and excitedly crossed the threshold of the school for the first time until they'd tearfully and optimistically crossed it for the last time. And, man, oh, man, was I a wreck that day watching this group go. It's one of the hardest and yet most fulfilling parts of being a teacher. I mean, we'd basically grown up together—I as a professional educator in a foreign country and they as blossoming young adults. Together we navigated and traversed the academic challenges and social perils of junior high school life and come through it all scathed but the better for it—at least we'd like to think so. We survived.

Within that class there were several students with whom I had forged special bonds. One student, named Baba-kun, never ceased to surprise me. In fact, I think he got off on it. He was the progeny of what could best be described as a human music library. His father, who I'd finally got to meet at the graduation ceremony, was something like my father. My dear old dad, may he rest in peace, was a truck driver in his head, but a Jazz guitarist in his heart. He had a music library of vinyl LPs—mostly jazz, R&B, classic soul and funk—that would make any collector drool.

When he and my mother separated, perhaps one of their biggest battles was over his treasure. *'Keep the kids, but give me my records please!'* They settled on half or so for each of them; he took off with most of the jazz and left her with the other genres. But, half was *a lot* of music. What he couldn't part with, I would later learn, he'd recorded onto giant reel-to-reel tapes that were about as big as movie reels. A hundred of them could probably fit on your average iPod. His collection was my introduction to music, and I tried to listen to everything he had, and studied the album covers and liner notes, as well. When I was a kid, I could tell you who the Ohio Players dedicated *I Want To Be Free* to.

Baba-kun was a Japanese version of me—a virtual walking encyclopedia of, shockingly, the same music I grew up on. He'd see me in the hallways, run up to me singing—in hardly comprehensible katakana English, of course—*Games People Play,* a Spinners hit from the early 70's, screaming "Shitteiru, shitteiru (do you know it, do you know it)?"

Back in his first year, I became aware of his vast musical knowledge. He knew the songs, the artists, the bands, the name of the band members, and even some of them by the instruments they played.

He was a senior at this time and I was really going to miss him. He'd given me so much and he will never know; for example, he'll never know how many times I walked into the school after a particularly rough train ride, just seething with animosity for all things Japanese, having revoked, in my heart, their membership card to the society of decent human beings, relegating them to a status that previously had only been obtainable by rapists, child molesters, corporate polluters, Nazis and the KKK. Then, I'd run into him in the hall with his *"shitteiru shitteiru"* song of the day, which would be something like *Hot Fun In the Summertime* by Sly and the Family Stone or *Try a Little Tenderness* by Otis Redding, and all would be forgiven, at least for the time being.

★ ★ ★ ★ ★

"What Christmas songs do you like?" I asked him in early November.

"Well, my favorite is The Jackson Five's *Give Love On Christmas Day.*"

I stood there astonished, as usual. This was a song from the Christmas album I loved most as a child.

"Do your classmates know it?"

"I don't think so. It's my mother's favorite. She loves Michael Jackson."

"You should tell them about it."

"Why?" Sharp kid, he smelled what Loco was cooking.

"We can sing it in class, maybe."

"You want *me* to suggest it to Kawaguchi-sensei?"

"Maybe. If your friends like it, it might be fun."

And, Baba-kun did just that. He brought in a Mini-Disc of the song and played it for all the class and, as a unit, they petitioned Kawaguchi-sensei.

Almost too simple.

We sang the song and the kids seemed to get off on it. Some were even doing the backups in baritone like Michael's brothers.

★ ★ ★ ★ ★

Takahashi-sensei, however, was not so simple. She had the first-year students, those little monsters, and they were not inclined to even sit down during class, let alone sing a song.

I had to be a little more devious.

I had prepared everything for an alternative song, The Jackson Five's *I Saw Mommy Kissing Santa Claus.* I presented my materials to Takahashi, but she'd already prepared everything for yet another year of Wham—the same material she'd used the previous year and which she had inherited from Kawaguchi, no doubt.

The day we were to introduce the new song, though, there was a problem. The CD wouldn't play for some strange reason. And, unfortunately, she didn't have a back up. She was panicked. This was a solid 15-20 minutes of the day's lesson plan.

"Let's use mine. I already have all the materials ready. They're on my desk."

"Oh, that's a great idea," she said, considering the alternative. I ran to the office, grabbed my CD and lyrics handouts with the Japanese translations off of my desk, all copied and ready to distribute, and returned to the class.

While I was in the office, she'd explained to the class that we were going to learn a different song.

Maybe it was Michael Jackson's childish yet soulful voice that appealed to them. I don't know. But, they loved the song.

Even Matsui-kun sang.

It never occurred to Takahashi-sensei that her CD could have been sabotaged. Such things are beyond conceivable here. However, halfway thorough the song she slid up beside me to tell me something, and I thought maybe somehow she'd gotten wise.

I relaxed and almost laughed when she asked, "how do you know George Michael is gay?"

Interlude

Small Accomplishable Goals

LOCO in YOKOHAMA

This conversation took place in a cafe in Yokohama with a private student of mine.

Student: So, what do you think makes you a good English teacher?
Me: At my job? Or with you?
Student: Is there a difference?
Me: Well, yeah.
Student: What's the difference?
Me: With you, I'm actually trying to help you improve your English speaking ability and listening comprehension. And I think I've been somewhat successful because, er, well, I'm patient, and I set small accomplishable goals for you which build up your confidence, I think. Your biggest problem when we started, if you remember, was, well, besides pronunciation, was your confidence. But, now, I think you can hold your own with any native English speaker and won't be stymied by a lack of confidence.
Student: You really think so?
Me: Oh yeah! You're leaps and bounds beyond where you were three years ago when we first started.
Student: Thanks.
Me: My pleasure.
Student: What about with your junior high school students?
Me: Well, that's a different story.
Student: Eee? You're not trying to improve their English ability and listening skills?
Me: Well, kinda, but actually, no.
Student: Why not?
Me: Well, I like to set small accomplishable goals for myself, as well.
Student: What do you mean?
Me: Getting my kids to actually speak and hear English—most of them—is virtually impossible. So, it's no longer my goal.
Student: So, you don't think you're a good teacher with the kids?
Me: I do, but I don't teach them English.

Students: Eeee! What do you teach them?
Me: I teach them not to be afraid of people who don't look like them, that speak a different language and may have different ideas, or do things a little differently.
Student: Ah!
Me: Yeah, I teach them how to interact with people they wouldn't otherwise have the chance to interact with. And I think every student that spends three years with me will go out into the world with little or no fear of those unlike themselves. To me, that is much more important than whatever English they might be able to retain from my lessons. I mean, most of them will never use English in their lives. But what I teach them will probably make them more inclined to open their minds. If I can even approach achieving that goal, then I feel I've done a world of good. I feel like I'm doing something worthwhile. And the students benefit, as well. It's a win-win.
Student: I agree. You are a really good teacher.
Me: Thanks

18

Loco Wuz Here

(Mendokusai Junior High)

LOCO in YOKOHAMA

On Valentine's day, some of my kids gave me chocolates and so, as tradition here dictates, I should return the favor come White Day. However, White Day was to fall on a Sunday. And, the majority of the students that gave me chocolates happened to be third-year students and would be graduating the next day and moving on to the next stage in their young lives in high school.

And to further complicate matters, all junior high schools in Yokohama have graduation at the same time on the same day. In other words, since it was impossible to be in two places at once, I had to choose between either attending the ceremony at Syouganai or Mendokusai. Naturally, I would have liked to attend both, but according to my schedule, I was to attend Syouganai's. I'd known the seniors at Mendokusai since they were first-year students so I decided I would attend theirs. But that meant I would need to have my schedule changed.

Which meant getting Silky himself on the line and pleading my case:

Me: . . . so, can you make it happen?
Tony: Anything for you, Loco, my man. My job is to make your job easier. I'll put your request in, but I'm sure it'll be approved.
Me: Glad to hear it
Tony: By the way, and in the spirit of making your job easier, I have some news.
Me: Let's have it.
Tony: Well the school pairings have changed and you won't be teaching at Mendokusai come April.
Me: I won't?
Tony: Nope. You'll still be at Syouganai, but now Syouganai has been paired with Yabai Junior High.
Me: Yabai? I see. Where's is that?
Tony: That's the good news! Yabai is also in Yokohama, but much closer to your home.

He told me where the school was.

Tony: Mendokusai is a hike for you, isn't it?
Me: I've gotten used to it.
Tony: Well this new school will cut your commute time in half, won't it?

Me:	Depends. Is Yabai near the station? Or do I have to walk 20 minutes from the station, or take a bus—
Tony:	Actually, I don't know. I'll check on that and get back to you.
Me:	Thanks. Wouldn't wanna go popping champagne without all the details.
Tony:	You're a funny guy, Loco. You should do stand-up or write a book or something.
Me:	Hmmm, that's a thought. Later Tony.

★ ★ ★ ★ ★

A couple of days later, Tony called back to follow-up, thorough guy that he was.

Tony:	You'd asked about Yabai? Well, it's actually a 10-minute walk from the station.
Me:	Thanks.
Tony:	You OK with this?
Me:	Don't have much of a choice, do I?
Tony:	No, not really. Sorry.
Me:	Yeah, well, Syouganai jyan (what you gonna do).
Tony:	Hey, Loco, man, one other thing.
Me:	Uh-huh?
Tony:	I know this is kinda fucked up but it's company policy not to discuss this with the teachers and staff over at Mendokusai.
Me:	What? Really?
Tony:	Yeah, I'm sorry but, well, that's how it is.
Me:	I see.
Tony:	Sorry Loco, but I gotta run, man.
Me:	Awright.

I'd gotten the call on my cell as I sat in the middle of the teacher's office at Mendokusai, where I'd spent the past three years of my life.

Takahashi was sitting over in the first-year teacher's area having a rather animated chat with Chichi Foofoo-san. I'd bet my last Black & Mild it was about Matsui-kun or Mika-chan. As I looked at the two of them, I thought about not only the time we'd spent in the trenches, struggling side-by-side to tame these beastie boys and girls, and the times she'd done some sneaky shit behind my back, but also her tenacity and patience as she'd faced these challenges, not to mention her general kindnesses. The Michael Jackson moment stood out as an act of kindness I was not likely to ever forget, and I felt myself forgiving her for her frailties. I certainly had my own shortcomings when it came to being the team member she needed, but eventually we'd found common ground, hadn't we?

And, seated beside me, Kawaguchi-sensei, my friend. I would, of course, tell her about my pending transfer, as she'd told me about hers a few days earlier, and how thrilled she was to be doing so. She, too, was headed for another school in Yokohama. I wasn't worried about Kawaguchi, though. I knew we'd stay in touch. I just felt my heart swell, as it did every time I thought about all she'd done to make my stay at Mendokusai a wonderful experience. From my first day there three years earlier, she'd been the one who made sure I knew everything I needed to know. It was something I'd taken for granted until I'd worked at other schools and learned that that wouldn't always be the case. She wasn't doing these things out of some kind of official obligation, or Japanese habitual courtesy, but out of a genuine desire to build a relationship.

Every time I walked past that poster of Africa on the wall on the third floor, I felt loved.

All over the office were teachers I'd had moments with. Some had even become my friends, in as much as we'd have good convos over coffee and a smoke in the shed out back sometimes. The following day, as it happened every year, most of them would ask me if I'd be returning in April with every expectation that I would. My answer the previous three times had been, "I don't know. I think so. I certainly hope so." This year I would have to look them in the eye and say the same.

Only, it'd be a lie. I did know.

I don't lie well, at least not to people I care about, anyway. And especially not at someone else's behest.

So, in addition to gearing up for the lie, emotionally that is, I'd started saying goodbye without actually saying goodbye.

Sugano-sensei was one of my smoking buddies, and one of the few teachers besides Takahashi and Kawaguchi that was actually totally comfortable around me. He'd studied abroad, and he'd married a woman who studied abroad, and though he couldn't speak English very well, that didn't stand in the way of his desire and effort to communicate. He accepted our differences and acknowledged our similarities. A rarity.

When I ran into him the next day in the smoke shed at our usual time after lunch, I handed him a lighter I'd had for years. It wasn't much. I just wanted to give him something. Something that made me feel real.

One of the things about living in Japan, namely the tendency on the part of most natives to other-ize foreigners, has a significant side effect: a feeling of invisibility. I know that sounds strange considering the behaviors I've described that occur in response to my presence, but, that's just it. It's not really *me* they are reacting to. It's just their perception of me. Some hodge-podge of stereotypes, rumors, misrepresentations, and misconceptions, mostly. Not me. Not Loco.

For most of my life here, I've been a canvas upon which the privileged paint as they please, or in the only ways they know how, while the real me exists beneath their paint jobs, essentially invisible. The result being a certain sense of not being. Thus, sometimes I behave as if I am invisible here. Even when some people have given me every indication that they were at least trying to see me, the preponderance of the paint-can-toting muck-slinging masses predisposed me, at times, to decline acting under the belief that their efforts would ultimately be in vain.

And, strangely, I was OK with this. I've rationalized that since this is an unavoidable case here I might as well enjoy the handful of advantages invisibility offers, and the inherent power of the paint job they've applied.

However, there were a few people whose efforts to see me, Sugano among them, that I wanted to acknowledge. And something as simple as the giving of something personal allowed this to happen. I envisioned my hand reaching out from beneath this muck, from this virtually solitary place where I existed, into the land of the Rising Sun.

I wanted to thank him, yes. But, it was also a selfish act. I simply wanted to be seen.

The only problem was that I couldn't tell him any of this. Because, actually, I didn't trust him enough, or really any of them, to say "between you and me, I won't be back next year, but I've been instructed by my company not to say anything so this has to remain on the QT, lips sealed, hush-hush. And, I wanted to say good-bye and thank you for being a really cool guy. So, here's a little something to remember me by."

Nope, sadly, I couldn't bring myself to do that, and I'm not sure why. So, instead. . .

"What's this?" Sugano-sensei asked.

"It's a lighter. You never seem to be able to find yours so I wanted to give you this."

"Oh, no, no, no, I can't take it. It's too—"

"No, take it. I want you to have it. I have plenty more. It's nothing special. I used to use it back in America, but I never use it anymore."

He looked it over, then looked me over, and, for a second, there was flash recognition of its significance. It shot across his face like a meteor. He'd glimpsed my eyes through the muck. It was just an instant, but in it a connection was made. Then he smiled, solemnly, and bowed deeply, as did I.

"Hontou ni doumo arigato gozaimasu (This is really kind of you. Thank you very much)!"

"Dou itashimashite (You're welcome)," I caught myself saying. I rarely use that phrase. I usually respond to all "thank yous" with "iie (not at all)" and a dismissive wave of the hand, but his solemnity almost made me show the full gravity of what I felt.

I had similar sessions with a couple of the other teachers, but I had to split them up. If they were to talk, as I knew they would, and all of them mentioned they'd received affectionate trinkets from me, it wouldn't take a genius to figure out what Loco was cooking.

The next day was my last at Mendokusai.

I held it together and lied on my company's behest. But, all day, I couldn't fight this feeling that I was going to disappear, like I'd never been there. It forged a throbbing pang in my heart.

I sat there at my desk, eating a special sushi lunch with all the other teachers, contemplating carving my name in my desk or spray painting it in graffiti on the wall in the smoke shed—LOCO WUZ HERE!

★ ★ ★ ★ ★

After lunch, I got another call from The Silky One:

Tony: Loco, my man, how's it going?

Me:	'Bout as well as can be expected.
Tony:	I understand. Any plans for your vacation?
Me:	I've got a project or two to work on.
Tony:	Really? What you working on?
Me:	Uhhh, nothing really. Just this and that.
Tony:	I see. None of my business. No problem. Well, the reason I—
Me:	I didn't mean it like that, Tony. I'm just not prepared to talk about it just yet.
Tony:	Nah, it's cool, Loco. I know you and I didn't get off on the right foot way back when. And it's been shaky ever since. I'm not sure why, but I guess that's how it goes. First impressions are lasting ones.
Me:	Well, you're right about that. We definitely got off on the wrong foot. But, to be honest, I don't even remember exactly what went down. That was years ago.
Tony:	I remember exactly what happened. You tried to squeeze *The Company* for a raise.
Me:	*What*??
Tony:	Ha, ha.. You don't remember, do you? You worked at an elementary school out in Fujisawa or somewhere for a few months while we were waiting for an opening at a school closer to your apartment. We wanted you to stay at that school because the teachers were raving about you, sending us letters and what not! But the 90-minute commute made it a no-brainer for you. It was two trains and a bus, if I remember correctly. Can't blame you. But, you told us you'd stay if you were to get a raise. I still have the email you wrote. I read it occasionally, just for kicks. It was the best piece of manipulation I've ever gotten from a teacher! Ha, ha!
Me:	Always happy to entertain you, Tony.
Tony:	Seriously, Loco, you got some skills, my man! You should be a writer!
Me:	From your lips to God's ears.
Tony:	I guess you blamed me when your request was denied?

LOCO in YOKOHAMA

Me: Nah. Nothing of the sort. Hell, it was a win-win for me. More money or more sleep. Why should I get uptight? Besides I know you're not the decision-maker over there when it comes to money. Why would I blame you?

Tony: I'm relieved to hear that. So, what's the deal?

Me: What deal?

Tony: Well, you never hang out with us. We usually go get drinks and shoot the shit at least once a month. Most of the other teachers have come out, but in three years you haven't come out, not even once. What are you? Anti-social?

Me: Not really. I guess I'm shy around foreigners.

Tony: Ha, ha, you've been here too long.

Me: Ya think?

Tony: Well, listen, this Friday we're going out for drinks and I'd really like it if you'd join us. I want to see what Loco is like after a couple of rounds. I'm sure some of the other teachers and staff would, too. They always ask about you at the Christmas and Halloween parties, and what-not. You are missed, you know.

Me: Lay it on thick, why don't you?

Tony: OK, well anyway, that was my pitch. It's your move. Hope you can make it.

Me: I'll seriously consider it. Seriously. Only because I appreciate your effort and I can feel the sincerity. But, I gotta tell you, I'm really not into hanging out with a bunch of drunken college grads. Most of the teachers are too young for me. I used to do that shit quite a bit back in my early days here, but nowadays, rarely.

Tony: I feel you on that! But, not all the teachers are kids. There are some in our age group. And who knows? You might make some new friends. Good conversation is hard to come by in these parts.

Me: Good conversation is hard to come by everywhere. Damn, Tone. I can see how you've gotten where you are.

Tony: I'm not sure how to take that.

Me: Cuz you're a smart man.

Tony: You're a funny guy, Loco.

Me:	I have my moments. Anyway, to what do I owe the pleasure of this call?
Tony:	Actually, that's what I called about. To let you know about Friday. A personal invitation, since you never reply to the emails, anyway.
Me:	Damn, I'm honored! How can I say no to that?
Tony:	Good! You're in?
Me:	Maybe. I got a question, though.
Tony:	Shoot.
Me:	Why couldn't I tell the teachers at Mendokusai I wouldn't be back in April? That forced lack of disclosure placed me under quite a bit of duress. I had friends there, you know.
Tony:	That came straight from the BOE. They have their reasons, and I'm afraid I'm not privy.
Me:	I see.
Tony:	I know how you—
Me:	Do you? Have you worked with the same people for three years, painstakingly cultivating relationships, only to be told you have to skip town without even a 'fuck you'?
Tony:	No, I don't mean I've been in your position. I just mean—
Me:	Well, anyway, listen. Mendokusai is having a goodbye party next week for the Japanese teachers who are transferring the old-fashioned way, you know, with speeches and handshakes and drinks and karaoke and all that conventional jazz. You think I'll be allowed to attend and pay my respects?
Tony:	Man, it really upset you, didn't it? I'm so sorry. It's not my fault you know?
Me:	I know, Tony. It's just, you represent "The Man". That's why you make the big bucks, and that's why you're catching it.
Tony:	I see. Well, let me check on that and I'll let you know.
Me:	You do that. Let me know by Friday . . . over a couple of cold ones. First round's on me. I'll wear my party mask.
Tony:	Really? You gonna come out? Excellent!
Me:	Yeah. You turned me around. Maybe you can convince me to be a writer, too.

19
Mental Instagrams
(Mendokusai Junior High)

I taught my last lessons at Mendokusai that afternoon with the first-year students. And, as per Silky and *The Company's* fucked up policy, I let no one know that that was the case.

But, of course, I knew.

I knew today when Mika was figuratively and literally showing her ass, sitting in her chair in such a way, chin resting on her knees, so as to expose her underwear beneath her uniform skirt. She did this on purpose, no doubt, perhaps trying to entice one of these future herbivores and metrosexuals over to the carnivore camp. And when Takahashi noticed and rushed over to plead with her to sit properly, receiving a sharp kick in her solar plexus for her efforts, I knew that I wouldn't be there next year to see how she blossomed and matured as I had with the students from the previous two years, some as mad as Mika.

And I knew during my last class with Matsui and Satou that I wouldn't be there next year when, ideally, they would take on the mantle of role models for the incoming first-year students because they will have matured a bit during the upcoming two-week spring holiday and realize their solemn responsibility to lead by example.

Yeah, I dreamed big, didn't I?

But, I held on to this dream because I'd seen it happen a number of times.

Some of the kids did develop a sense of obligation to the grades below theirs. Granted, some felt nothing but, by virtue of the school's culture and the social constructs in place here in Japan, were thrust into the role of mentors; for example, for "Sports Day", one of many national holidays in Japan, it was not so much the responsibility of the teachers to help the lower grades prepare for the festivities, as it was the upper grades who'd performed the dances and various other routines previously. And this dignified duty successfully brought out the best in some causes I thought to be lost. So, I held my hopes high.

Despite all the evidence to the contrary.

★ ★ ★ ★ ★

Earlier that day, I ran into Matsui and his lieutenant, Satou, fighting in the hallway with the erasers from the classroom. And both had powdered the other's face in white chalk. Matsui's had more, obviously not quite holding his own in eraser-to-eraser combat against his faithful sidekick. He was laughing madly, evidently enjoying every second of the fight, but with his face chalked up, he looked like a character from one of the scariest movies I'd ever seen—a Japanese horror flick called, *Ju-on*.

A ju-on is a curse that occurs when a person dies with a deep and burning grudge. This curse inhabits a place and kills anyone who dares to enter. I'm not sure what it was about this movie that was able to tap into my fear center and unlock feelings I thought were shut away for good. But, it did.

When I was a kid, horror movies were more Gothic and were scary as shit! *The Exorcist*, *The Omen*, *Rosemary's Baby*—I know I'm dating myself. They just don't make good goth like that anymore. But, the eighties ended all that. My susceptibility to horror movies was alleviated by the likes of Michael Myers, Jason Voorhees, and Freddie Krueger. I lost the capacity to suspend disbelief for horror, and gained the ability to laugh my ass off and root for the villain. And, *Evil Dead* 1 and 2 turned it all into camp. *The Sixth Sense* and *Blair Witch Project* made admirable efforts, but to no avail. My days of getting the heebie-jeebies at a movie were gone for good. I was invulnerable to horror.

Yeah, not so much.

Ju-on was my first Japanese horror film, and it popped my cherry wide open. Most of that susceptibility to horror returned quite suddenly, and inconveniently, while I was at the theater with my girlfriend at the time who'd insisted on going to see it. That creepy fucking boy scared the bejesus outta me. I was jumping in my seat and looking away like I had while watching *The Exorcist* and seeing Linda Blair—possessed and vomiting some awful shit on priests and shoving a crucifix up her coochie—cry out "help me, mommy, help me." I loathed the boy's next appearance on-screen and I even had the willies for a couple of days after.

Seeing Matsui and Satou with their faces chalked up brought it all back for a hot second—that dark theater, that chalky blue-white skin, that screeching sound he made before the kill, the powerlessness of his victims. Even Matsui's screech, when I grabbed them both by their scruffs, was similar to the ju-on's.

I let go of them, told them to cut it out and go wash their faces, and went into the bathroom. While I took a piss, I tried to regroup, but not a moment later they came into the bathroom after me.

LOCO in YOKOHAMA

"Loco-sensei no junya mite ii (let me see your junior)?" Matsui screeched through his laughter. I figured he meant my dick. The kids always wanted to see my dick if I found myself in their bathroom.

"Piss off, you little demons!" I said in Japanese.

"Eeeee!" He yelled, followed by. . . nothing. They let me be, surprising the hell out of me, and left. Maybe I scared them, I wondered.

Nope.

When I came out of the bathroom, the two of them ambushed me. From either side of the entrance they leapt on my legs like half a pack of hyenas hankering for scrotum. I picked tiny Matsui up over my shoulder and swung his flailing legs around to keep his partner off of me. My back, which used to get a kick out of this kind of horseplay, twinged a little and scared me back to reality.

Your days of manhandling teens are numbered, it whispered sharply in my ear, via my lower back, and I responded by gingerly placing Matsui back on his feet, exposing my nuts, and giving his partner the opening he'd been waiting for. He pounced on my crotch and grabbed at it savagely, a vicious little smirk on his face.

Fortunately, he'd had more pants in his hand than anything else or I'd probably be warding off yakuza trying to tattoo my ass right now in Yokohama Penitentiary.

I kneed Satou away, a little harder than I would have normally, in an attempt to let him know he'd crossed the line. He understood, or so it seemed, and backed off. Matsui looked at him as if to say, "What are you waiting for? You're not afraid of this motherfucker, are you?"

But, neither of them budged.

Matsui, still chalky, and panting with a blood-lusty expression beneath it, and Satou's blank morbidity, inspired my *Ju-on* vision to return. I turned and walked away. I didn't look back. I didn't want them to see my apprehension.

Later that day, as I approached their classroom, to teach them for the final time, they bum-rushed me again.

"Junya-misete (show me your dick)!" cried Matsui as he launched himself at me, filled with gleeful abandon. Gotta love his perseverance, I thought, as I swatted his little ass away. Satou joined in, but not so aggressively. I could see he was a little wary of my knee. Every time I raised it defensively, he leapt two feet away. But his eyes remained cold and unwavering.

I hope he doesn't take this grudge to the grave with him.

The bell to begin class began to chime, but it meant absolutely nothing to these two. Satou's leeriness about being kneed by me, I could see, was dissipating little by little as he and Matsui, apparently, had studied my defensive moves and adapted like a couple of pint-sized velociraptors. They were easily weaving around my maneuvers and garnering hungry handfuls of my jewels.

The bell had rung a full minute ago, but still they were on me. Takahashi had her hands full with a couple of other disruptive students.

"Suwari nasai (sit down)!" I shouted at the two knuckleheads harassing my scrotum. And, abruptly, they stopped, turned and headed for their seats. I was as amazed as the other students. That was too easy. What did I miss? I looked around for booby traps or maybe a "kick my ass!" sign, in Japanese, stuck on my back. Nada. Then, I heard some of the well-behaved students in the class giggling. I looked for the source. It was Matsui, of course, with a brown leather wallet in his hands, rummaging through the contents, pulling out money! I patted my back pocket. Empty.

No the fuck he didn't!

"You motherfucker!" I yelled, and took off after him. He was laughing and evading my capture with the speed and agility of a chicken. Man, I was lucky I didn't get my hands on him on my initial effort to do so. I definitely would've been placed in custody. I could have caught him, but I would have had to make a total berserker of myself to do so—jump over students, toss aside desks, and what not. Luckily I had the presence of mind to catch myself, take a deep breath, and remember that I was the teacher.

But, my wallet!

This kind of disregard for personal privacy and breach of the teacher-student covenant had to be addressed, and that right soon!

Matsui was watching me and he must have seen the emotions playing out on my face because he suddenly flipped the script, came over to me, handed me my wallet, and said, so sweetly, "Honto ni gomen nasai, Loco-sensei (I'm really sorry)," brandishing that slightly naive, slightly precocious smile of his—like this was all beyond him and he was just a

LOCO in YOKOHAMA

kid being a kid and having a little fun at his teacher's expense. No harm, no foul.

He strolled over to his seat, his eyes never leaving me—nor mine him—and sat down. Satou and his boys were patting him on the head and congratulating him on this epic ruse; it was one that would go down in the history books. Total classic! And he couldn't help himself, but gloat a little, basking in the glow of their adoration and respect.

But, he kept a wary eye on me through all this. He knew he'd, once again, crossed a line, and he had the awareness to be scared.

When I could pull my eyes off of him, I noticed that Takahashi was oblivious to all of this. She was still trying to get the student in the back to put away his Rubik's Cube. He had the top two rows completed and was struggling with the final maneuvers. I used to be able to finish it in a minute when I was in high school. Fond memories of being popular due to this ability flooded me, and I stood there in reminiscence.

When I glanced back Matsui's way, I saw him closing a knife.

The girl seated behind him, Saori-chan, one of the few remaining well-behaved students in the class, was watching him do this with about as much interest as one might have watching a carpenter put a hammer away in his tool belt.

They say a picture speaks a thousand words. Well, the picture playing out in my head was not the glimpse of the knife but, the image of Saori's reaction to the knife. It spoke to the normality of this act and to its utter lack of newsworthiness. I mean, I've been here a while, but I haven't completely lost touch with the reality of the world outside of Japan. And a Swiss Army knife wouldn't have even raised an eyebrow back in my school days. But, I was under the distinct impression that here—in the land of all that is cute and small and safe beyond all recognition—I thought that, here, this kind of thing would send shock waves of repulsion and fear racing at tsunami speed around the entire school—across the entire fucking prefecture, in fact.

Anyway, I was wrong. And that was an enlightening moment for me. It was a moment not to be outshone, at least not in the next 15 minutes, I thought.

Wrong, yet again.

When Takahashi finally got the student to put the Rubik's away—which coincided with his having finished it—and she came back to the

325

front of the room to join me, I whispered in her ear, "Matsui's got a knife in his desk."

She reacted the way I had expected Saori to react, but the damage was done. The image of Saori's nonchalance had already been uploaded to my mental instagram page.

"Really?"

I shot her a look.

She went over to his desk, got down on her knees the way waiters and waitresses sometimes do here in restaurants, had a little exchange with him, and then began picking through his desk. She came up empty-handed, came back over to me and shrugged with a look like 'maybe you imagined it', and for a second, I imagined I had. A micro fucking second. I knew a knife when I saw one.

"Listen, he's got a knife!" I snapped, trying to keep the urgency out of my voice for the sake of the students watching all of this with the curiosity one might watch a street illusionist.

"I'll check for it later," she said a little dismissively, and started going through the motions of teaching a lesson. We hadn't been able to get through a lesson in this class in months. So, I did the same, but I kept my peripherals trained on Matsui. After a few minutes, I relaxed as much as a teacher can when you know that a wily student seated near you was playing with a knife after having had an altercation with you a few moments earlier. The most comforting thought was that, judging from Saori's reaction to it, he had probably brought this thing to school and brandished it many times and he hadn't stabbed me or anyone else yet, so chances are that he has a little self-control.

I was walking around the room assisting the manageable students with the lesson I had planned when I heard a loud pop from behind me. I wheeled around to see Matsui aiming a gun at a guy seated near him.

Columbine, and a dozen other school shootings, raced though my head. But only for a second. The sound and look of the gun cried fake, but the image of Matsui aiming it intently at another student joined the image of Saori's apathetic expression on my mental Instagram: hashtag #Revelations.

I swallowed my apprehension and walked towards Matsui-kun, and watched as his aim slowly adjusted from being leveled at the student's head to being leveled at me. I sped up and just as it would have been aimed at my gut, grabbed his arm and wrenched the gun from his hand, his tiny index finger tight on the trigger.

I looked around, armed with this toy, at the students in the vicinity to see their reactions to this. More apathy; the possession of toy guns and Swiss Army knives had entered the realm of the prosaic here in Mendokusai Junior High.

At least, in Matsui's hand it had.

So, I decided not to overreact. It was just a toy. And the knife was just a Boy Scout's utility blade, good for cutting ropes and carving "Matsui Loves Saori" in the bark of some hapless cherry blossom tree.

I examined the gun closely to confirm without a doubt that it was indeed a toy and then I handed it back to him.

"Put it away!" I said. He just looked at me with those guileless innocent eyes of his, smiled that warm, enchanting smile, and complied.

When I returned to the front of the room, I realized that Takahashi hadn't seen any of that episode either.

"He has a toy gun, too," I said, softly, so only she could hear. Again, she looked at me incredulously.

The bell began to ring and, half way through it, I watched as Matsui slid the gun out of his desk and was about to put it in his book bag.

"Look!" I snapped at Takahashi. She turned in time to catch a glimpse of it before it disappeared into his bag. Her eyes bulged.

My work was done. I grabbed my teaching material and headed for the door. I needed some air. Outside the door, Satou bushwhacked me. He'd sprung at my crotch the moment I exited, shouting for Matsui. Matsui came a-running, wrapped himself around my leg, and seated himself on my foot so that I would have to drag him in order to escape.

He looked up at me with that same expression he'd had the first time we'd met, when he'd run and jumped in my arms, hugged me around the neck, and made me feel like I'd found a home here among the Japanese— little did he know.

So this was it. Our last class. Our last day. I tried to go through the motions of fighting them off, but my heart wasn't in it. I basically let them assault my balls. It took them a moment to notice I wasn't putting up a fight, but once they did, they ceased hostilities and gave me very concerned looks.

"Are you OK, Loco-sensei?" It was Satou's voice, and as soon as I heard it, I realized it was a voice I'd never heard before. Strangely enough, I felt kind of honored. Teachers had been trying to get him to talk since the beginning of the school year. I wasn't even sure if he spoke to Matsui.

"I'm fine, thank you."

I didn't know what else to say.

I had started walking away from them when Takahashi came out of the classroom. On the down-low she showed me what she had hidden beneath her teaching materials; it was the toy gun and the pocket knife.

"While you had him distracted, I got them!" she exclaimed very excitedly, like she'd planned this heist and pulled it off without a hitch.

"That's nice," I replied as we headed for the staircase. As we descended, I looked back. Matsui and Satou stood at the top of the staircase, watching me.

I thought, there stand the mentors for the incoming first-year students. . .

And yet, somehow, I remained hopeful

★ ★ ★ ★ ★

That evening after work, I left the school grounds for the last time, closed the gate behind me, and began the 15-minute walk to the train station. About a block away, I sparked up a stogie, my usual. Also, as usual, I walked with my head down, trying not to notice people. It was the best way I'd found to keep my peace of mind.

In my peripheral vision I could see the front wheel of a bike rolling almost besides me, only it was in the street. Japanese people tend to do all kinds of weird shit when they find themselves near me, and my not paying them any mind tends to embolden them. But, stalking alongside me would be extreme even for Japanese. So, I took a look.

It was Matsui-kun.

He was dressed in his street clothes: flannel shirt, blue jeans, and Pro-keds. I'd never seen him out of uniform. He must have gone home first. He was smiling at me in a very friendly way—which made me suspicious. It was the smile he'd feign before he launched one of his offensives on my nuts.

"Loco-sensei, I surprise you?" He asked in English. I was more surprised by the use of English than the stalking.

"Yep."

"I'm sorry."

"No problem," I said, but I was still on-guard against a sudden assault.

"I didn't know you smoked," he said in Japanese, after a thoughtful beat. I guess he'd drained his English conversation reservoir. "Is that a cigar?"

"Yeah, kinda," I replied, switching to Japanese.

"It smells good," he said.

I started getting a little self-conscious because he was paying the Black & Mild so much attention. I was very concerned about setting a bad example for the kids, especially a wayward one like Matsui. So, I clipped it and put the clip back in the box. His eyes were glued to my every movement.

"Are you going home now?" He asked.

"Yes."

"Can I come home with you?" He had the most earnest look on his face that he could muster. For a moment, I thought he was dead-ass serious and it spooked me. Then, noticing he had me, he let out that infectious laugh of his.

"No," I laughed. "Where are you going?"

"I'm going to meet my friend."

"At the game center?" I often see some of the students at the game center near the station as I pass by on my way home.

"Yep. How did you know?"

"Just guessed." I kept walking. There was an awkward silence for a few moments—at least I felt awkward. It was a silence in which I figured he'd race ahead and go about his business like most of the other students do when they ran into me outside of the school. But, I glanced to my side and, sure enough, he was still there, and still smiling.

"You want some candy?" he asked me.

I gave him a double take. "Sure."

He stopped, opened the knapsack he had in his bicycle's basket, and pulled out a pouch with all kinds of cartoony characters and Japanese written all over it. I still have trouble reading katakana, but I could make out "suppai (sour)". He opened the pouch and offered it to me. I took one out and, despite my trust issues, placed it in my mouth. He did the same.

"It's sour, right," he said, like he'd expected me to find the taste disagreeable.

"Yeah, but delicious," I said. And it was—like some of the the candies I used to enjoy as a kid myself, like Lemonheads and certain flavors of "Now & Later".

We resumed, me walking, him riding alongside me, sucking on our candies, and chit-chatting. He told me he lived not far from the station so he often came to this game center. I mentioned that I often saw fliers stuck to the ground in that area. When the Yokohama bike patrol officers confiscate your bike for parking it illegally, they'll often "glue" a flier to the sidewalk in the area where your bike was parked so that you'll know that it was not stolen, but thrown on the back of a truck and taken to a yard. The flier explains where, when, and how you could get it back.

"Oh, I know a place to put it. Don't worry," he said.

"OK."

"Well, Loco-sensei, see you in April!" he said, cheerfully, as we reached the game center. I glanced at him and he must have seen the lie in my eyes. "Eeeee? You're not coming back, are you? Why? Because of me?"

"What? I didn't say that!" I gasped, knowing I'd somehow just confirmed his suspicions. Clever kid.

"Well, why aren't you coming back?"

"I have no choice."

"I see," he said, looking like the joy had been sucked out of him. "Will you come visit?"

"Why? So you and Satou can attack jun-ya?"

His smile returned from wherever my bad news had banished it, just that quick. The resilience of kids is remarkable. But it looked different. It was neither precocious nor guileless. Prepubescent experience was etched into it. It was like he'd aged right before my eyes, transforming from a child into an adolescent in real time.

I shot my last mental Instagram of Matsui at that moment.

"So, you can watch me play baseball! I've joined the baseball club!"

"Really?" I said, surprised as hell. The baseball club is one of the more demanding and disciplined clubs in the school. "Congratulations!"

"Thanks," he said, blushing.

He certainly had more than enough energy for it! Something told me he was going to be alright.

"Well, then I'll definitely come and visit you. Do your best!"

I chucked him on the arm.

"I will," he said, gave me a quick bow and turned to leave. "Loco-sensei, ki wo tsukete ne (be careful out there)!"

I was half-hoping he'd come and leap in my arms one last time—probably the one thing I'll miss about him most—but looking at him, suddenly all grown up, I would have been disappointed if he had.

He kept looking back as he walked his bike into an alleyway, emerging seconds later without it. He noticed I was still standing in the same spot.

"Byeeee!" he shouted, jumping up and down excitedly, then he ran into the game center.

20
Distant, Aloof, but Alive
(Syouganai Junior High)

On Mrs. Betty's last day, in the morning meeting, she bid us all farewell. I could tell that most of the other teachers would not be impacted by her departure at all. Most seemed preoccupied, even during her brief speech thanking everyone for their kindness and support. After lifeless, almost robotic applause, during which Akiyama's and mine were conspicuously the loudest and longest, she returned to her desk across from us, her eyes misted over yet steely as ever. Apparently, she was aware of the lukewarmness of the farewell, too. Akiyama and I, however, being the beneficiaries of most of what Mrs. Betty had to offer, were afflicted.

"Y'all cut that out, now, hear?" she scolded sternly

"This place won't be the same without you, and these fools don't even know it," I said, trying to temper my feelings on the matter. I felt out of sorts. "We're gonna miss having you around."

Akiyama solemnly nodded her agreement.

Mrs. Betty just waved my words away, and smiled that crooked smile of hers, obviously moved.

"Let's go out and have a little party tonight!" Akiyama suggested. "Just the three of us."

Yamada-sensei was still MIA, and Okubo was at her desk mumbling and grinning to herself. I felt kind of bad about the way Akiyama had just automatically excluded them, though, but only a little.

"Oh, nooo. Mrs. Betty's too old and too tired to be going out at night," she protested, and I was kinda relieved. I wasn't keen on having Mrs. Betty make one more step than she had to. "But, if y'all'd like, y'all could come over to my house. I'd love to have ya! And my grandson's always asking about you, Mr. Loco. Seems you made quite an impression on the boy. He'd love to see you!"

My spirits rose swiftly. "Great idea! I'm in!"

Akiyama agreed.

★ ★ ★ ★ ★

Mrs. Betty might be old, but she could put away some Japanese moonshine. We went—or, rather, they— Akiyama and she, went through two bottles while I was still nursing my second glass. I wasn't aware at the time, but I had begun to refrain from getting drunk with co-workers.

This was because, once drunk, I had a tendency to answer questions honestly and directly—answers that tended to change the mood, and not in a way conducive to a party atmosphere.

For example, to a relatively innocent question like, "how long do you plan to stay in Japan," under the influence, I might answer, "until I stop believing that whatever doesn't kill you makes you stronger," followed by a scoffing chuckle or a grim smile. Of course, that would instigate follow-up questions, and lead into a Q&A in which Japan and Japanese would be criticized in the subtlest ways an inebriated person can manage. Unless I found I was being too subtle and they'd missed the point, whereupon I may or may not pump up the volume depending on my mood or blood alcohol content. My criticisms were rarely challenged, at least not substantially. Instead, they would be diplomatically responded to, perhaps even agreed with. This would be followed by a bout of shame on my part for having been a selfish killjoy with my "negativity."

And, being that I could hardly address these kinds of issues with the perpetrators among the nameless masses, aside from my fellow foreigners—whom I've long since learned are usually a futile waste of time to get into such things with—my closest friends and colleagues here are the only Japanese ears I have at my disposal.

Yeah, I knew me. I could be a real earnest dick if I didn't keep my wits about me. So, yeah, sober was best.

We sat around a table on the tatami-mat covered floor in Mrs. Betty's spacious living room, surrounded by a roomful of mementos from around the world, relics of her extraordinary life. She'd explained once in the office that she brought back something from everywhere she'd ever gone, but I had imagined an attic or maybe a trunk filled with souvenirs. I had not been able to imagine what hundreds of little random pieces of her life adorning a single room would look like; or the impact their combined bouquet would have on that room, the seizing of the senses that ensued. Nothing appeared to have been bought. These were not airport gift shop knickknacks but actual pieces of the places she'd traveled to; quartz from Argentina somewhere, a playbill from some obscure playhouse in Paris. They were all acquired somehow, chosen to capture a moment in time, which somehow consumed the whole room in her slightly eerie personal space-time continuum.

Unable to fully relax, and drawn to the abundance of curios, I spent 20 minutes just roaming through Mrs. Betty's life, before they both implored me to have a seat.

We sat and talked for over an hour about the good times we had spent together, and laughed at some of the adventures we shared with the first-year students. We also chatted about some of the more serious issues that the school had yet to address, like the outrageous and borderline dangerous behavior of some of the third-year kids.

It was around that time that Mrs. Betty suddenly asked, "So, what's bothering you, Mr. Loco?"

"Huh?"

"You're so quiet."

They were both looking at me, like they'd been talking about me.

"Yeah, you haven't really said anything," Akiyama added. "Are you OK?"

I couldn't understand what they were talking about. And they were speaking English!

"Not just tonight, by God! I declare, for a few weeks you've been sho'nuff keeping to your lonesome," Mrs. Betty said, her voice a little higher than usual, and slurring a bit. I'd never seen her drunk. "That ain't like you!"

"What?" I yelped. "I've been talking. Just now I said, umm, I said . . ."

They just smiled at me and waited patiently. I couldn't remember what I'd said last, or even when I'd said it. Everything that crossed my mind was thoughts I'd had while they were talking. They were thoughts about how difficult it was going to be without a presence like Mrs. Betty's around—somebody who was courageous enough to speak truth to power, confident enough to speak her mind without an overabundance of censorship and diplomacy, and could speak my language in more ways than one.

But, it was true. I hadn't verbally been saying much at all.

"Hora (see, I told you)!" Akiyama shouted and laughed. She was shit-faced. Mrs. Betty's cheeks were as red as a Japanese plum on a mound of rice, but her eyes were clear and sharp as always.

"I bet you're thinking," Mrs. Betty said, dissecting me with a stare, tilting her head to the side. "I bet yous just a-thinking all the time, thinking so much you can't even talk, ain't you?"

"I guess."

"That's good, though," Mrs. Betty snapped. "Ain't nothing wrong with thinking. Ain't that right, Akiyama?"

"Sou desu yo ne (sure is)," Akiyama slurred.

"Why ain't you drinking, though?" Mrs. Betty asked, shrewdly. "You've been sucking on that glass for about an hour. What's going on with you?"

"I have too been drinking. I—"

"Come, come now, son," she snapped. "No need to start fibbin'. When a man got problems too big for drink, those be the most serious problems. Yes, indeed. And when that man starts lying about those problems, well, now you has me worried!"

Akiyama glanced at Mrs. Betty's concern, then down at my half-filled glass, then at me, compassionately.

"It's nothing," I lied, again, as Mrs. Betty shook her head. "I'm just gonna miss you."

"Why? I'm right here, and you's welcome here anytime. Anytime! Nah, it's more than that! Right, Akiyama?"

"I've been meaning to say something, but," Akiyama cried, sincerity in her whole disposition. "You have been different, lately."

"Ain't that the truth!" Mrs. Betty said. "You used to chat with us during your free time. Nowadays, all you do is write. You don't even so much as smile anymore. I ain't one to be prying in a man's business. God knows my late husband, may he rest in peace, wouldn't have none of that. Dear man would sooner die than talk about his troubles. But you has us concerned, you understand? We just wanna know you awright, sugar."

They were teaming up on me. It felt like an intervention. I pictured some junkie scratching, sniveling, and rubbing his nose on his sleeve, surrounded by loved ones who he'd mistreated or betrayed or even robbed at some point, coming together in one last ditch effort to save his ass from his worst enemy—himself!

And I laughed. Hard.

"Ha!" Mrs. Betty shouted. "There you are! I knew you was in there. Come on out and have a drink with us! Please."

"Sounds like a plan," I said and threw down that half a glass of shochu I'd been nursing and slid the empty glass across the table to Akiyama. She promptly refilled it. Before I knew it, we'd finished the bottle and had cracked another. Apparently Mrs. Betty kept an ample supply around, just like my grandmother used to keep her bar well-stocked. Mrs. Betty was from the old school.

    I started feeling it kick in around the fifth glass. After that, I lost count. I was drinking it like water.

    "What are you writing about these days," Akiyama asked, in Japanese, alcohol having adhered a permanent droopy smirk on her face.

    "I'm writing about how I started hating Japanese people."

    They both broke out laughing. Akiyama fell back on the tatami, her dress flew up exposing her underwear. Mrs. Betty cackled like some strange bird. I'd never heard her laugh that way before. Akiyama sat back up after a few moments, realized her undies were in full view and quickly brushed her dress down. I pretended not to have noticed.

    "I'm serious, y'all," I said, slurring a little, hardly containing my own laughter. "Crazy, huh?"

    "Ain't nothing crazy about that!" Mrs. Betty said, still giggling. "Shit, I hate them, too, sometimes!"

    I dropped my glass.

    Luckily, it was empty except for some ice cube chips.

    "Me too," Akiyama chimed in, her lips over-moist.

    "I'm serious!" I repeated, trying to pick up the ice slivers with my fingers, but dropping them over and over. Then I gave up. A little water ain't gonna hurt that tatami none. When I looked up, they were both watching me, and I wondered if I had stuck my foot in it and killed the mood yet again.

    That part of my brain that never gets too drunk to remember what time that last train to Yokohama is, and counts my drinks and dollars, and secures my wallet, and tells me not to flirt with co-workers when my dick says, "she wants you, man, go for it!" That part of my brain came to full alert as it was apt to do when ' be careful' is the order of the moment.

    "Mr. Loco," Mrs. Betty said, having caught the catch in my voice. "Is that what's been bothering you? You think you hate Japanese people?"

    "Well, yeah, kinda, I guess," I wasn't even sure anymore. I felt so ridiculous. "Not the kids, of course, but . . ."

    "Listen," she said, and paused. She glanced at Akiyama who hiccupped and blushed. Then back to me. "You listening?"

"Yes ma'am," I said, and she smiled. I'd never called her "ma'am" before. I must have sounded so serious.

"You're what I call a thinker," she said, and I could hear a hundred other people I've known over the years, saying the same. Some saying it as a good thing, as in it was opposed to someone whose brain is only gray matter that takes up space. And others said so for not so complimentary a reason, as in, "but you need to get off your lazy ass and put those thoughts to good use 'cause thinking is only half the battle!"

". . . and that's a good thing! Lord knows, we need more thinkers in the world, but, most people ain't thinkers. No, sir. Most people just do. All they know is "do". Thinking is like, uh, like, a luxury. You know what I mean? And, you, my dearest, are a rich man.

"You're a dreamer, too. I know. I watch you. I listen to you. The way you teach a lesson. How generous you are with children. The way you're unafraid to share your ideas. Cuz, that's the way you see the world. A place where people share ideas. Yes, indeed, you have a rich imagination."

Akiyama was swaying back and forth, like if Mrs. Betty were singing a beloved hymn, but she was attentive.

"I've been all over the world, as you know. And when I travel, I don't just go to see the sights. I mean, sure, I like tourist attractions as much as the next woman, but that's not why I travel. I think I'm a lot like you. I wanna learn something about the people I meet, the places I go. I wanna grow from the experience, share ideas, share myself. Almost every place I've gone, I've made friends. I avoid hotels and restaurants as much as possible. I'd much rather have dinner in people's homes, sleep in their guest rooms or in small local inns—talk with real people about their lives, about real things.

"Sometimes, it's dangerous, of course. And my husband used to catch fits all the time, bless his heart, but that's Betty, and he knew what he was getting into when he asked for my hand in matrimony. I've always been this way.

"You know the worst part of traveling? And I don't talk about this much. Maybe never. But, God knows, it's always in my mind. The worst part is when you run into people with closed-minds, or minds that only open for the familiar, which is basically the same thing. It's easy to feel pity for these people, but pity is a horrible thing. Horrible. Never feel pity. Even hate is better than pity.

"But, remember this, it's not the people you hate, it's the idea. Don't get stuck on the people. I'm not saying you shouldn't hate. Hell, hate is as natural—as *human*, as love. All I'm saying is, if you must hate, hate the idea! The idea is the enemy; the people are just a vessel for the idea. Just as *you're* a vessel for an idea.

"You're so lucky, Mr. Loco. So blessed," she said, her eyes watering up. "You love hard, and you hate hard, and that's the measure of a full emotional life. Anybody tells you different is a saint or full of shit! You'll never be content to just do, or to just think. And that's what makes you who you are. It's also what makes you hate!

"But, that's why I'm so fond of you! I love you, Mr. Loco, cuz you. . ." and she paused, again, and pursed her wet lips. "You, my dear, are a human being—a man at-large!"

I was sitting there just watching this woman—her mannerisms and her powerful yet soothing way of making her point. She reminded me so much of my Aiko. Like, if Aiko had lived to be as old as Mrs. Betty, she'd be just like her. I know she would have.

"I want to be these things you see in me," I said to her, looking right in her eyes. "I'm just going through some changes now . . . some rough changes. Some of these changes feel like they are out of my hands. I think that's why I write so much. Writing makes me feel like I've got my life under control. Documenting this chaos I call a life *is* my life these days. You know?

"I look out my eyes and I see a world of fear and ignorance, hidden beneath a whole lot of smiling faces. And it scares me, sometimes. I wanna change it, for the better. Be part of a movement that removes the fake surface so we can all see what's beneath, and *deal* with it. You know? Maybe then, together, we can begin to remove that layer, too. . .But I don't know what's beneath the fear and ignorance. Is there another layer? If there is, I've never seen it. I've never even read about it except in fiction. Maybe that's all there is. Maybe I'll be helping to remove the only measure of joy most people will ever have in this world . . . And for what?"

I sat there shaking my head, waiting for an answer that will probably never come.

"Maybe I think too much. Or maybe I lie to myself too well. Maybe I'm just losing it. I don't know."

"I'm here to tell ya, ain't nothing wrong with losing it," Mrs. Betty snapped abruptly, eyes narrowed and red, and a vein appearing down the center of her forehead. "Nothing at all. Especially for writers. Hell, you gotta be a little loco to be a writer, anyway. The best ones usually are, yes indeed. You're a very sensitive soul, honey, and this world is a rough place for your kind. But, you're gonna be just fine. You hear me? Trust me. I know things. You are much stronger than you feel right now."

As she spoke I could see the wisdom of the ages etched in her withered face. And when combined with the sensory assault of all the history of her world that surrounded us, it felt almost like listening to immortality, like everyone I've ever loved, and has ever loved me, both living and in the beyond, were reverberating through her in one sage and majestic voice.

Akiyama seemed to notice, as well. Or maybe it was the moonshine that applied that queer expression to her face. But, her concentration appeared to be dramatically increased suddenly.

"You know, Mr. Loco. I read a lot. And, *personally*, I prefer writers who don't try so hard, don't try to change things. You know what I mean? Maybe because deep down I'm just a conservative woman . . . but I feel like change doesn't need writers. Not necessarily. Change is inevitable. This movement you speak of is a natural occurrence. It's the *writers* who need change.

"I like writers who can just ride the currents of life, encounter things they would try to change, but have the wisdom, the audacity, to just glide through, sharing stories along the way. Like Gods—distant, aloof, but alive! Know what I mean?"

I did . . . kinda. But I said nothing. I just watched her as she sat there in her chair, a glass of shochu grasped within her fingers. They were weathered with age spots and wrinkles, and a little shaky. She raised the glass up to her mouth, resting it on her lip, and poured the remaining moonshine down her throat. Then she held up the glass, looking at it, almost child-like, and seemed surprised to find it empty. Some private thought drew a grin to her face. Then she placed the glass on the table, looked at me, and winked her eye."

'But, you see, I'm a dreamer, too.'

ABOUT THE AUTHOR

Baye McNeil is an author, freelance writer, teacher, blogger and street photographer from Brooklyn, New York. His critically-acclaimed first book, *Hi! My Name is Loco and I am a Racist* was named one of the 10 Best Black Books of 2012. He spends his free time taking photos, playing basketball, cycling and reading. He currently resides in Yokohama, Japan.

Websites:
www.locoinyokohama.com
www.himynameisloco.com

Facebook:
www.facebook/locoinyokohama.com

Twitter:
@locohama

Printed in Great Britain
by Amazon.co.uk, Ltd.,
Marston Gate.